Michael Kidron is a political economist and has been general editor of Pluto Projects.
Amongst other books, he has written *Western Capitalism Since the War* and *The War Atlas*
(with Dan Smith).

Ronald Segal has written very widely, including *Political Africa*, a dictionary of African politics;
The Race War, a study of racial conflict in history; a major biography of Leon Trotsky;
and books on America, India and the Middle East.

A recent product of the authors' fruitful collaboration is *The Book of Business, Money and Power*.

THE NEW
STATE OF THE WORLD ATLAS

REVISED AND UPDATED
MICHAEL KIDRON & RONALD SEGAL
A PLUTO PROJECT

Pan Books LONDON AND SYDNEY

The State of the World Atlas first published 1981 and
The New State of the World Atlas first published 1984
by Pan Books Limited and Heinemann Educational Books Limited.

This revised edition first published 1987 by
Pan Books Limited, Cavaye Place, London SW10 9PG
and simultaneously in hardback by
Heinemann Educational Books Limited,
22 Bedford Square, London WC1B 3HH.

ISBN   0 330 30145 4

Artwork by Swanston Graphics, Derby
Printed and bound in Hong Kong by
Mandarin Offset

CONTENTS

INTRODUCTION ■

In our Introduction to *The New State of the World Atlas*, published in 1984, we drew attention to a definite drop in the statistical standards provided by the United Nations and by other international organizations. Far from being able, on this occasion, to report some improvement, we are persuaded that such standards have, if anything, continued to decline, as governments increasingly employ statistics for cosmetic purposes, while the offices responsible for gathering and processing information show all the signs of financial undernourishment.

More than ever, we have had recourse to privileged institutions, of business or the state, which have progressively become the proprietors of high quality information; to the investigative press; to officials within the data-gathering agencies of international bodies and individual states, who have guided us through the maze of often misleading statistics; to representatives of pressure groups, whose interest lies in understanding and revealing socially and politically potent information.

All this constitutes the sharpest contrast with our recent experience in producing *The Book of Business, Money and Power*. For in the preparation of that, our problem was not the poverty of available information but the very riches. Speeded by the new technology and by a huge investment of skills, talent, time and money, statistics gush into the marketplace on every subject that concerns the search for profit.

It is the primacy of this motivation which informs the essential paradoxes of so much that happens in our world and which promotes the very problems it pretends to solve.

When oil prices rose sharply in the 1970s, there was widespread clamour in the rich industrial states against the Organization of Petroleum Exporting Countries for acting as a predatory cartel, and much was made of the damage that was being done to the economies of the poor states. Then, as oil prices began collapsing in the mid-1980s, with accompanying pressures on the financial system, there was widespread clamour in the rich industrial states for OPEC to get its act together as a cartel and agree on production cuts to raise the price of oil. The rapid enrichment of many oil-exporters in the 1970s led to a recycling of the huge sums involved through the major international banks, which pressed the governments of poor states to borrow more and more. When the debt crisis emerged in the early 1980s, with the evident inability of many poor states to repay their debts or even meet the service charges, the major international banks agreed to various rescheduling schemes, that merely postponed the problem, and reduced the flow of new money, just when such money was most needed.

All along, the rich states have eloquently demanded the liberation of world trade from protectionist devices, so that lagging economies can grow faster, and the poor states can earn enough from expanding exports to repay their debts. But the same rich states have increasingly resorted to protectionist devices that restrain the expansion of exports from the poor, so as to secure the domestic market for their own products. Not least, malnutrition and even famine have spread and strengthened their hold over much of the poor world, while the financial cost of storing enormous surplus stocks in the rich world constitute such an embarrassment that butter is being fed to power stations.

Even as this introduction is being written, stock markets boom alongside high unemployment and spreading deprivation in the rich states, while competitive consumption there is heedlessly pursued alongside the squalor and despair that grip the states of the poor. It is difficult to escape the analogy of our world with the Lebanon of the early 1970s, when private palaces and exclusive boutiques, alongside overflowing sewers and suffocating slums, gave their peculiar distinction to the then celebrated Switzerland of the Middle East.

Matching this mood of a triumphant marketplace, in which an aggressive accumulation has come to be acclaimed as the protection and even the source of individual freedom, there is widespread demoralization in the once assertive constituency of support for an alternative system of values. As we pointed out in the introduction to the last edition of this atlas, single-issue movements, of women, gays, greens and other campaigners, had displaced the broad coalitions of the past that, with all their shortcomings and inadequacies, at least expressed a more coherent challenge to the irrational and divisive ordering of our world.

There is as yet little evidence that such coalitions, of a kind and a concern consistent with the scale of the dangers confronting us all, are in the making; still less, that there is a serious recognition of the need to confront, in a creative internationalist spirit, the division of humanity in separate states of self-serving sovereignty. But there is evidence at least, within the single-issue movements themselves, of frustration with the narrow confines of single-issue politics. The women's movement is fiercely debating the value of mere equal treatment for men and women, in a period when men and women are alike suffering the impact. Gays, where they are not once again seeking safety in the closet, are reaching out to understand the nature and values of a world at large that seeks to contaminate them with responsibility for the AIDS epidemic. Greens, excited by their increasing public acceptance, particularly in West Germany, are in ever-widening inner dispute over which political alignments and alliances they should adopt. Across the variety of single-issue concerns, there is a growing, sometimes anguished, realization that the issues are intrinsically interrelated.

And the global dimension of alternative values is being increasingly served by events. The cloud of nuclear poison from the Chernobyl disaster did not stop at the borders of state sovereignty to have its passport stamped. The pollution that kills the lakes in Canada and the trees in West Germany rains down regardless of its birthplace and citizenship elsewhere on the map. The invasion of space by the arms race derides the delimitations of political geography on our spinning planet. If this atlas does no more than demonstrate the injustices, dangers and irrelevancies of our state-ridden system, it will have served its purpose.

This atlas could not have been created without a large number of people and their institutions. We thank them for their generosity, their seriousness of purpose and, where appropriate, their spirit. Those that may be mentioned are recognized on the maps themselves, or in the acknowledgements. Those that need or wish to remain unnamed must be satisfied with this blanket expression of indebtedness.

We owe a debt as well to the many people who took seriously the purposes and the spirit of the earlier editions and laced their criticism with positive suggestions for improvement. Some of these friends we have heeded. We are grateful to them all. And we would single out for our appreciation Steven Seidenberg who helped with additional research.

Many of the strengths of this atlas derive directly from the spirit of Pluto Projects. Anne Benewick and Nina Kidron are owed particular thanks, as is Malcolm Swanston and his team, for their several and unique contributions. Above all, this book is a collaboration between authors who have gained through the years an increasingly productive mutual trust and tolerance. We have, therefore, especially each other to thank.

Michael Kidron
Ronald Segal

March 1987

Sovereign states in and since 1945

	sovereign in 1945
	sovereign since 1945
	colonies/'overseas departments'/occupied territories and other anomalies

Sources: Statesman's Year-Book; US Department of State; Wint; press reports

45
1947
1948
1951
1956
1958
1960
1962
1963

JORDAN
MONGOLIA
PHILIPPINES

BHUTAN
INDIA
PAKISTAN

BURMA
ISRAEL
N KOREA
S KOREA
SRI LANKA

EAST GERMANY
WEST GERMANY
INDONESIA
KAMPUCHEA
LAOS TAIWAN
VIETNAM

LIBYA

MOROCCO
SUDAN
TUNISIA

GHANA
MALAYSIA

GUINEA

BENIN CAMEROON
CAR CHAD CONGO CYPRUS
GABON IVORY COAST MADAGASCAR
MALI MAURITANIA NIGER
NIGERIA SENEGAL SOMALIA
TOGO BURKINA ZAIRE

KUWAIT
SIERRA LEONE
TANZANIA

ALGERIA BURUNDI
JAMAICA RWANDA
TRINIDAD AND TOBAGO
UGANDA WESTERN SAMOA

KENYA

MALAWI
MALTA S
ZAMBIA

1. The World of States

Since the Second World War the number of
independent states has grown from 72 to 168.
The proliferation continues.

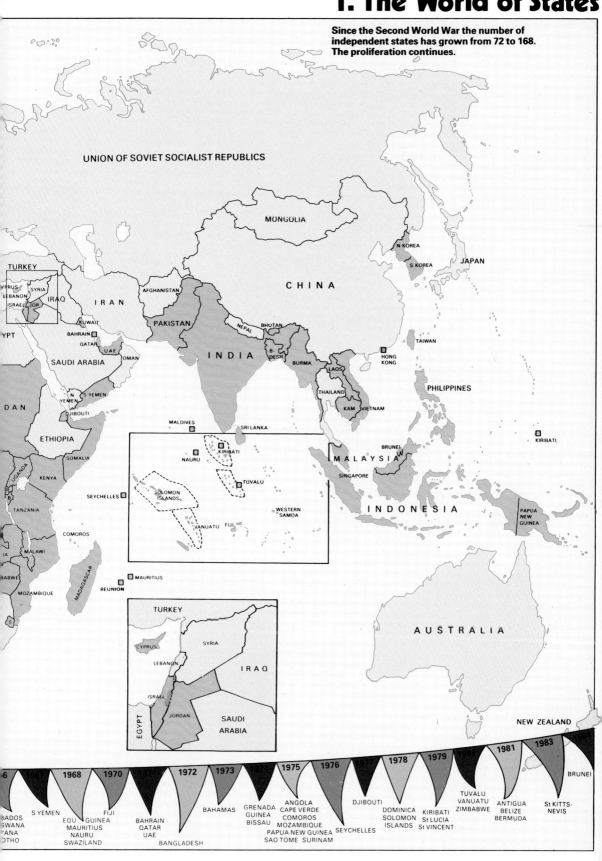

UNION OF SOVIET SOCIALIST REPUBLICS

MONGOLIA

N KOREA

S KOREA

JAPAN

TURKEY

CYPRUS
LEBANON   SYRIA
ISRAEL JOR   IRAQ

IRAN

CHINA

AFGHANISTAN

KUWAIT

BAHRAIN
QATAR
UAE   OMAN

PAKISTAN

NEPAL

BHUTAN

TAIWAN

SAUDI ARABIA

INDIA

B.
DESH

BURMA

HONG
KONG

YPT

N
YEMEN   S YEMEN

DJIBOUTI

LAOS

PHILIPPINES

DAN

ETHIOPIA

SOMALIA

THAILAND

KAM   VIETNAM

MALDIVES

SRI LANKA

UGANDA

KENYA

NAURU

KIRIBATI

BRUNEI

MALAYSIA

KIRIBATI

B)

SEYCHELLES

TUVALU

SINGAPORE

TANZANIA

SOLOMON
ISLANDS

WESTERN
SAMOA

INDONESIA

PAPUA
NEW
GUINEA

COMOROS

VANUATU   FIJI

MALAWI

ABWE

MOZAMBIQUE

MAURITIUS

REUNION

MADAGASCAR

TURKEY

CYPRUS

SYRIA

LEBANON

IRAQ

AUSTRALIA

ISRAEL

EGYPT

JORDAN

SAUDI
ARABIA

NEW ZEALAND

BRUNEI

6	1968	1970	1972	1973	1975	1976	1978	1979	1981	1983

BADOS
SWANA
YANA
OTHO

S YEMEN

EQU GUINEA
MAURITIUS
NAURU
SWAZILAND

FIJI

BAHRAIN
QATAR
UAE

BANGLADESH

BAHAMAS

GRENADA
GUINEA
BISSAU

ANGOLA
CAPE VERDE
COMOROS
MOZAMBIQUE
PAPUA NEW GUINEA
SAO TOME SURINAM

DJIBOUTI

SEYCHELLES

DOMINICA
SOLOMON
ISLANDS

KIRIBATI
St LUCIA
St VINCENT

TUVALU
VANUATU
ZIMBABWE

ANTIGUA
BELIZE
BERMUDA

St KITTS-
NEVIS

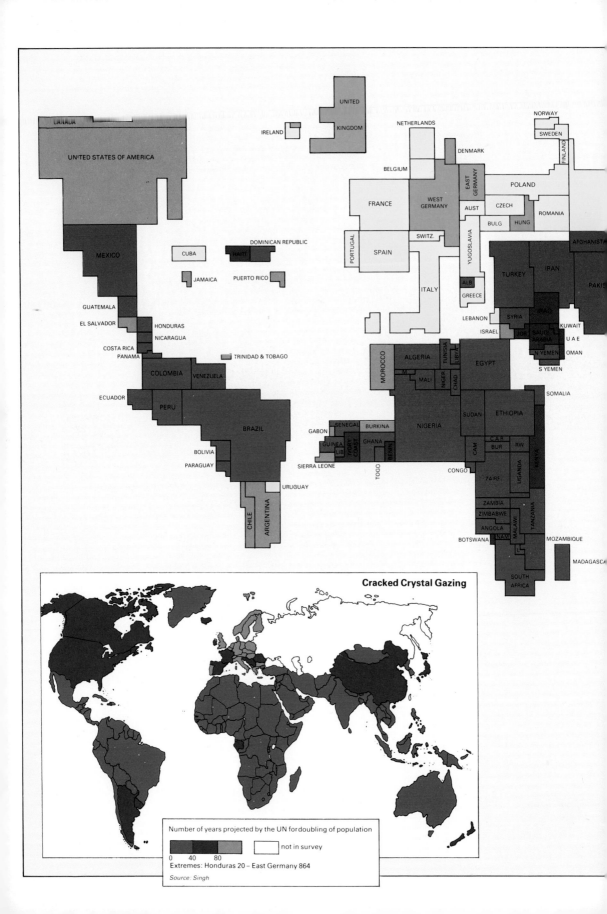

Cracked Crystal Gazing

Number of years projected by the UN for doubling of population

0   40   80   not in survey

Extremes: Honduras 20 – East Germany 864

Source: Singh

By the year 2050 the population of the world will be some 14 billion, or more than three times its present size. The increase will be overwhelmingly among the poor. Yet the poor are poor not because they are many but because resources are disproportionately concentrated among the rich.

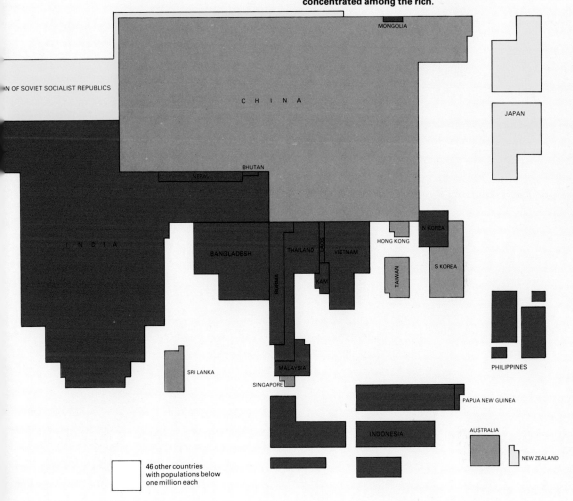

46 other countries
with populations below
one million each

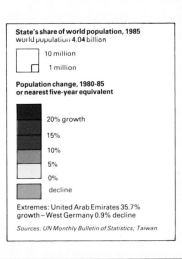

State's share of world population, 1985
world population 4.04 billion

☐ 10 million
☐ 1 million

**Population change, 1980-85
or nearest five-year equivalent**

20% growth
15%
10%
5%
0%
decline

Extremes: United Arab Emirates 35.7%
growth – West Germany 0.9% decline

Sources: UN Monthly Bulletin of Statistics; Taiwan

The Lure of Wealth

Antarctica, one hundred million years ago, showing what were until then continuous mountain ranges; the Transantarctic Mountains connected to the Andes in South America; the Central Antarctic Mountains connected to the Rand in South Africa and to mineral rich areas in Australia.
Vast reserves of coal as well as deposits of oil and natural gas are known to exist in Antarctica, though as yet it is uneconomic to exploit.

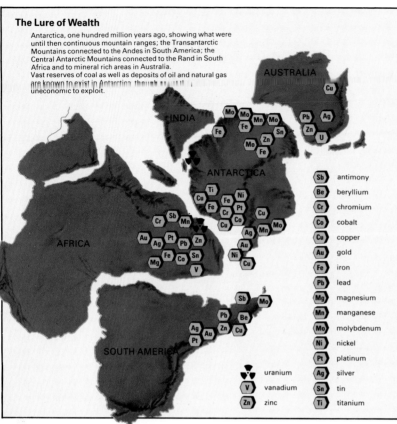

AUSTRALIA

INDIA

ANTARCTICA

AFRICA

SOUTH AMERICA

Sb	antimony
Be	beryllium
Cr	chromium
Co	cobalt
Cu	copper
Au	gold
Fe	iron
Pb	lead
Mg	magnesium
Mn	manganese
Mo	molybdenum
Ni	nickel
Pt	platinum
☢	uranium	Ag	silver
V	vanadium	Sn	tin
Zn	zinc	Ti	titanium

Claimants and Neighbours

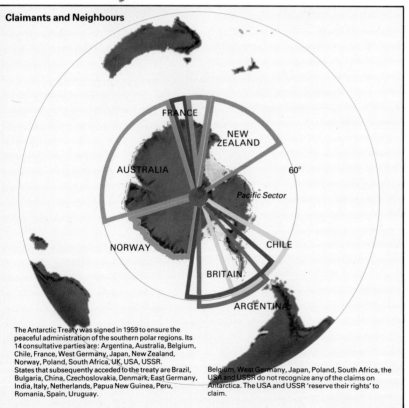

FRANCE

NEW ZEALAND

AUSTRALIA

60°

Pacific Sector

NORWAY

CHILE

BRITAIN

ARGENTINA

The Antarctic Treaty was signed in 1959 to ensure the peaceful administration of the southern polar regions. Its 14 consultative parties are: Argentina, Australia, Belgium, Chile, France, West Germany, Japan, New Zealand, Norway, Poland, South Africa, UK, USA, USSR.
States that subsequently acceded to the treaty are Brazil, Bulgaria, China, Czechoslovakia, Denmark, East Germany, India, Italy, Netherlands, Papua New Guinea, Peru, Romania, Spain, Uruguay.

Belgium, West Germany, Japan, Poland, South Africa, the USA and USSR do not recognize any of the claims on Antarctica. The USA and USSR 'reserve their rights' to claim.

AUST
Casey

USSR
Mirny

AUSTRALIA
Davis

AUSTRALIA
Mawson

USSR
Molodezhnaya

JAPAN
Mizuho

JAPAN
Syowa

US
Novolazarevsk

The Settlers
Scientific stations operating south of the 60th parallel, mid-1980s

Sources: Earthscan; SCAR Bulletin

3. The State Invades Antarctica

In the scramble for Antarctica, it is not geographical proximity but technological superiority and material power that will determine which state ultimately gets what. The scientific station is an assertion of this.

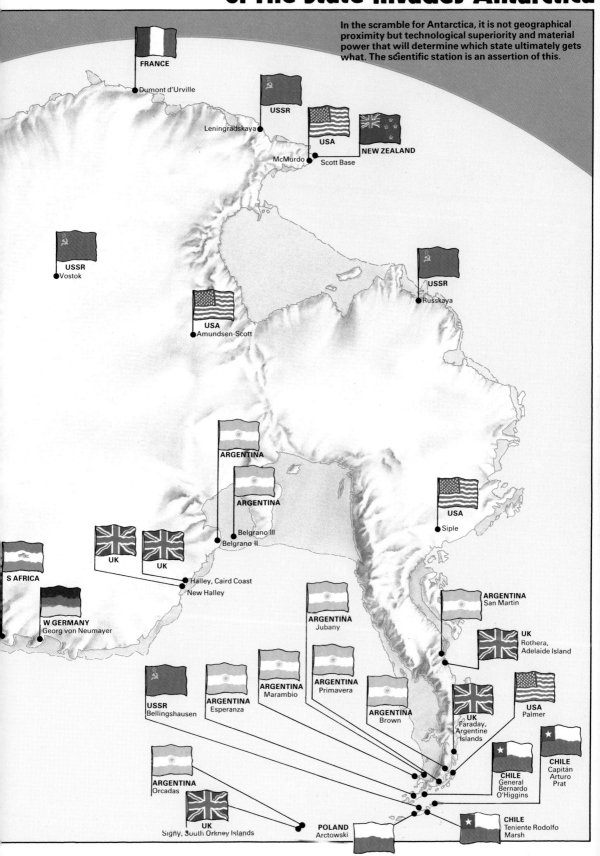

FRANCE Dumont d'Urville

USSR Leningradskaya

USA McMurdo / Scott Base

NEW ZEALAND

USSR Vostok

USA Amundsen-Scott

USSR Russkaya

ARGENTINA

ARGENTINA Belgrano III / Belgrano II

USA Siple

UK Halley, Caird Coast / New Halley

S AFRICA

W GERMANY Georg von Neumayer

ARGENTINA San Martin

UK Rothera, Adelaide Island

ARGENTINA Jubany

ARGENTINA Marambio

ARGENTINA Primavera

ARGENTINA Brown

UK Faraday, Argentine Islands

USA Palmer

USSR Bellingshausen

ARGENTINA Esperanza

CHILE General Bernardo O'Higgins

CHILE Capitán Arturo Prat

ARGENTINA Orcadas

UK Signy, South Orkney Islands

POLAND Arctowski

CHILE Teniente Rodolfo Marsh

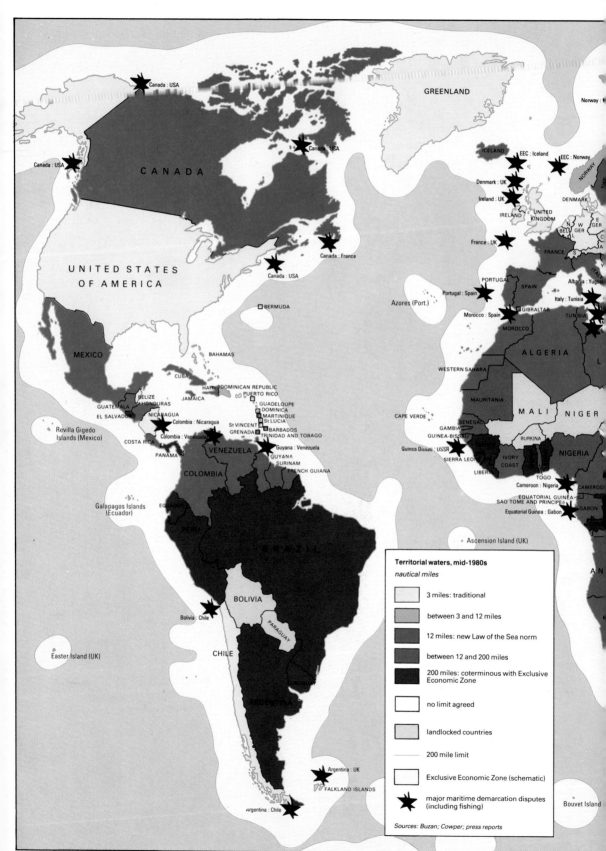

Canada : USA

GREENLAND

Norway :

Canada : USA

Canada : USA

CANADA

ICELAND
EEC : Iceland
EEC : Norway

NORWAY

Denmark : UK

DENMARK

Ireland : UK

IRELAND
UNITED
KINGDOM

N W E
BEL GER
GER

Canada : France

France : UK

FRANCE

S

Canada : USA

UNITED STATES
OF AMERICA

BERMUDA

Azores (Port.)

PORTUGAL

Portugal : Spain

SPAIN

Albania : Yugos

ITALY

Italy : Tunisia

Morocco : Spain

GIBRALTAR

TUNISIA

MOROCCO

MEXICO

BAHAMAS

CUBA

WESTERN SAHARA

ALGERIA

L

Revilla Gigedo
Islands (Mexico)

GUATEMALA
BELIZE
HONDURAS
EL SALVADOR
NICARAGUA
COSTA RICA
PANAMA

HAITI
DOMINICAN REPUBLIC
PUERTO RICO
JAMAICA
GUADELOUPE
DOMINICA
MARTINIQUE
St LUCIA
BARBADOS
TRINIDAD AND TOBAGO

Colombia : Nicaragua

St VINCENT
GRENADA

Colombia : Venezuela

Guyana : Venezuela

CAPE VERDE

MAURITANIA

M A L I

N I G E R

SENEGAL
GAMBIA
GUINEA-BISSAU

Guinea Bissau : USSR

BURKINA

NIGERIA

VENEZUELA

COLOMBIA

GUYANA
SURINAM
FRENCH GUIANA

SIERRA LEON

IVORY
COAST

LIBERIA

TOGO

Galapagos Islands
(Ecuador)

ECUADOR

PERU

B R A Z I L

Ascension Island (UK)

Cameroon : Nigeria

CAMEROO

EQUATORIAL GUINEA
SAO TOME AND PRINCIPE

Equatorial Guinea : Gabon

GABON

AN

Easter Island (UK)

BOLIVIA

Bolivia : Chile

PARAGUAY

CHILE

URUGUAY

ARGENTINA

Argentina : UK

FALKLAND ISLANDS

Argentina : Chile

Bouvet Island

Territorial waters, mid-1980s

nautical miles

3 miles: traditional

between 3 and 12 miles

12 miles: new Law of the Sea norm

between 12 and 200 miles

200 miles: coterminous with Exclusive
Economic Zone

no limit agreed

landlocked countries

200 mile limit

Exclusive Economic Zone (schematic)

★ major maritime demarcation disputes
(including fishing)

Sources: Buzan; Cowper; press reports

4. The State Invades the Sea

The scramble to extend state control over one-third of the world's sea area continues. In 1987, the UK asserted total jurisdiction over the waters surrounding the Falkland Islands, in conflict with Argentina's claims. By then, the Third UN Convention on the Law of the Sea, signed by 138 states in 1982, had been ratified by only 14, or 46 fewer than required.

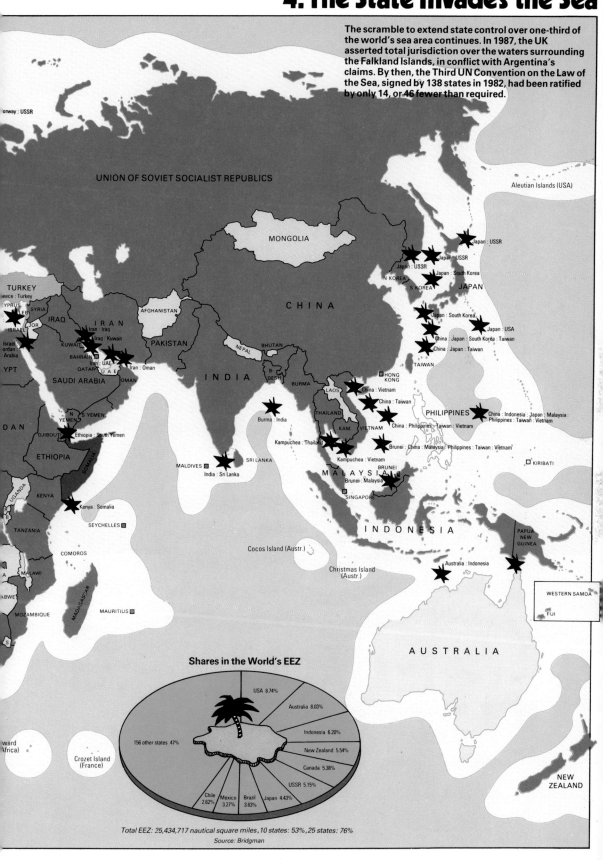

orway : USSR

Aleutian Islands (USA)

UNION OF SOVIET SOCIALIST REPUBLICS

MONGOLIA

Japan : USSR

Japan : USSR

Japan : USSR

Japan : South Korea

N KOREA

S KOREA

JAPAN

TURKEY

eece : Turkey

YPRUS

LEB

SYRIA

IRAQ

JOR

ISRAEL

Israel : Jordan : Arabia

YPT

SAUDI ARABIA

AFGHANISTAN

IRAN

Iran : Iraq

Iraq : Kuwait

KUWAIT

BAHRAIN

QATAR

U A E

Iran : UAE

Iran : Oman

OMAN

PAKISTAN

NEPAL

BHUTAN

INDIA

B DESH

BURMA

CHINA

Japan : South Korea

Japan : USA

China : Japan : South Korea : Taiwan

China : Japan : Taiwan

TAIWAN

HONG KONG

PHILIPPINES

China : Indonesia : Japan : Malaysia : Philippines : Taiwan : Vietnam

DAN

N YEMEN

S YEMEN

DJIBOUTI

Ethiopia : South Yemen

ETHIOPIA

SOMALIA

Burma : India

SRI LANKA

Kampuchea : Thailand

LAOS

THAILAND

KAM

VIETNAM

China : Vietnam

China : Taiwan

China : Philippines : Taiwan : Vietnam

Brunei : China : Malaysia : Philippines : Taiwan : Vietnam

KIRIBATI

MALDIVES

India : Sri Lanka

Kampuchea : Vietnam

BRUNEI

Brunei : Malaysia

UGANDA

KENYA

Kenya : Somalia

SEYCHELLES

TANZANIA

COMOROS

MADAGASCAR

MAURITIUS

MALAWI

ABWE

MOZAMBIQUE

M A L A Y S I A

SINGAPORE

I N D O N E S I A

Cocos Island (Austr.)

Christmas Island (Austr.)

Australia : Indonesia

PAPUA NEW GUINEA

WESTERN SAMOA

FIJI

A U S T R A L I A

NEW ZEALAND

ward (Africa)

Crozet Island (France)

Shares in the World's EEZ

USA 8.74%

Australia 8.03%

Indonesia 6.20%

New Zealand 5.54%

Canada 5.38%

USSR 5.15%

156 other states 47%

Chile 2.62%

Mexico 3.27%

Brazil 3.63%

Japan 4.43%

Total EEZ: 25,434,717 nautical square miles, 10 states: 53%, 25 states: 76%

Source: Bridgman

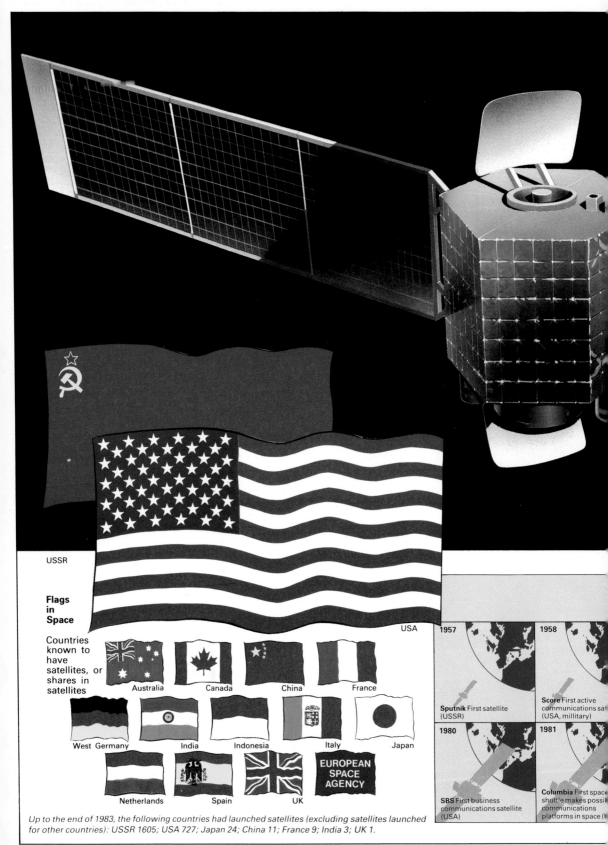

USSR

Flags in Space

Countries known to have satellites, or shares in satellites

Australia Canada China France

West Germany India Indonesia Italy Japan

Netherlands Spain UK EUROPEAN SPACE AGENCY

USA

1957
Sputnik First satellite (USSR)

1958
Score First active communications sat (USA, military)

1980
SBS First business communications satellite (USA)

1981
Columbia First space shuttle makes possi communications platforms in space (U

Up to the end of 1983, the following countries had launched satellites (excluding satellites launched for other countries): USSR 1605; USA 727; Japan 24; China 11; France 9; India 3; UK 1.

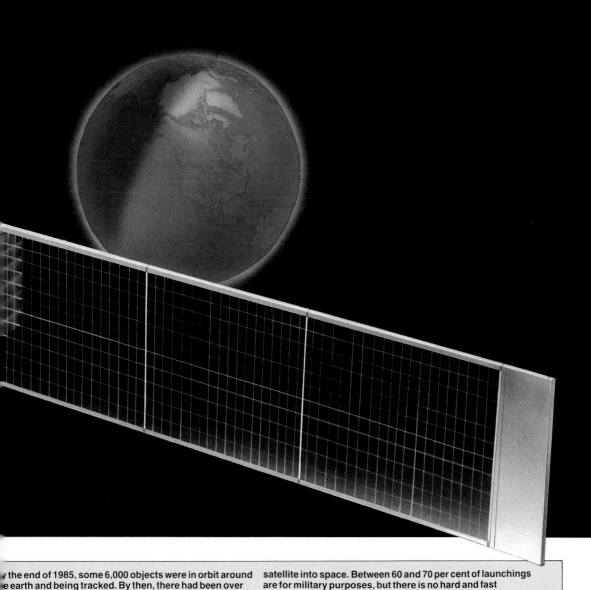

y the end of 1985, some 6,000 objects were in orbit around e earth and being tracked. By then, there had been over 300 launchings, some of them putting more than one satellite into space. Between 60 and 70 per cent of launchings are for military purposes, but there is no hard and fast division between military and commercial uses.

	1963	1965	1966	1972	1979
st active al ations satellite	**Syncom II** First 'parked' satellite for continuous use (USA)	**Early Bird** First commercial communications satellite (USA)	**Intelsat** First international communications satellite, providing telephone circuits	**Telesat** First communications satellite launched by USA for another country (Canada)	**Ariane** First European Space Agency satellite launched

	1984	1985		1986	
te to handle, usly, meteorology casting (India)	**Arianespace** First commercial launch (France/Europe) **NASA** First flight of shuttle, Discovery (USA)	**NASA** Shuttle disaster on launch, Challenger (USA) **Arianespace** Ariane failure loses two communications satellites (France/Europe) **China** Announces intention of entering space haulage business		**Arianespace** Failure of two launches grounds Ariane until 1987 (France/Europe) **NASA** Delta rocket explodes on launch (USA) NASA withdraws from commercial satellite launching business (USA) **China** Contracts to launch two satellites for Teresat, Houston, Texas **MCI** Annouces replacement of satellite-borne telephone circuits with submarine fibre-optic cables (USA)	

Sources: Kidron & Smith; Royal Aircraft Establishment; press reports

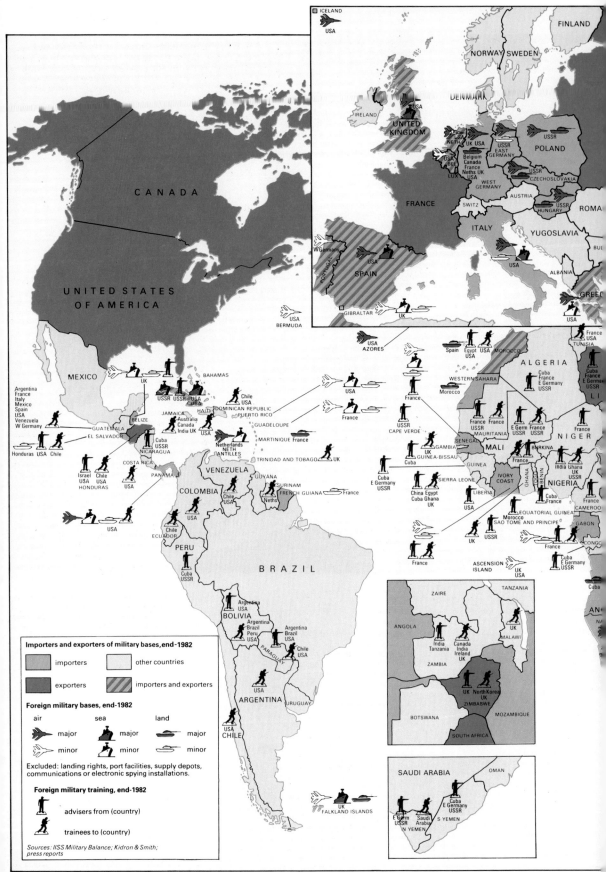

The international military order has spawned about 3,000 foreign military bases and installations along with innumerable military advisers and trainees. By the mid-1980s, some two million military personnel were serving abroad in 91 foreign countries and territories.

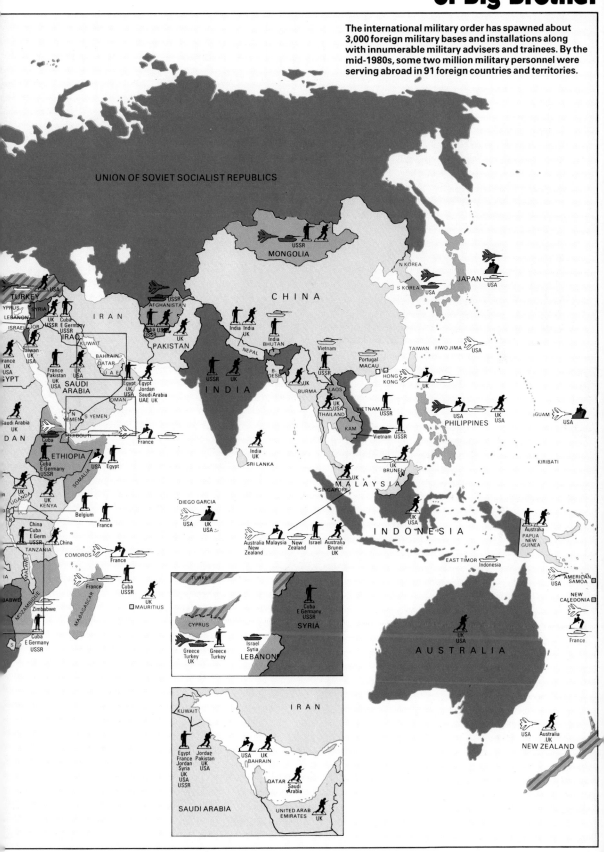

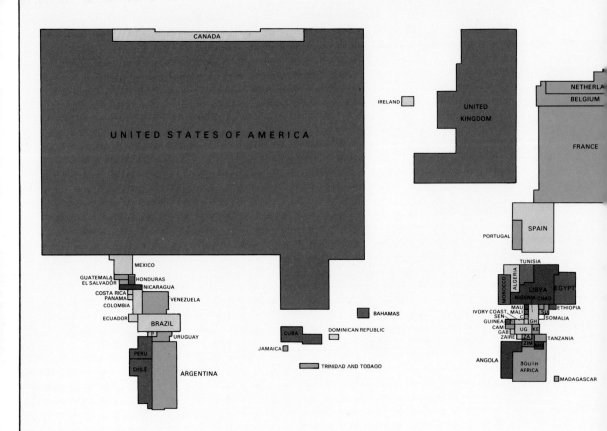

CANADA

IRELAND

UNITED
KINGDOM

NETHERLA

BELGIUM

FRANCE

UNITED STATES OF AMERICA

PORTUGAL

SPAIN

TUNISIA

MEXICO

GUATEMALA
EL SALVADOR
HONDURAS
NICARAGUA

MOROCCO
ALGERIA
LIBYA
EGYPT

COSTA RICA
PANAMA
COLOMBIA

VENEZUELA

NIGERIA
CHAD
ETHIOPIA

ECUADOR

BRAZIL

BAHAMAS

MAU
MALI
IVORY COAST
SEN
SOMALIA

URUGUAY

DOMINICAN REPUBLIC

GUINEA
GH
CAM
GAB
UG
KE

PERU

CUBA

ZAIRE
ZA
ZIM
TANZANIA

JAMAICA

CHILE

ARGENTINA

TRINIDAD AND TOBAGO

ANGOLA

SOUTH
AFRICA

MADAGASCAR

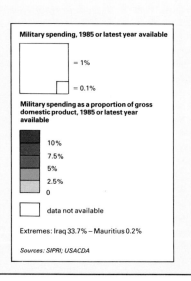

Military spending, 1985 or latest year available

☐ = 1%

☐ = 0.1%

Military spending as a proportion of gross domestic product, 1985 or latest year available

■ 10%

■ 7.5%

■ 5%

■ 2.5%

☐ 0

☐ data not available

Extremes: Iraq 33.7% – Mauritius 0.2%

Sources: SIPRI; USACDA

About $US 800 billion were spent on the military in 1985, substantially more than all the wealth generated by the 2,200 million people living in China, India and Black Africa. The USA and USSR together account for more than half of all military spending.

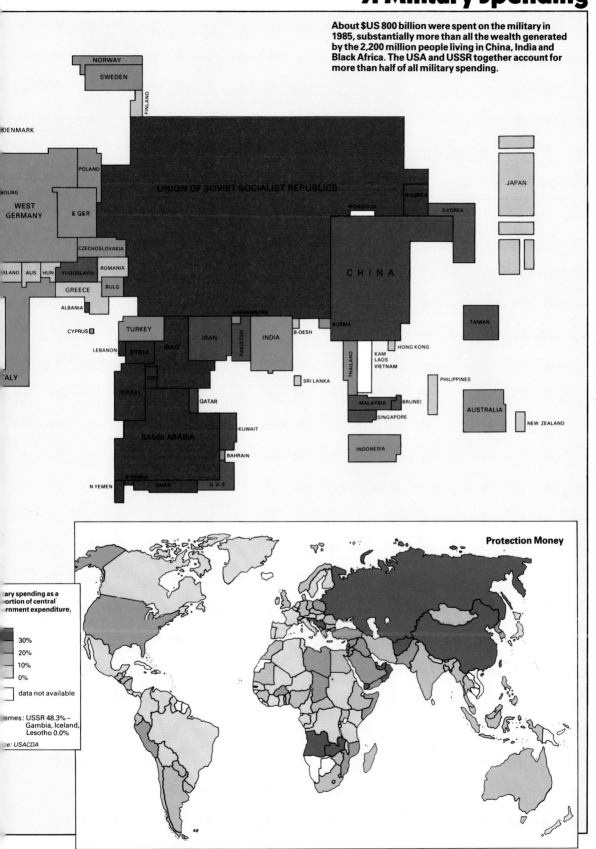

NORWAY
SWEDEN
FINLAND
DENMARK
POLAND
NOURG
WEST GERMANY
E GER
UNION OF SOVIET SOCIALIST REPUBLICS
N KOREA
JAPAN
MONGOLIA
S KOREA
CZECHOSLOVAKIA
RLAND AUS HUN YUGOSLAVIA ROMANIA
GREECE BULG
CHINA
ALBANIA
TALY
CYPRUS
TURKEY
AFGHANISTAN
TAIWAN
LEBANON SYRIA IRAQ IRAN PAKISTAN INDIA B-DESH BURMA
HONG KONG
JOR
THAILAND
KAM
LAOS
VIETNAM
ISRAEL
QATAR
SRI LANKA
PHILIPPINES
KUWAIT
MALAYSIA BRUNEI
AUSTRALIA
NEW ZEALAND
SINGAPORE
SAUDI ARABIA
BAHRAIN
S YEMEN
INDONESIA
N YEMEN OMAN U A E

Protection Money

ary spending as a
ortion of central
rnment expenditure,

30%
20%
10%
0%

data not available

emes: USSR 48.3% –
Gambia, Iceland,
Lesotho 0.0%

ce: USACDA

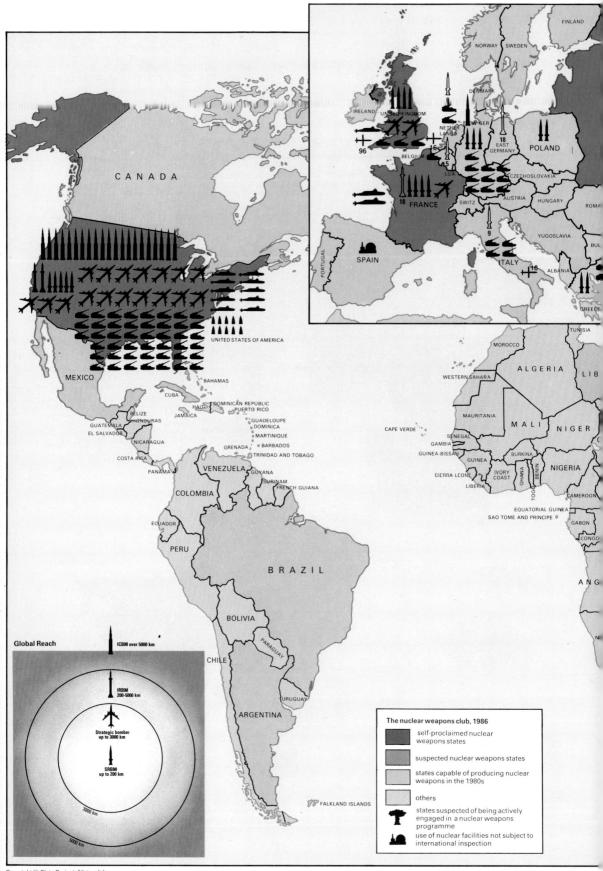

CANADA

UNITED STATES OF AMERICA

MEXICO

BELIZE
GUATEMALA   HONDURAS
EL SALVADOR
NICARAGUA
COSTA RICA
PANAMA

CUBA
BAHAMAS
JAMAICA   HAITI   DOMINICAN REPUBLIC
PUERTO RICO
GUADELOUPE
DOMINICA
MARTINIQUE
GRENADA   BARBADOS
TRINIDAD AND TOBAGO

VENEZUELA
GUYANA
COLOMBIA   SURINAM
FRENCH GUIANA
ECUADOR

PERU

BRAZIL

BOLIVIA

PARAGUAY

CHILE

URUGUAY

ARGENTINA

FALKLAND ISLANDS

IRELAND   UNITED KINGDOM
96
NETHER
LANDS
16
BELGIUM
LUX
5
18   FRANCE
SWITZ
SPAIN
PORTUGAL

NORWAY   SWEDEN   FINLAND

DENMARK
W. GER
18
EAST
GERMANY   POLAND
CZECHOSLOVAKIA
AUSTRIA   HUNGARY
ROMA
9
YUGOSLAVIA
BUL
ITALY   16   ALBANIA
GREECE

TUNISIA
MOROCCO
ALGERIA   LIB
WESTERN SAHARA
MAURITANIA
MALI   NIGER
CAPE VERDE
SENEGAL
GAMBIA
GUINEA-BISSAU
GUINEA   BURKINA   NIGERIA
SIERRA LEONE   IVORY
COAST   GHANA   BENIN
LIBERIA   TOGO   CAMEROON
EQUATORIAL GUINEA   GABON
SAO TOME AND PRINCIPE   CONGO
ANG

Global Reach

ICBM over 5000 km

IRBM
200-5000 km

Strategic bomber
up to 3000 km

SRBM
up to 200 km

3000 km

5000 km

The nuclear weapons club, 1986

self-proclaimed nuclear
weapons states

suspected nuclear weapons states

states capable of producing nuclear
weapons in the 1980s

others

states suspected of being actively
engaged in a nuclear weapons
programme

use of nuclear facilities not subject to
international inspection

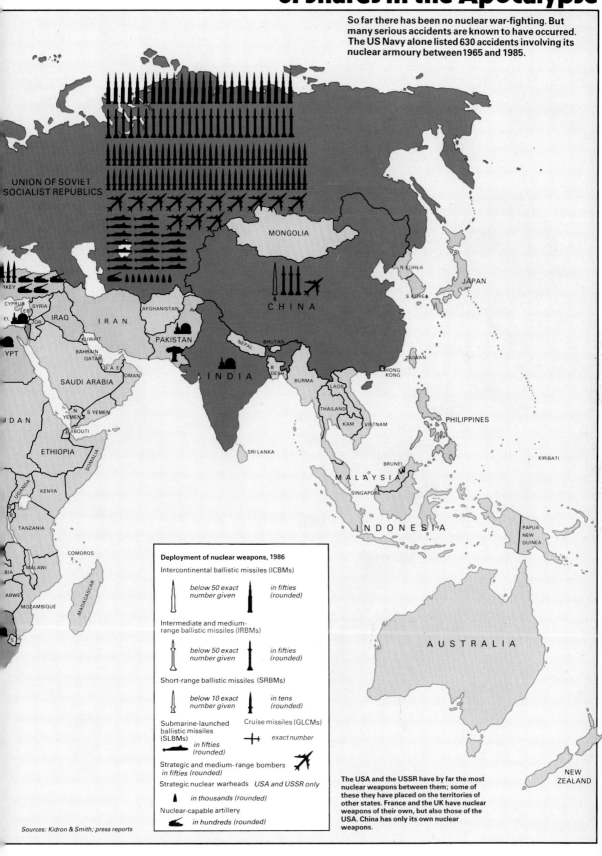

So far there has been no nuclear war-fighting. But many serious accidents are known to have occurred. The US Navy alone listed 630 accidents involving its nuclear armoury between 1965 and 1985.

UNION OF SOVIET SOCIALIST REPUBLICS

MONGOLIA

N KOREA

JAPAN

S KOREA

CHINA

TURKEY

CYPRUS
SYRIA
LEB
EL
OR
IRAQ
IRAN
AFGHANISTAN

YPT

KUWAIT
BAHRAIN
QATAR
U.A.E
OMAN
PAKISTAN

NEPAL
BHUTAN
B DESH

TAIWAN

HONG KONG

SAUDI ARABIA

INDIA

BURMA

LAOS

N YEMEN
S YEMEN
DJIBOUTI

THAILAND

KAM VIETNAM

PHILIPPINES

UDAN

ETHIOPIA

SOMALIA

SRI LANKA

UGANDA
KENYA
B

BRUNEI

KIRIBATI

MALAYSIA

TANZANIA

COMOROS

SINGAPORE

INDONESIA

PAPUA NEW GUINEA

BIA
MALAWI

MADAGASCAR

ABWE
MOZAMBIQUE

S

AUSTRALIA

Deployment of nuclear weapons, 1986

Intercontinental ballistic missiles (ICBMs)

below 50 exact number given   *in fifties (rounded)*

Intermediate and medium-range ballistic missiles (IRBMs)

below 50 exact number given   *in fifties (rounded)*

Short-range ballistic missiles (SRBMs)

below 10 exact number given   *in tens (rounded)*

Submarine-launched ballistic missiles (SLBMs)

Cruise missiles (GLCMs)

exact number

in fifties (rounded)

Strategic and medium-range bombers *in fifties (rounded)*

Strategic nuclear warheads   *USA and USSR only*

in thousands (rounded)

Nuclear-capable artillery

in hundreds (rounded)

NEW ZEALAND

The USA and the USSR have by far the most nuclear weapons between them; some of these they have placed on the territories of other states. France and the UK have nuclear weapons of their own, but also those of the USA. China has only its own nuclear weapons.

Sources: Kidron & Smith; press reports

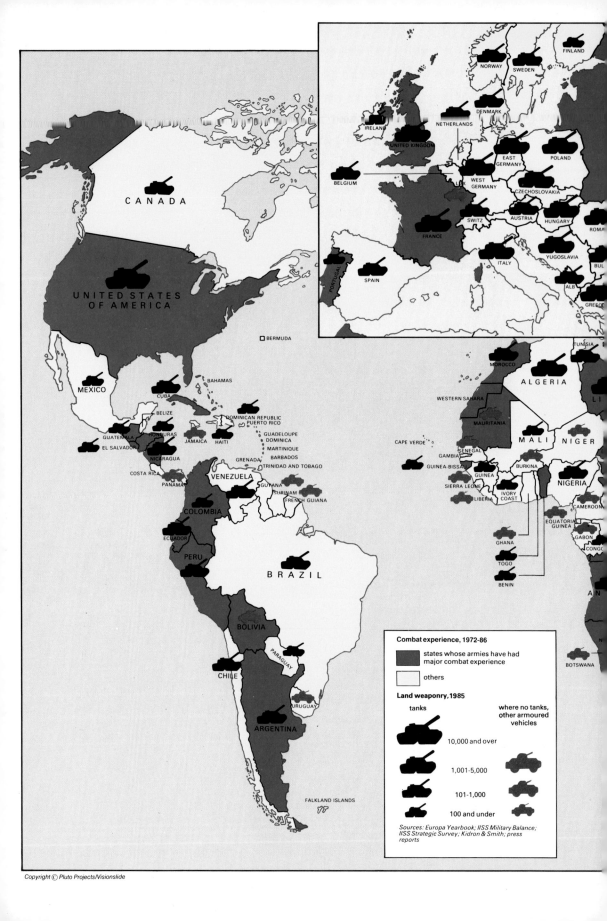

CANADA

UNITED STATES
OF AMERICA

BERMUDA

MEXICO

BAHAMAS

CUBA

BELIZE

DOMINICAN REPUBLIC
PUERTO RICO

GUATEMALA
HONDURAS
EL SALVADOR
NICARAGUA

JAMAICA   HAITI

GUADELOUPE
DOMINICA

MARTINIQUE

COSTA RICA

GRENADA   BARBADOS
TRINIDAD AND TOBAGO

PANAMA

VENEZUELA

GUYANA

SURINAM
FRENCH GUIANA

COLOMBIA

ECUADOR

PERU

BRAZIL

BOLIVIA

PARAGUAY

CHILE

URUGUAY

ARGENTINA

FALKLAND ISLANDS

NORWAY   SWEDEN   FINLAND

DENMARK

IRELAND   NETHERLANDS

UNITED KINGDOM

EAST
GERMANY   POLAND

BELGIUM   LUX.

WEST
GERMANY   CZECHOSLOVAKIA

SWITZ.   AUSTRIA   HUNGARY   ROMA

FRANCE

ITALY   YUGOSLAVIA   BUL

PORTUGAL   SPAIN   ALB

GREECE

MOROCCO   TUNISIA

ALGERIA   LI

WESTERN SAHARA

MAURITANIA

MALI   NIGER

CAPE VERDE

SENEGAL

GAMBIA

GUINEA-BISSAU   GUINEA   BURKINA   NIGERIA

SIERRA LEONE

LIBERIA   IVORY
COAST

CAMEROON

EQUATORIAL
GUINEA

GHANA   GABON   CONGO

TOGO

BENIN   AN

BOTSWANA

N

Copyright © Pluto Projects/Visionslide

Combat experience, 1972-86

states whose armies have had
major combat experience

others

Land weaponry, 1985

tanks   where no tanks,
                               other armoured
                               vehicles

10,000 and over

1,001-5,000

101-1,000

100 and under

*Sources: Europa Yearbook; IISS Military Balance;
IISS Strategic Survey; Kidron & Smith; press
reports*

9. Conventional Killing

There are about 26 million people in the military forces of the world; and another 52 million who keep them supplied.

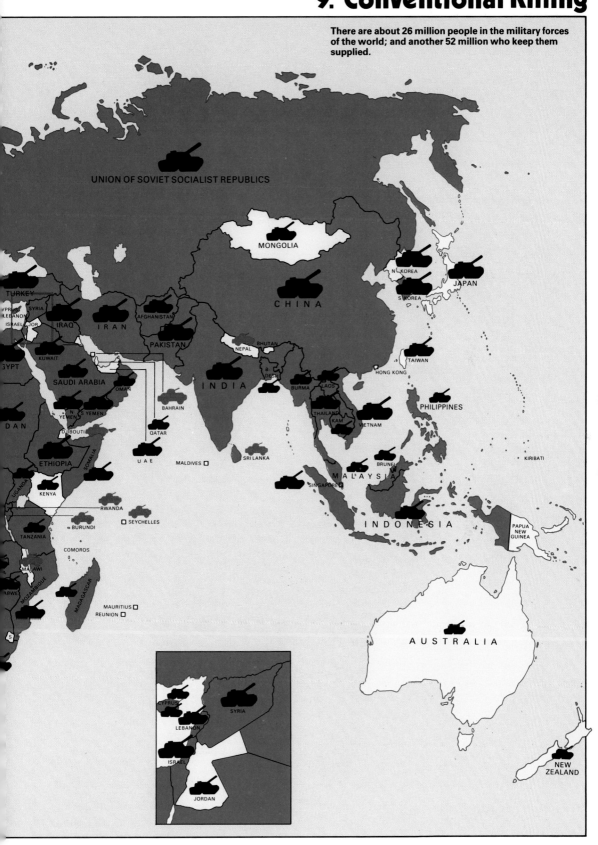

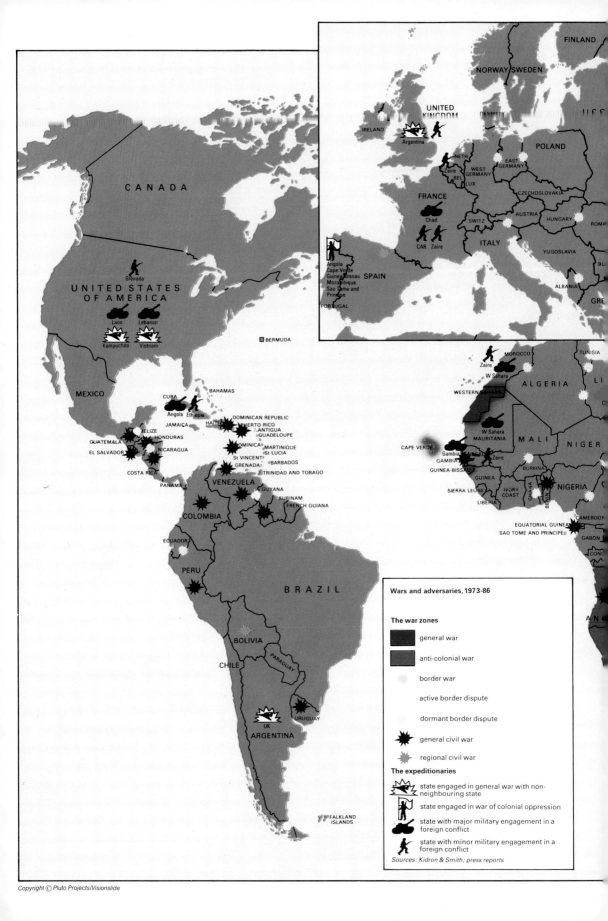

The war zones map showing:

CANADA

UNITED STATES OF AMERICA
- Grenada
- Laos
- Lebanon
- Kampuchea
- Vietnam

BERMUDA

MEXICO

CUBA
Angola / Ethiopia
JAMAICA
HAITI
BAHAMAS
BELIZE
HONDURAS
GUATEMALA
EL SALVADOR
NICARAGUA
COSTA RICA
PANAMA

DOMINICAN REPUBLIC
PUERTO RICO
ANTIGUA
GUADELOUPE
DOMINICA
MARTINIQUE
St LUCIA
St VINCENT
GRENADA
BARBADOS
TRINIDAD AND TOBAGO

VENEZUELA
GUYANA
SURINAM
FRENCH GUIANA

COLOMBIA

ECUADOR

PERU

BRAZIL

BOLIVIA

CHILE
PARAGUAY

URUGUAY

UK
ARGENTINA

FALKLAND ISLANDS

Europe inset:

FINLAND
NORWAY / SWEDEN
UNITED KINGDOM
Argentina
IRELAND
DENMARK
NETH
Zaire
BEL
LUX
WEST GERMANY
EAST GERMANY
POLAND
FRANCE
Chad
CAR / Zaire
SWITZ
AUSTRIA
CZECHOSLOVAKIA
HUNGARY
ITALY
YUGOSLAVIA
ALBANIA
ROMA
GRE

Angola
Cape Verde
Guinea Bissau
Mozambique
Sao Tome and Principe
SPAIN
PORTUGAL

Africa:

MOROCCO
Zaire
W Sahara
TUNISIA
WESTERN SAHARA
ALGERIA
LI
W Sahara
MAURITANIA
MALI
NIGER
CAPE VERDE
Gambia / Zaire
GAMBIA
GUINEA-BISSAU
GUINEA
BURKINA
SIERRA LEONE
IVORY COAST
GHANA
BENIN
NIGERIA
LIBERIA
EQUATORIAL GUINEA
SAO TOME AND PRINCIPE
CAMEROON
GABON
CONG
AN
N

Legend:

Wars and adversaries, 1973-86

The war zones

- general war
- anti-colonial war
- border war
- active border dispute
- dormant border dispute
- general civil war
- regional civil war

The expeditionaries

- state engaged in general war with non-neighbouring state
- state engaged in war of colonial oppression
- state with major military engagement in a foreign conflict
- state with minor military engagement in a foreign conflict

Sources: Kidron & Smith; press reports

The apologists say that expenditure on arms has helped to keep the peace. Some peace!

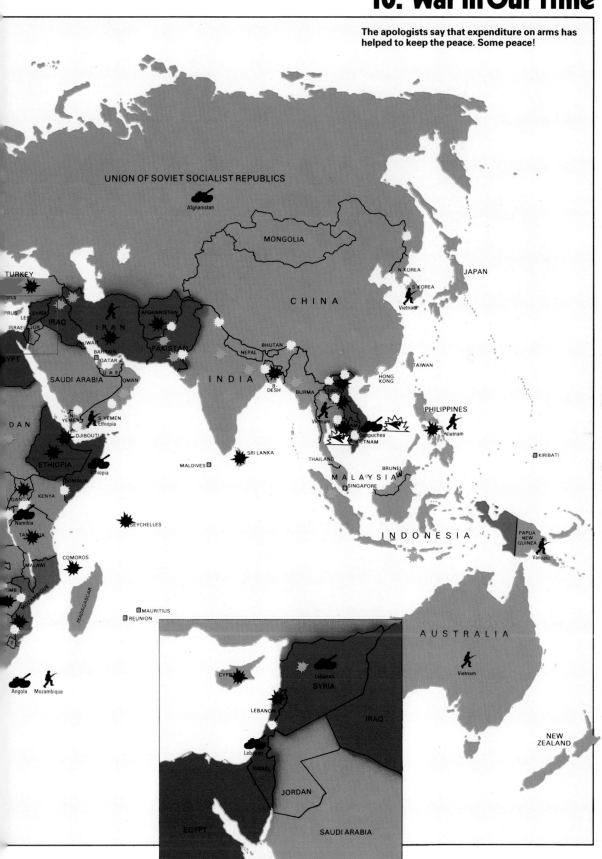

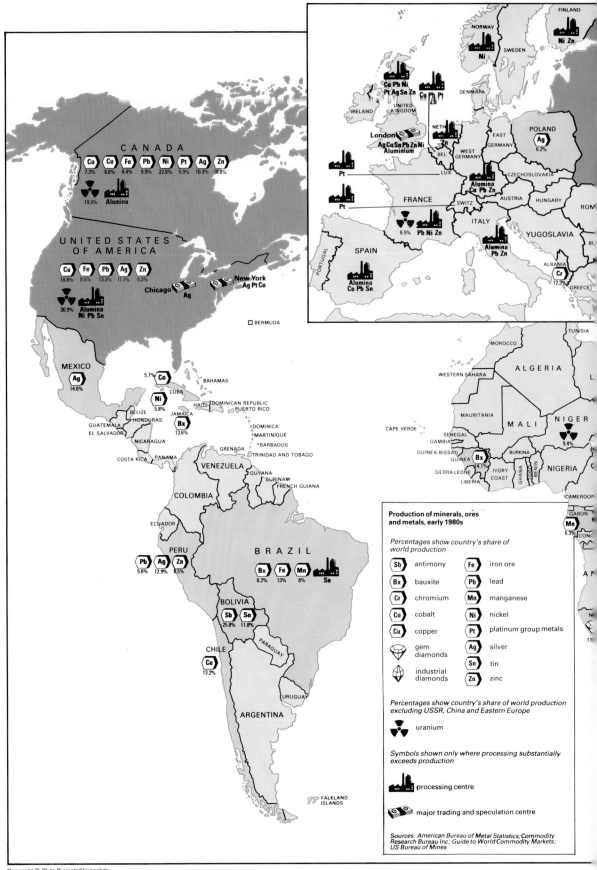

Production of minerals, ores and metals, early 1980s

Percentages show country's share of world production

Sb	antimony	**Fe**	iron ore
Bx	bauxite	**Pb**	lead
Cr	chromium	**Mn**	manganese
Co	cobalt	**Ni**	nickel
Cu	copper	**Pt**	platinum group metals
	gem diamonds	**Ag**	silver
	industrial diamonds	**Sn**	tin
		Zn	zinc

Percentages show country's share of world production excluding USSR, China and Eastern Europe

uranium

Symbols shown only where processing substantially exceeds production

processing centre

major trading and speculation centre

Sources: American Bureau of Metal Statistics; Commodity Research Bureau Inc; Guide to World Commodity Markets; US Bureau of Mines

Copyright © Pluto Projects/Visionslide

Minerals are the raw material of economic power.
States that possess them do not necessarily own them
or control their use. Those states that both possess
them and exercise such control are major mineral
powers.

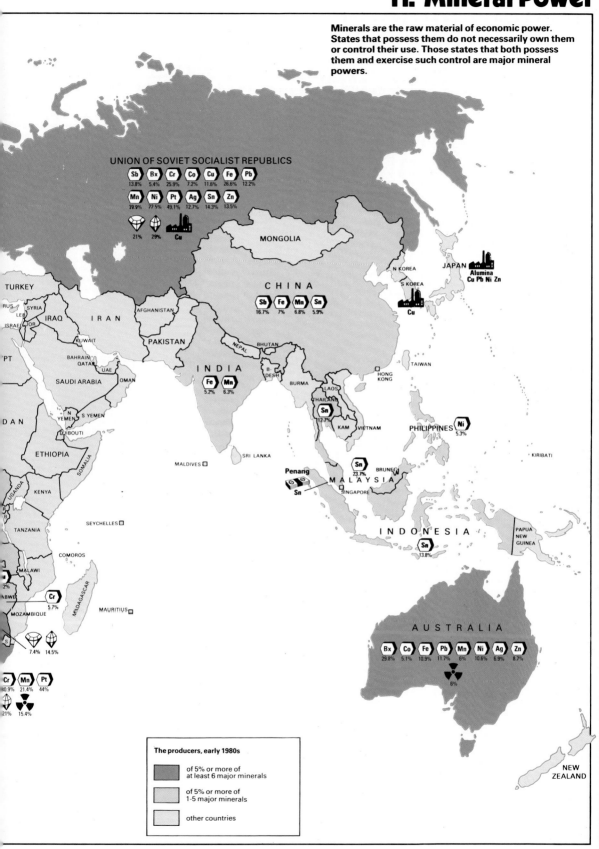

UNION OF SOVIET SOCIALIST REPUBLICS

Sb	Bx	Cr	Co	Cu	Fe	Pb
13.8%	5.4%	25.9%	7.2%	11.6%	26.6%	12.2%

Mn	Ni	Pt	Ag	Sn	Zn
39.9%	77.5%	49.1%	12.7%	14.3%	13.5%

21% 29% Cu

MONGOLIA

JAPAN Alumina Cu Pb Ni Zn

N KOREA
S KOREA   Cu

CHINA

Sb	Fe	Mn	Sn
16.7%	7%	6.8%	5.9%

TURKEY
RUS SYRIA
LEB
ISRAEL JOR   IRAQ   I R A N   AFGHANISTAN
KUWAIT   PAKISTAN
BAHRAIN
PT   QATAR
SAUDI ARABIA   UAE   OMAN

NEPAL   BHUTAN
B-DESH
I N D I A

Fe	Mn
5.2%	6.3%

BURMA   TAIWAN

HONG KONG

LAOS
THAILAND

Sn
12.7%

KAM VIETNAM

PHILIPPINES

Ni
5.3%

KIRIBATI

DAN
N YEMEN S YEMEN
DJIBOUTI

ETHIOPIA

SOMALIA

UGANDA
KENYA

SEYCHELLES ▢

MALDIVES ▢

SRI LANKA

Penang
Sn

MALAYSIA

Sn
23.7%

BRUNEI
N

SINGAPORE

TANZANIA

COMOROS

MALAWI

ZBWE

Cr
5.7%

MADAGASCAR

MAURITIUS ▢

MOZAMBIQUE

7.4% 14.5%

I N D O N E S I A

Sn
13.8%

PAPUA
NEW
GUINEA

A U S T R A L I A

Bx	Co	Fe	Pb	Mn	Ni	Ag	Zn
29.8%	5.1%	10.9%	11.7%	6%	10.6%	6.9%	8.7%

6%

Cr	Mn	Pt
40.9%	21.4%	44%

21% 15.4%

**NEW
ZEALAND**

The producers, early 1980s

of 5% or more of
at least 6 major minerals

of 5% or more of
1-5 major minerals

other countries

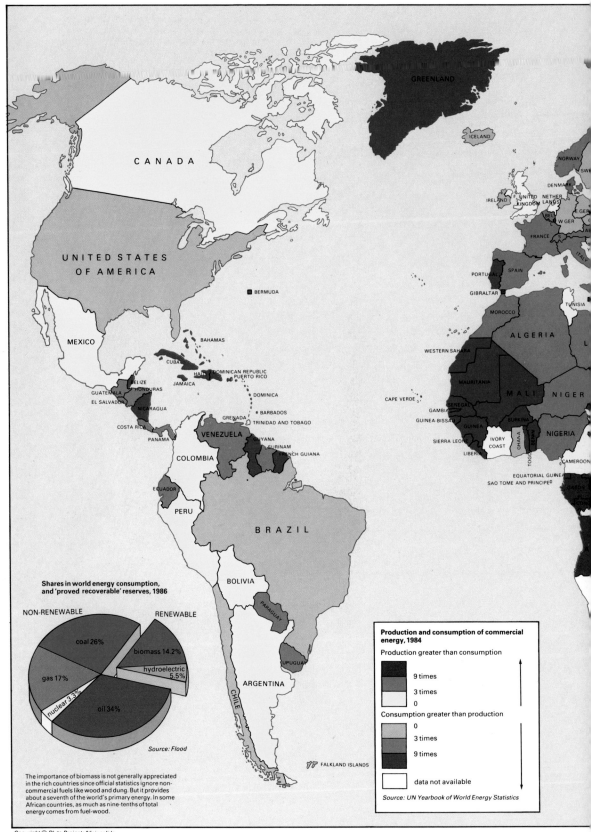

Shares in world energy consumption, and 'proved recoverable' reserves, 1986

Source: Flood

The importance of biomass is not generally appreciated in the rich countries since official statistics ignore non-commercial fuels like wood and dung. But it provides about a seventh of the world's primary energy. In some African countries, as much as nine-tenths of total energy comes from fuel-wood.

Production and consumption of commercial energy, 1984

Source: UN Yearbook of World Energy Statistics

More energy reaches us from the sun than can conceivably be put to human use. Yet many states are energy paupers, and most are energy poor.

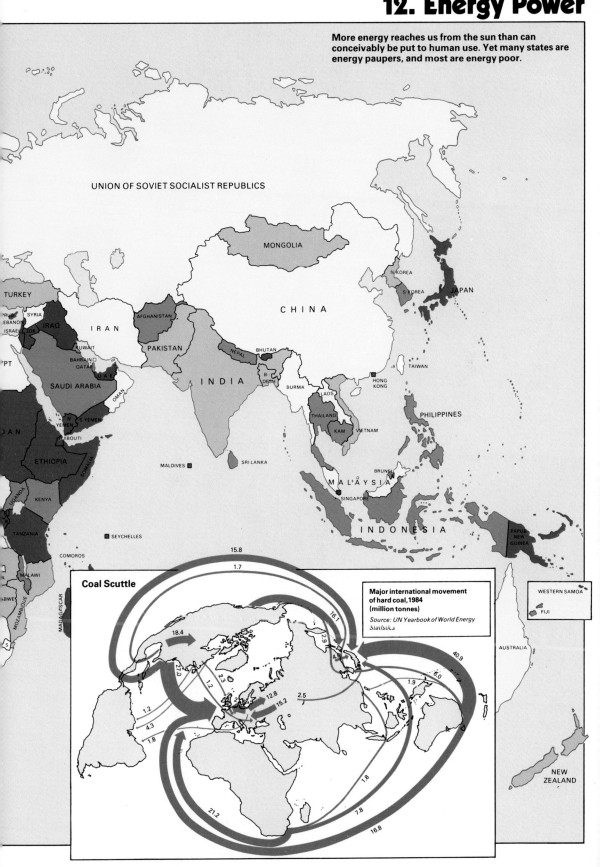

UNION OF SOVIET SOCIALIST REPUBLICS

MONGOLIA

N.KOREA

S.KOREA

JAPAN

CHINA

TURKEY

YPRUS
LEBANON
SYRIA
ISRAEL
JOR
IRAQ
IRAN
AFGHANISTAN
KUWAIT
BAHRAIN
QATAR
U.A.E.
SAUDI ARABIA
OMAN
PAKISTAN
NEPAL
BHUTAN
B'DESH
TAIWAN

HONG KONG

PT

N.YEMEN
S.YEMEN
DJIBOUTI
ETHIOPIA
SOMALIA

DAN

INDIA

BURMA
LAOS
THAILAND
KAM
VIETNAM
PHILIPPINES

UGANDA
KENYA

MALDIVES

SRI LANKA

BRUNEI

MALAYSIA

SINGAPORE

TANZANIA

SEYCHELLES

INDONESIA

PAPUA NEW GUINEA

COMOROS

MADAGASCAR

MALAWI

WESTERN SAMOA

FIJI

ABWE

MOZAMBIQUE

S

Coal Scuttle

Major international movement of hard coal, 1984 (million tonnes)

Source: UN Yearbook of World Energy Statistics

15.8
1.7
16.1
2.9
40.9
18.4
27.0
2.3
1.2
8.0
1.9
1.2
12.8
2.5
15.2
1.2
4.3
1.8
1.8
7.8
21.2
16.8

AUSTRALIA

NEW ZEALAND

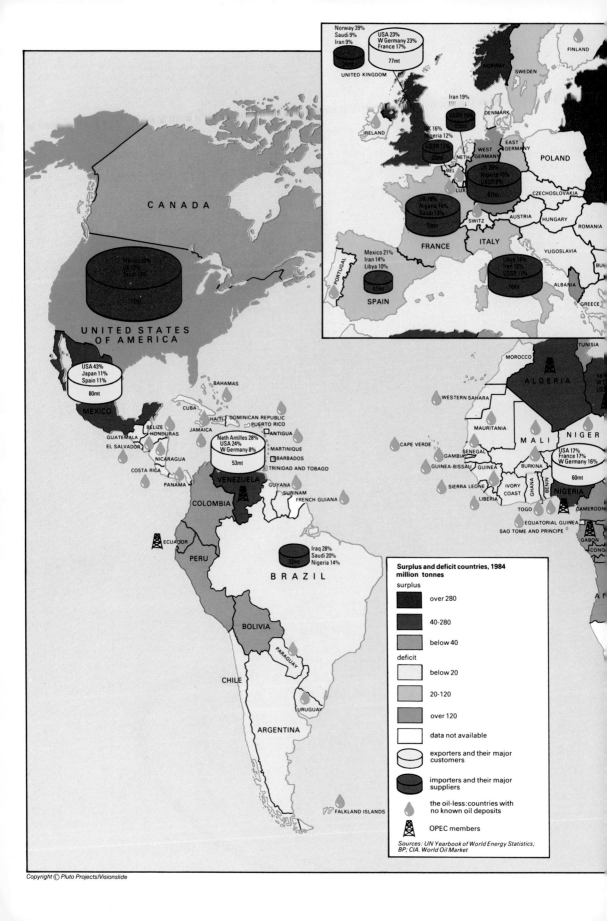

Norway 39%
Saudi 9%
Iran 9%
56mt
UNITED KINGDOM

USA 23%
W Germany 23%
France 17%
77mt

Iran 19%
42mt

UK 16%
Nigeria 12%
USSR 11%
23mt
NETH
BEL
LUX

USSR 10%
32mt
DENMARK

WEST
GERMANY
UK 25%
Nigeria 15%
USSR 9%
87mt
EAST
GERMANY

POLAND

CZECHOSLOVAKIA

UK 19%
Nigeria 14%
Saudi 13%
70mt
FRANCE

AUSTRIA
HUNGARY
SWITZ
ROMANIA
ITALY

Mexico 21%
Iran 14%
Libya 10%
41mt
SPAIN

PORTUGAL

Libya 14%
Iran 12%
USSR 11%
76mt

YUGOSLAVIA
ALBANIA
GREECE

FINLAND
SWEDEN
NORWAY
IRELAND

CANADA

UNITED STATES
OF AMERICA

Mexico 20%
UK 10%
Saudi 10%
172mt

USA 43%
Japan 11%
Spain 11%
80mt
MEXICO

BAHAMAS
CUBA
HAITI DOMINICAN REPUBLIC
PUERTO RICO
BELIZE
HONDURAS JAMAICA
GUATEMALA
EL SALVADOR
NICARAGUA
COSTA RICA
PANAMA
ANTIGUA

Neth Antilles 28%
USA 24%
W Germany 8%
53mt

MARTINIQUE
BARBADOS
TRINIDAD AND TOBAGO

VENEZUELA
COLOMBIA
GUYANA
SURINAM
FRENCH GUIANA

ECUADOR
PERU

Iraq 28%
Saudi 20%
Nigeria 14%
32mt

B R A Z I L

BOLIVIA

PARAGUAY

CHILE

URUGUAY

ARGENTINA

FALKLAND ISLANDS

TUNISIA
MOROCCO
ALGERIA

WESTERN SAHARA

MAURITANIA
CAPE VERDE
SENEGAL
GAMBIA
GUINEA-BISSAU GUINEA
SIERRA LEONE
LIBERIA IVORY
COAST
MALI
BURKINA
GHANA
BENIN
TOGO

NIGER

USA 17%
France 17%
W Germany 16%
60mt
NIGERIA

CAMEROON
EQUATORIAL GUINEA
SAO TOME AND PRINCIPE
GABON
CONGO

Surplus and deficit countries, 1984 million tonnes

surplus

over 280

40-280

below 40

deficit

below 20

20-120

over 120

data not available

exporters and their major customers

importers and their major suppliers

the oil-less:countries with no known oil deposits

OPEC members

Sources: UN Yearbook of World Energy Statistics; BP; CIA. World Oil Market

Two countries, Japan and the USA, use more than a quarter of world oil production; and two countries, the USSR and Saudi Arabia, provide just under a quarter of world oil exports.

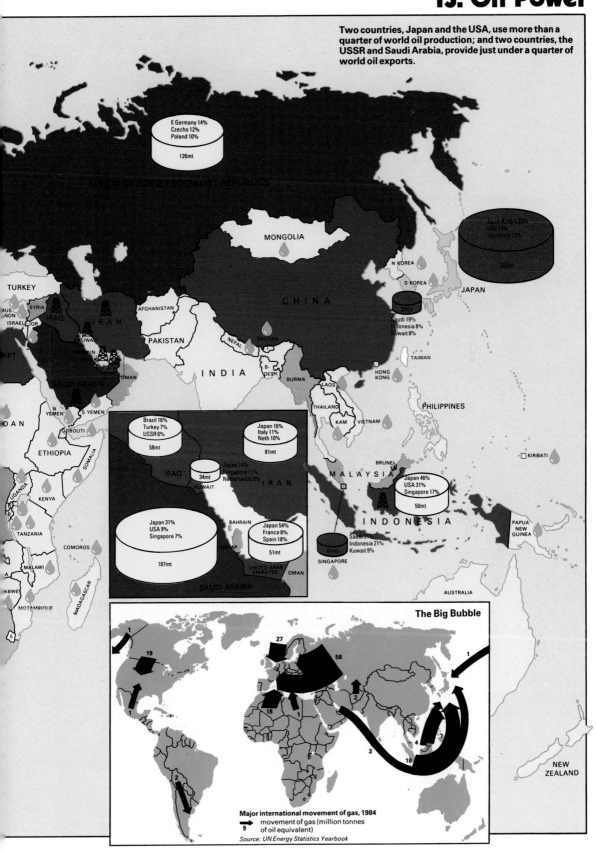

E Germany 14%
Czecho 12%
Poland 10%
126mt

Saudi Arabia 32%
UAE 16%
Indonesia 13%
182mt

Saudi 19%
Indonesia 8%
Kuwait 8%
27mt

Brazil 16%
Turkey 7%
USSR 6%
58mt

Japan 16%
Italy 11%
Neth 10%
81mt

Japan 14%
Singapore 11%
Netherlands 9%
34mt
KUWAIT

Japan 31%
USA 9%
Singapore 7%
187mt

Japan 54%
France 8%
Spain 18%
51mt

Japan 46%
USA 31%
Singapore 17%
50mt

Saudi 31%
Indonesia 21%
Kuwait 9%
41mt
SINGAPORE

The Big Bubble

Major international movement of gas, 1984

→ movement of gas (million tonnes
9   of oil equivalent)

Source: UN Energy Statistics Yearbook

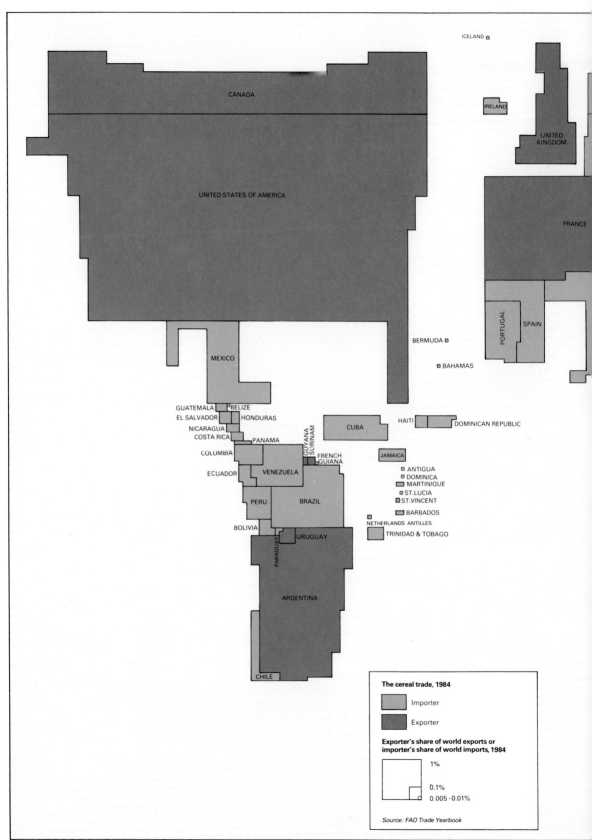

ICELAND

IRELAND

UNITED KINGDOM

CANADA

FRANCE

UNITED STATES OF AMERICA

PORTUGAL SPAIN

BERMUDA

BAHAMAS

MEXICO

GUATEMALA BELIZE
EL SALVADOR HONDURAS
NICARAGUA
COSTA RICA PANAMA

HAITI DOMINICAN REPUBLIC

CUBA

COLUMBIA

GUYANA
SURINAM
FRENCH
GUIANA

JAMAICA

ANTIGUA
DOMINICA
MARTINIQUE
ST.LUCIA
ST.VINCENT
BARBADOS
NETHERLANDS ANTILLES
TRINIDAD & TOBAGO

ECUADOR VENEZUELA

PERU BRAZIL

BOLIVIA

PARAGUAY URUGUAY

ARGENTINA

CHILE

The cereal trade, 1984

   Importer

   Exporter

**Exporter's share of world exports or
importer's share of world imports, 1984**

1%

0.1%

0.005 - 0.01%

Source: FAO Trade Yearbook

14. Food Power

'Food is a weapon. It is now one of the principal weapons in our negotiating kit.' Earl Butz, when US Secretary of State for Agriculture.

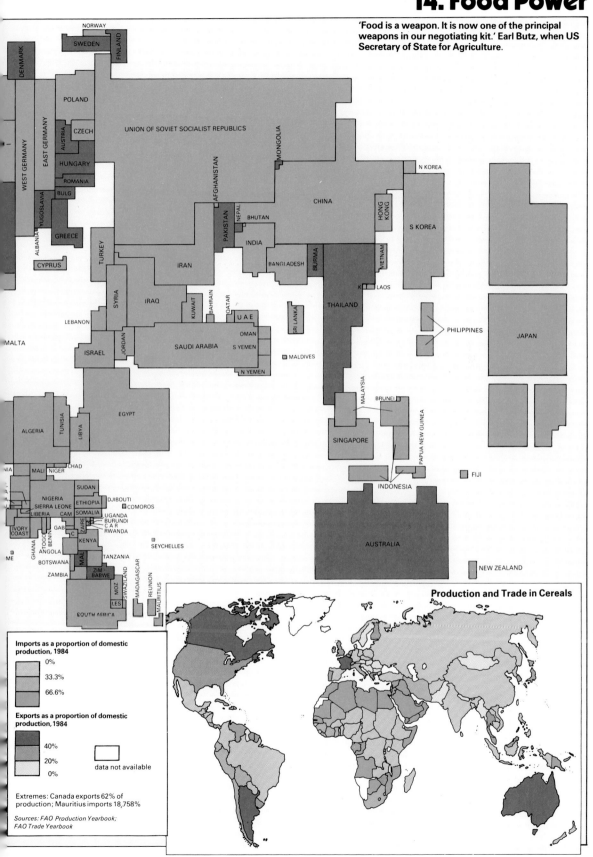

Production and Trade in Cereals

Imports as a proportion of domestic production, 1984
0%
33.3%
66.6%

Exports as a proportion of domestic production, 1984
40%
20%
0%
data not available

Extremes: Canada exports 62% of production; Mauritius imports 18,758%

Sources: FAO Production Yearbook; FAO Trade Yearbook

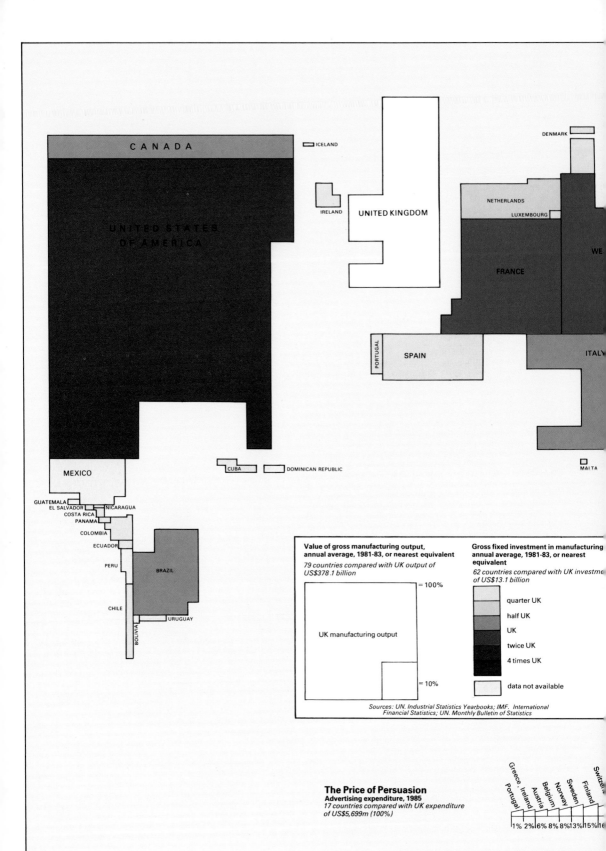

CANADA

ICELAND

DENMARK

UNITED STATES
OF AMERICA

IRELAND

UNITED KINGDOM

NETHERLANDS

LUXEMBOURG

FRANCE

WE

PORTUGAL

SPAIN

ITALY

MEXICO

CUBA

DOMINICAN REPUBLIC

MALTA

GUATEMALA
EL SALVADOR
COSTA RICA
PANAMA

NICARAGUA

COLOMBIA

ECUADOR

PERU

BRAZIL

CHILE

URUGUAY

BOLIVIA

**Value of gross manufacturing output,
annual average, 1981-83, or nearest equivalent**

*79 countries compared with UK output of
US$378.1 billion*

= 100%

UK manufacturing output

= 10%

**Gross fixed investment in manufacturing
annual average, 1981-83, or nearest
equivalent**

*62 countries compared with UK investme
of US$13.1 billion*

quarter UK

half UK

UK

twice UK

4 times UK

data not available

*Sources: UN. Industrial Statistics Yearbooks; IMF. International
Financial Statistics; UN. Monthly Bulletin of Statistics*

The Price of Persuasion
Advertising expenditure, 1985
*17 countries compared with UK expenditure
of US$5,699m (100%)*

Greece, Ireland
Portugal
Austria
Belgium
Norway
Sweden
Finland
Switzerl

1% 2% 6% 8% 8% 13% 15% 16

As the history of the UK in the last century or so
illustrates, industry is the basis for the relative power
of the modern state and investment a means of
achieving or securing it.

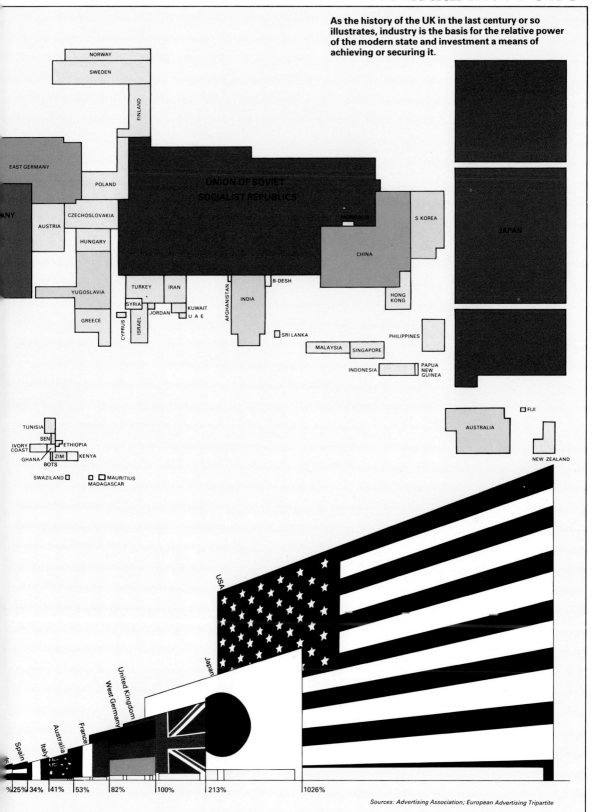

%25% 34% 41% 53% 82% 100% 213% 1026%

Sources: Advertising Association; European Advertising Tripartite

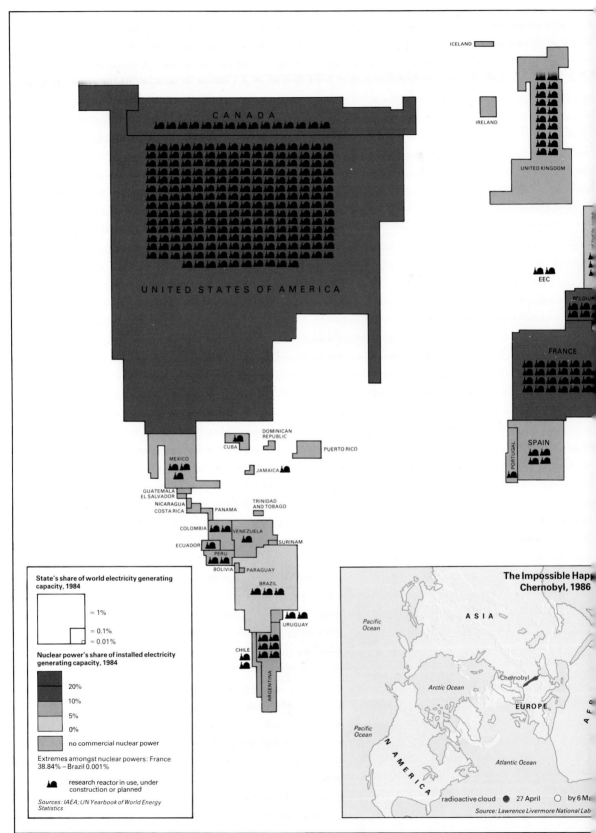

ICELAND

IRELAND

UNITED KINGDOM

CANADA

UNITED STATES OF AMERICA

EEC

BELGIUM

FRANCE

DOMINICAN
REPUBLIC

CUBA

PUERTO RICO

MEXICO

JAMAICA

SPAIN

PORTUGAL

GUATEMALA
EL SALVADOR
NICARAGUA
COSTA RICA

PANAMA

TRINIDAD
AND TOBAGO

COLOMBIA

VENEZUELA

ECUADOR

SURINAM

PERU

BOLIVIA

PARAGUAY

BRAZIL

URUGUAY

CHILE

ARGENTINA

State's share of world electricity generating capacity, 1984

= 1%

= 0.1%

= 0.01%

Nuclear power's share of installed electricity generating capacity, 1984

20%

10%

5%

0%

no commercial nuclear power

Extremes amongst nuclear powers: France 38.84% – Brazil 0.001%

research reactor in use, under construction or planned

Sources: IAEA; UN Yearbook of World Energy Statistics

The Impossible Happens: Chernobyl, 1986

ASIA

Pacific
Ocean

Arctic Ocean

Chernobyl

EUROPE

AFRICA

Pacific
Ocean

N AMERICA

Atlantic Ocean

radioactive cloud ● 27 April ○ by 6 May

Source: Lawrence Livermore National Lab

Some states use nuclear power; some are nuclear
powers. All began with research reactors.

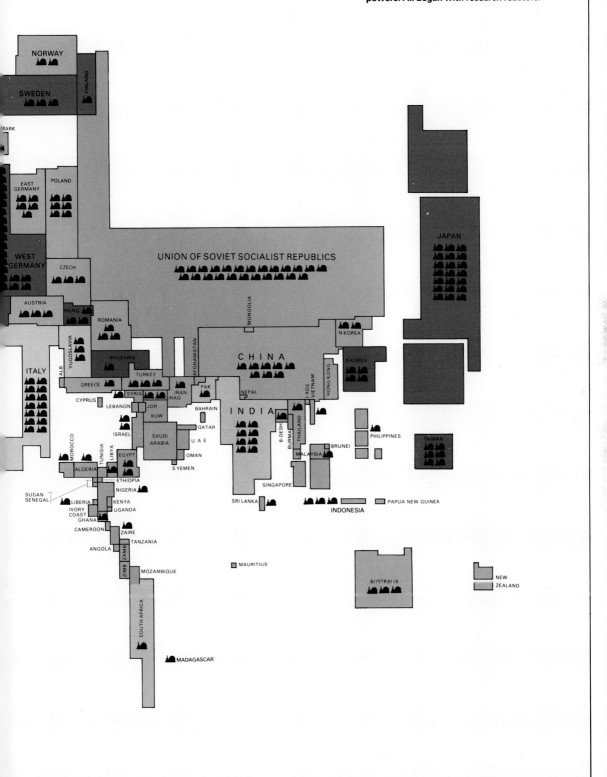

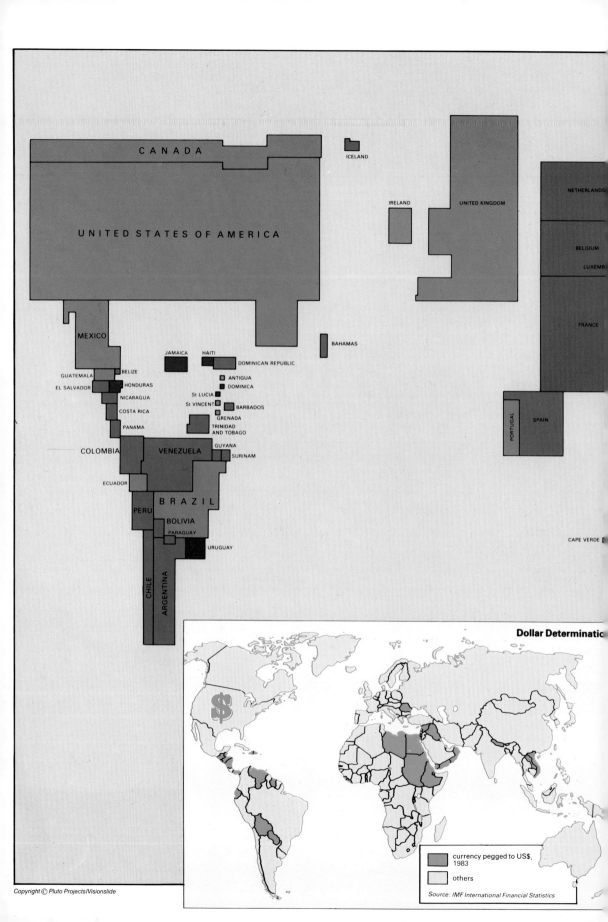

CANADA

UNITED STATES OF AMERICA

ICELAND

IRELAND   UNITED KINGDOM

NETHERLANDS

BELGIUM

LUXEMB

FRANCE

MEXICO

JAMAICA   HAITI

DOMINICAN REPUBLIC

BAHAMAS

GUATEMALA   BELIZE

EL SALVADOR   HONDURAS

NICARAGUA

COSTA RICA

PANAMA

ANTIGUA

DOMINICA

St LUCIA

St VINCENT   BARBADOS

GRENADA

TRINIDAD
AND TOBAGO

COLOMBIA   VENEZUELA   GUYANA

SURINAM

ECUADOR

BRAZIL

PERU   BOLIVIA

PARAGUAY

URUGUAY

CHILE   ARGENTINA

PORTUGAL   SPAIN

CAPE VERDE

Dollar Determinatio

currency pegged to US$,
1983

others

Source: IMF International Financial Statistics

17. Financial Power

The IMF (International Monetary Fund) is the world's leading interstate financial organization. Only a few countries – notably the USSR and Switzerland – do not belong to it.

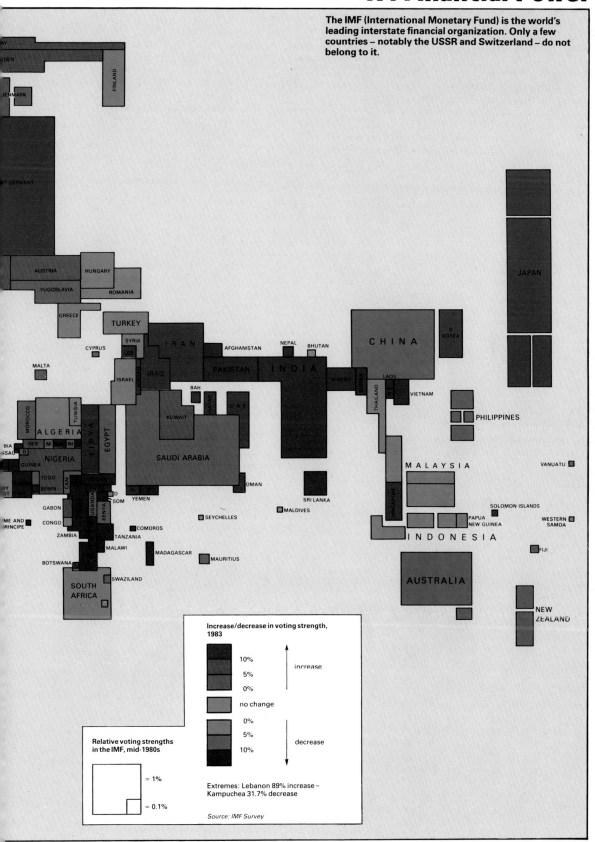

Increase/decrease in voting strength, 1983

- 10% } increase
- 5%
- 0%
- no change
- 0% } decrease
- 5%
- 10%

Extremes: Lebanon 89% increase – Kampuchea 31.7% decrease

Relative voting strengths in the IMF, mid-1980s

- ☐ = 1%
- ▫ = 0.1%

Source: IMF Survey

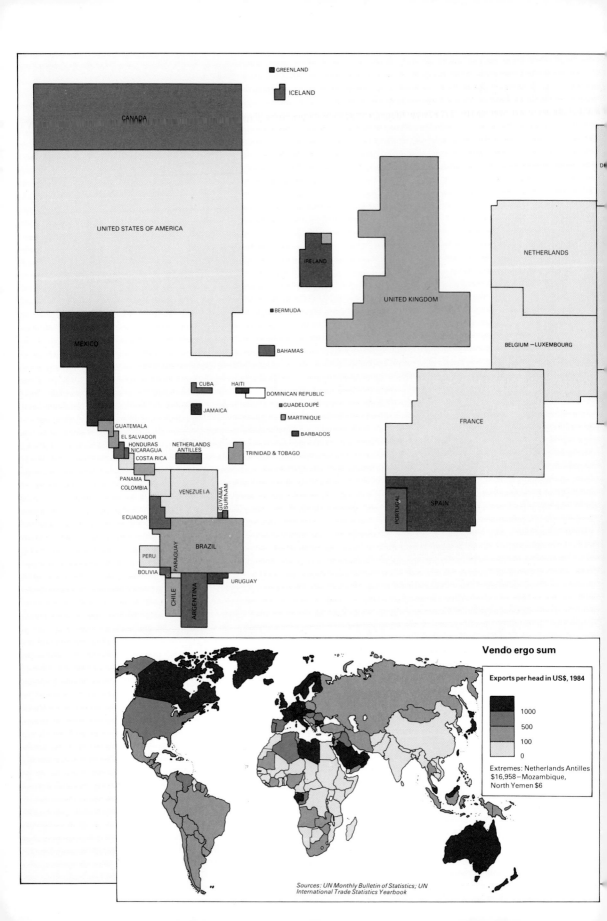

GREENLAND

ICELAND

CANADA

UNITED STATES OF AMERICA

NETHERLANDS

IRELAND

BERMUDA

UNITED KINGDOM

BELGIUM—LUXEMBOURG

MEXICO

BAHAMAS

CUBA   HAITI

DOMINICAN REPUBLIC

GUADELOUPÉ

JAMAICA

MARTINIQUE

FRANCE

BARBADOS

GUATEMALA

EL SALVADOR

HONDURAS

NETHERLANDS
ANTILLES

NICARAGUA

TRINIDAD & TOBAGO

COSTA RICA

PANAMA

COLOMBIA

VENEZUELA

GUYANA
SURINAM

ECUADOR

PORTUGAL

SPAIN

BRAZIL

PERU

PARAGUAY

BOLIVIA

URUGUAY

CHILE

ARGENTINA

Vendo ergo sum

Exports per head in US$, 1984

1000

500

100

0

Extremes: Netherlands Antilles
$16,958—Mozambique,
North Yemen $6

*Sources: UN Monthly Bulletin of Statistics; UN
International Trade Statistics Yearbook*

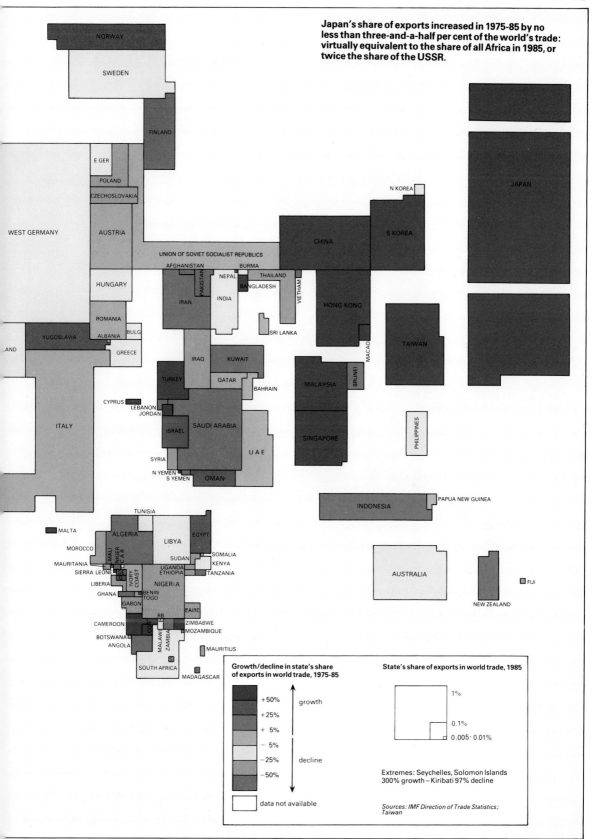

Japan's share of exports increased in 1975-85 by no less than three-and-a-half per cent of the world's trade: virtually equivalent to the share of all Africa in 1985, or twice the share of the USSR.

Growth/decline in state's share of exports in world trade, 1975-85

+50%
+25%
+ 5%   growth
− 5%
−25%   decline
−50%

data not available

State's share of exports in world trade, 1985

1%
0.1%
0.005- 0.01%

Extremes: Seychelles, Solomon Islands
300% growth – Kiribati 97% decline

Sources: IMF Direction of Trade Statistics; Taiwan

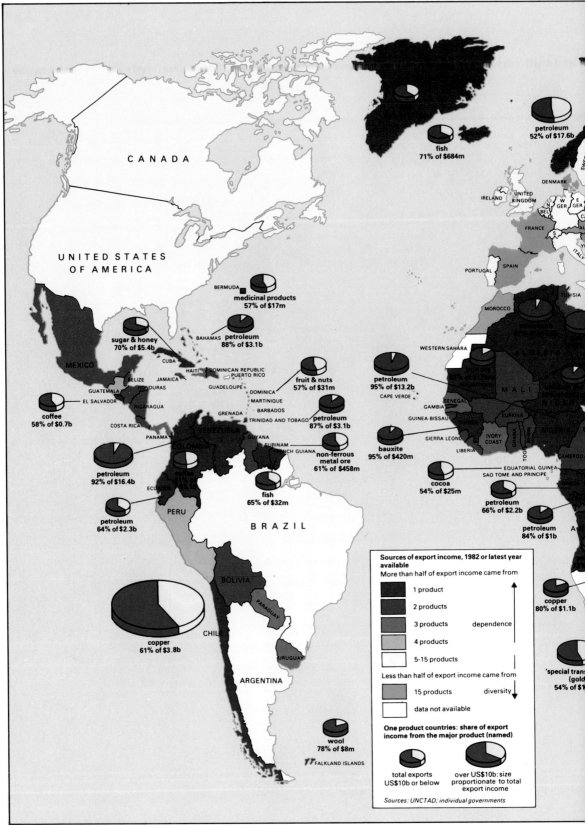

CANADA

UNITED STATES
OF AMERICA

MEXICO

BELIZE
GUATEMALA
EL SALVADOR
HONDURAS
NICARAGUA
COSTA RICA
PANAMA

coffee
58% of $0.7b

CUBA
JAMAICA
HAITI
DOMINICAN REPUBLIC
PUERTO RICO
GUADELOUPE
DOMINICA
MARTINIQUE
BARBADOS
GRENADA
TRINIDAD AND TOBAGO

BERMUDA
medicinal products
57% of $17m

BAHAMAS
petroleum
88% of $3.1b

sugar & honey
70% of $5.4b

fruit & nuts
57% of $31m

petroleum
87% of $3.1b

VENEZUELA
COLOMBIA
GUYANA
SURINAM
FRENCH GUIANA

non-ferrous
metal ore
61% of $458m

petroleum
92% of $16.4b

ECUADOR

PERU

fish
65% of $32m

BRAZIL

petroleum
64% of $2.3b

BOLIVIA

PARAGUAY

copper
61% of $3.8b

CHILE

URUGUAY

ARGENTINA

wool
78% of $8m

FALKLAND ISLANDS

fish
71% of $684m

petroleum
52% of $17.6b

DENMARK
IRELAND
UNITED KINGDOM
W GER
E GER
BEL
CZ
AU
FRANCE
S
YL
ITALY

PORTUGAL
SPAIN

TUNISIA

MOROCCO

WESTERN SAHARA

petroleum
95% of $13.2b

CAPE VERDE

SENEGAL
GAMBIA
GUINEA-BISSAU
GUINEA
SIERRA LEONE
LIBERIA
IVORY COAST
MALI
BURKINA
GHANA
TOGO
BENIN
NIGERIA
CAMEROON

bauxite
95% of $420m

cocoa
54% of $25m

EQUATORIAL GUINEA
SAO TOME AND PRINCIPE

petroleum
66% of $2.2b

petroleum
84% of $1b

copper
80% of $1.1b

'special trans
(gold
54% of $1

Sources of export income, 1982 or latest year available

More than half of export income came from

■	1 product
	2 products
	3 products dependence
	4 products
	5-15 products

Less than half of export income came from

	15 products diversity
	data not available

One product countries: share of export income from the major product (named)

total exports
US$10b or below

over US$10b: size
proportionate to total
export income

Sources: UNCTAD; individual governments

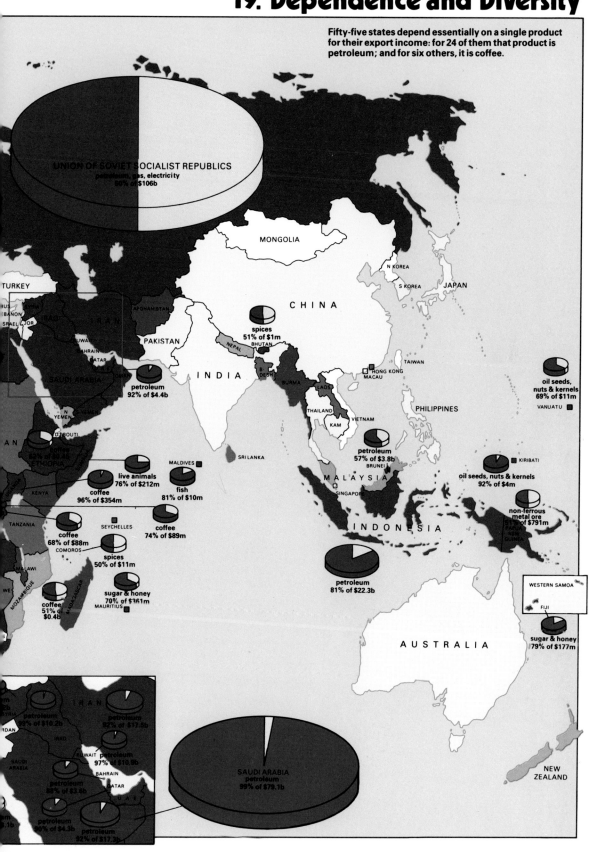

19. Dependence and Diversity

Fifty-five states depend essentially on a single product for their export income: for 24 of them that product is petroleum; and for six others, it is coffee.

UNION OF SOVIET SOCIALIST REPUBLICS
petroleum, gas, electricity
60% of $106b

MONGOLIA

N KOREA

S KOREA

JAPAN

CHINA

spices
51% of $1m

TURKEY

AFGHANISTAN

PAKISTAN

TAIWAN

HONG KONG
MACAU

INDIA

BHUTAN

B-
DESH

BURMA

LAOS

petroleum
92% of $4.4b

SAUDI ARABIA

KUWAIT

BAHRAIN

QATAR

N
YEMEN

DJIBOUTI

ETHIOPIA

coffee
82% of $0.4b

live animals
76% of $212m

coffee
96% of $354m

MALDIVES

fish
81% of $10m

THAILAND

KAM

VIETNAM

PHILIPPINES

oil seeds,
nuts & kernels
69% of $11m

VANUATU

KENYA

SEYCHELLES

coffee
68% of $88m

COMOROS

spices
50% of $11m

coffee
74% of $89m

SRI LANKA

petroleum
57% of $3.8b

BRUNEI

MALAYSIA

SINGAPORE

oil seeds, nuts & kernels
92% of $4m

KIRIBATI

non-ferrous
metal ore
51% of $791m

PAPUA
NEW
GUINEA

TANZANIA

MALAWI

MOZAMBIQUE

coffee
51% of
$0.4b

MADAGASCAR

MAURITIUS

sugar & honey
70% of $361m

INDONESIA

petroleum
81% of $22.3b

AUSTRALIA

WESTERN SAMOA

FIJI

sugar & honey
79% of $177m

NEW
ZEALAND

IRAN

petroleum
99% of $10.2b

IRAQ

petroleum
92% of $17.5b

KUWAIT

petroleum
97% of $10.9b

BAHRAIN

QATAR

petroleum
88% of $3.6b

SAUDI ARABIA
petroleum
99% of $79.1b

petroleum
90% of $4.3b

petroleum
92% of $17.3b

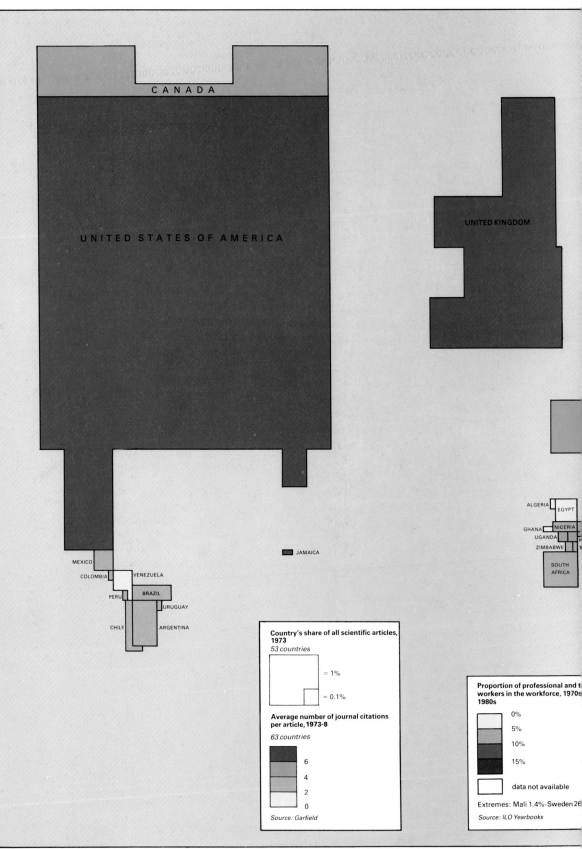

CANADA

UNITED STATES OF AMERICA

UNITED KINGDOM

ALGERIA
EGYPT
GHANA NIGERIA
UGANDA
ZIMBABWE
SOUTH
AFRICA

JAMAICA

MEXICO
COLOMBIA VENEZUELA
PERU BRAZIL
URUGUAY
CHILE ARGENTINA

Country's share of all scientific articles, 1973
53 countries

= 1%

= 0.1%

Average number of journal citations per article, 1973-8
63 countries

6
4
2
0

Source: Garfield

**Proportion of professional and t
workers in the workforce, 1970s
1980s**

0%
5%
10%
15%

data not available

Extremes: Mali 1.4%-Sweden 26

Source: ILO Yearbooks

Copyright © Pluto Projects/Visionslide

Science is fashioned in very few countries, and scientific fashions are disseminated by a handful of journals, 80 of which account for one quarter of all citations in science journals.

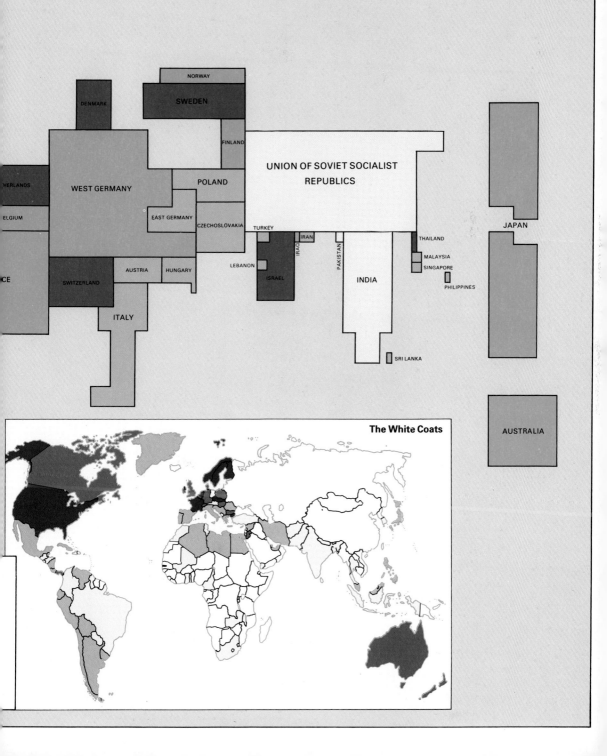

NORWAY

SWEDEN

DENMARK

FINLAND

WEST GERMANY

POLAND

UNION OF SOVIET SOCIALIST REPUBLICS

HERLANDS

ELGIUM

EAST GERMANY

CZECHOSLOVAKIA

TURKEY

IRAN

IRAQ

PAKISTAN

THAILAND

JAPAN

MALAYSIA

SINGAPORE

ICE

SWITZERLAND

AUSTRIA

HUNGARY

LEBANON

ISRAEL

INDIA

PHILIPPINES

ITALY

SRI LANKA

The White Coats

AUSTRALIA

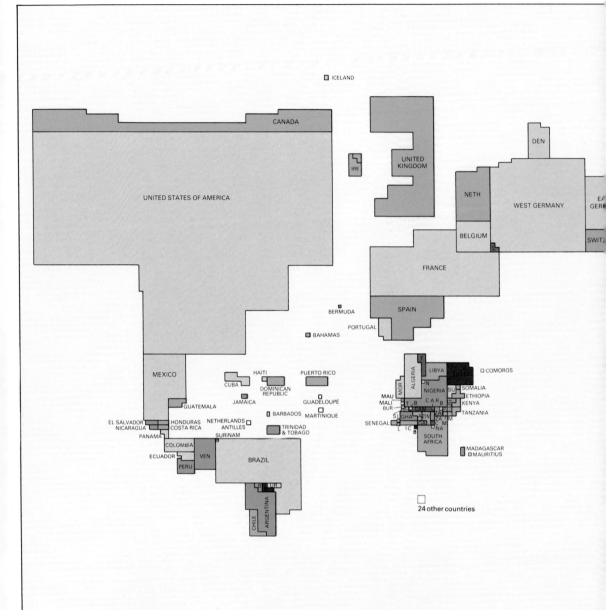

ICELAND

CANADA

DEN

UNITED
KINGDOM

IRE

NETH

WEST GERMANY

EA
GER

UNITED STATES OF AMERICA

BELGIUM

SWIT.

FRANCE

BERMUDA

SPAIN

PORTUGAL

BAHAMAS

MEXICO

HAITI

PUERTO RICO

ALGERIA

LIBYA

COMOROS

CUBA

DOMINICAN
REPUBLIC

MOR

N

SOMALIA

JAMAICA

GUADELOUPÉ

MAU

NIGERIA

SU

ETHIOPIA

MARTINIQUE

MALI

C A R

KENYA

GUATEMALA

BARBADOS

BUR

T

B

CAM UM

B

TANZANIA

EL SALVADOR
NICARAGUA

HONDURAS
COSTA RICA

NETHERLANDS
ANTILLES

SENEGAL

S

GHA

AZIM

CA

MI

PANAMA

SURINAM

TRINIDAD
& TOBAGO

L

IC

GAL

CA

NA

M

COLOMBIA

B

SOUTH
AFRICA

ECUADOR

VEN

MADAGASCAR

PERU

BRAZIL

MAURITIUS

24 other countries

CHILE

ARGENTINA

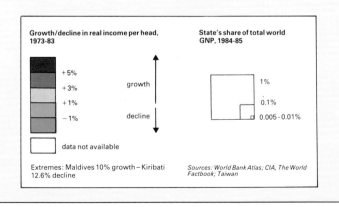

Growth/decline in real income per head, 1973-83

+5%

+3%

growth

+1%

−1%

decline

data not available

Extremes: Maldives 10% growth – Kiribati 12.6% decline

State's share of total world GNP, 1984-85

1%

0.1%

0.005 - 0.01%

Sources: World Bank Atlas; CIA, The World Factbook; Taiwan

Together, only three states – the USA, USSR and Japan – account for more than half the gross national product of the whole world.

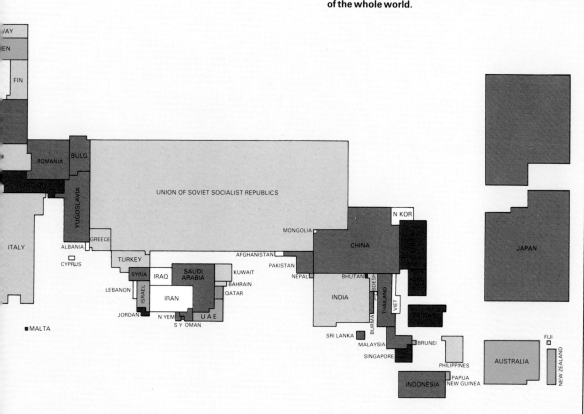

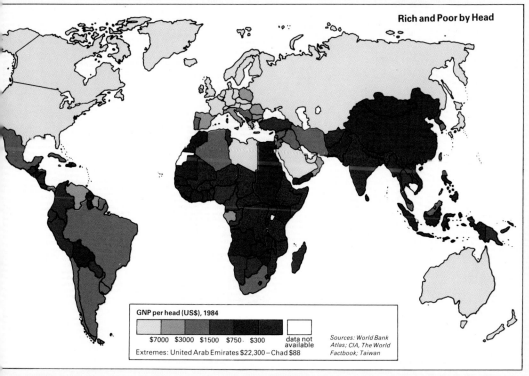

Rich and Poor by Head

GNP per head (US$), 1984

$7000 $3000 $1500 $750 $300   data not available

Extremes: United Arab Emirates $22,300 – Chad $88

Sources: World Bank Atlas; CIA, The World Factbook; Taiwan

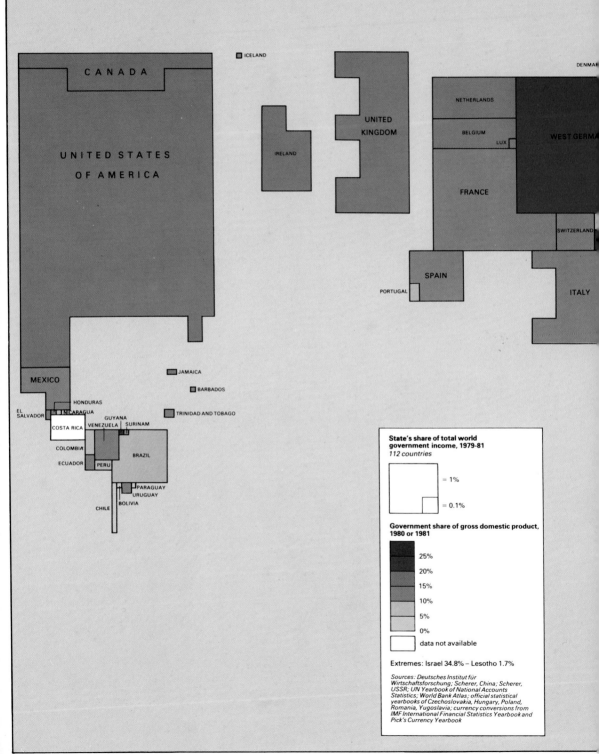

CANADA

UNITED STATES

OF AMERICA

ICELAND

DENMARK

UNITED
KINGDOM

IRELAND

NETHERLANDS

BELGIUM

LUX

WEST GERMANY

FRANCE

SWITZERLAND

SPAIN

PORTUGAL

ITALY

MEXICO

JAMAICA

BARBADOS

HONDURAS

EL
SALVADOR

NICARAGUA

COSTA RICA

GUYANA

VENEZUELA

SURINAM

TRINIDAD AND TOBAGO

COLOMBIA

ECUADOR

PERU

BRAZIL

PARAGUAY

URUGUAY

CHILE

BOLIVIA

**State's share of total world
government income, 1979-81**
112 countries

= 1%

= 0.1%

**Government share of gross domestic product,
1980 or 1981**

25%

20%

15%

10%

5%

0%

data not available

Extremes: Israel 34.8% – Lesotho 1.7%

*Sources: Deutsches Institut für
Wirtschaftsforschung; Scherer, China; Scherer,
USSR; UN Yearbook of National Accounts
Statistics; World Bank Atlas; official statistical
yearbooks of Czechoslovakia, Hungary, Poland,
Romania, Yugoslavia; currency conversions from
IMF International Financial Statistics Yearbook and
Pick's Currency Yearbook*

22. The First Slice of the Cake

A government's wealth does not necessarily reflect the wealth of the people it rules.

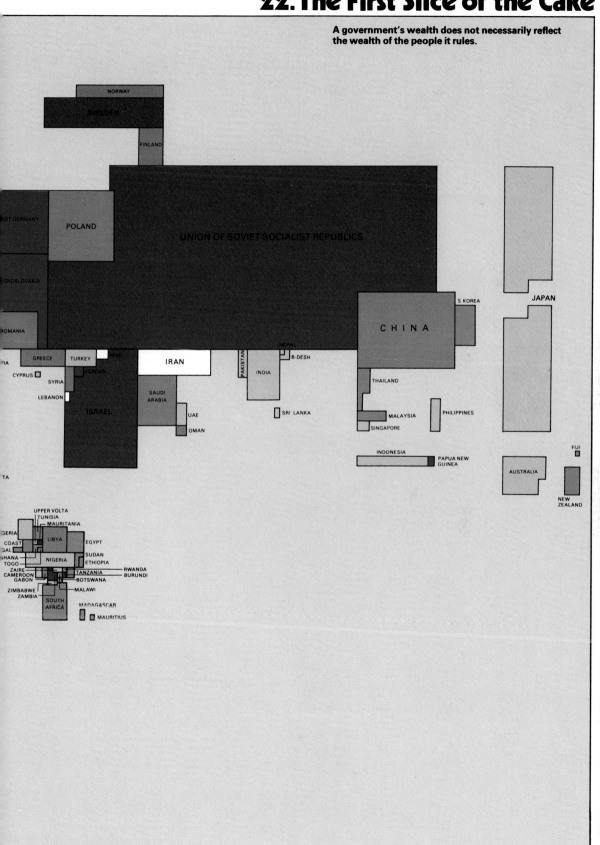

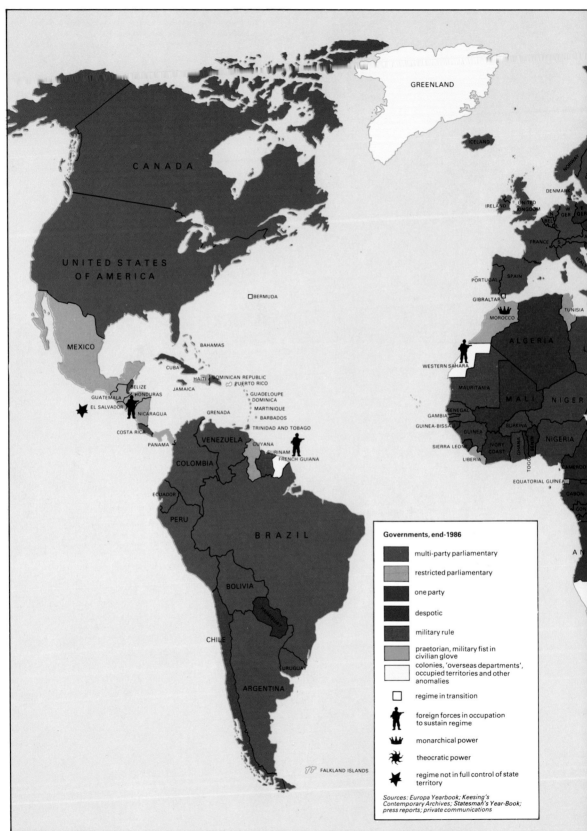

GREENLAND

ICELAND

CANADA

NORWAY

DENMARK

IRELAND UNITED KINGDOM
W GER E GER
BEL
FRANCE S
UNITED STATES
OF AMERICA
ITALY

PORTUGAL SPAIN

BERMUDA

GIBRALTAR

MOROCCO TUNISIA

MEXICO

BAHAMAS

WESTERN SAHARA

ALGERIA L

CUBA

HAITI DOMINICAN REPUBLIC
PUERTO RICO

MAURITANIA

BELIZE
GUATEMALA HONDURAS
EL SALVADOR NICARAGUA

JAMAICA

GUADELOUPE
DOMINICA

MARTINIQUE

BARBADOS

MALI NIGER

SENEGAL

GAMBIA

BURKINA

GUINEA-BISSAU

COSTA RICA

GRENADA

TRINIDAD AND TOBAGO

NIGERIA

GUINEA

SIERRA LEONE

IVORY
COAST

GHANA

PANAMA

VENEZUELA

GUYANA

SURINAM

FRENCH GUIANA

LIBERIA

TOGO

CAMEROON

COLOMBIA

EQUATORIAL GUINEA

ECUADOR

GABON

CO

PERU

B R A Z I L

AN

BOLIVIA

Governments, end-1986

multi-party parliamentary

restricted parliamentary

PARAGUAY

one party

CHILE

despotic

military rule

URUGUAY

praetorian, military fist in
civilian glove

ARGENTINA

colonies, 'overseas departments',
occupied territories and other
anomalies

regime in transition

foreign forces in occupation
to sustain regime

monarchical power

theocratic power

FALKLAND ISLANDS

regime not in full control of state
territory

Sources: Europa Yearbook; Keesing's
Contemporary Archives; Statesman's Year-Book;
press reports; private communications

23. Complexions of Government

However different governments may be, all are ultimately concerned with the control of the many by the few. In this respect, governments have more in common with one another than with their own citizens.

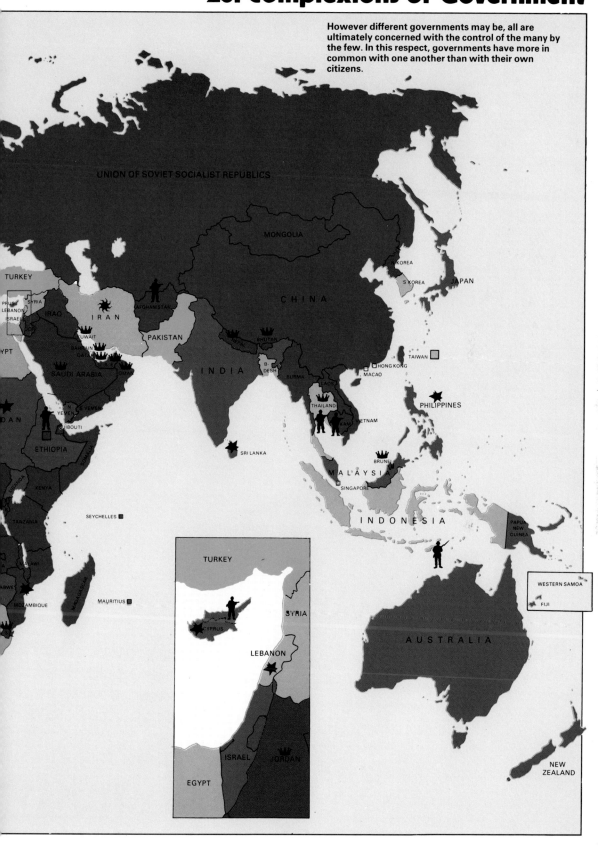

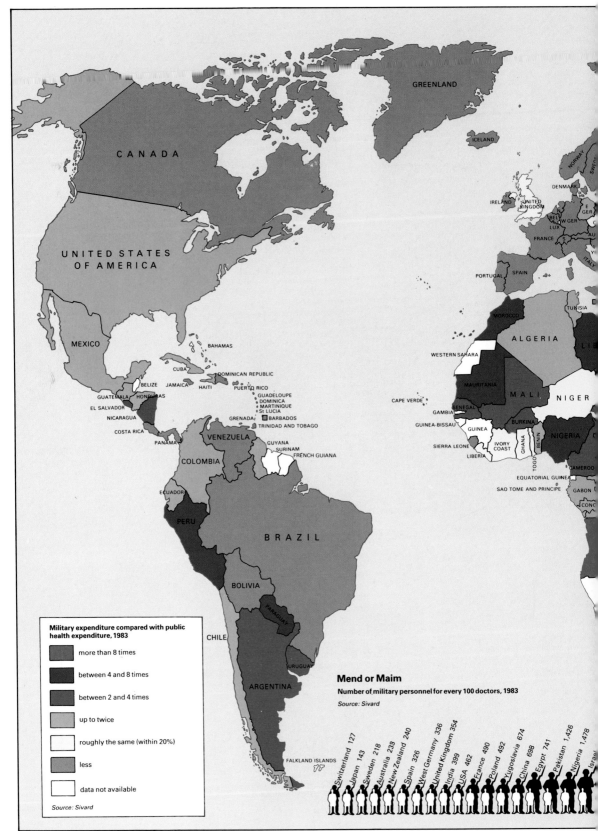

GREENLAND

ICELAND

CANADA

UNITED STATES
OF AMERICA

NORWAY

DENMARK
IRELAND UNITED
KINGDOM
BELG OWGER
LUX
FRANCE S
AU
ITALY

PORTUGAL SPAIN

TUNISIA

MOROCCO

MEXICO

BAHAMAS

WESTERN SAHARA

ALGERIA

LIB

CUBA

CAPE VERDE

MAURITANIA

MALI

NIGER

BELIZE JAMAICA
GUATEMALA HONDURAS
EL SALVADOR
NICARAGUA
COSTA RICA
PANAMA

DOMINICAN REPUBLIC
HAITI
PUERTO RICO
GUADELOUPE
DOMINICA
MARTINIQUE
St LUCIA
GRENADA BARBADOS
TRINIDAD AND TOBAGO

SENEGAL
GAMBIA
GUINEA-BISSAU GUINEA
SIERRA LEONE
LIBERIA IVORY
COAST

BURKINA

GHANA
TOGO
BENIN

NIGERIA

CAMEROO

VENEZUELA

GUYANA
SURINAM
FRENCH GUIANA

EQUATORIAL GUINEA
SAO TOME AND PRINCIPE

GABON

COLOMBIA

ECUADOR

CONG

PERU

BRAZIL

BOLIVIA

PARAGUAY

CHILE

URUGUAY

ARGENTINA

**Military expenditure compared with public
health expenditure, 1983**

more than 8 times

between 4 and 8 times

between 2 and 4 times

up to twice

roughly the same (within 20%)

less

data not available

Source: Sivard

FALKLAND ISLANDS

Mend or Maim

Number of military personnel for every 100 doctors, 1983

Source: Sivard

Switzerland 127
Japan 143
Sweden 218
Australia 233
New Zealand 240
Spain 326
West Germany 336
United Kingdom 354
India 399
USA 462
France 490
Poland 492
Yugoslavia 674
China 698
Egypt 741
Pakistan 1,426
Nigeria 1,478
Israel

Copyright © Pluto Projects/Visionslide

24. Harmworkers and Healthworkers

There are six times as many military people as physicians in the world; and governments spend 40 per cent more supplying them than on health care.

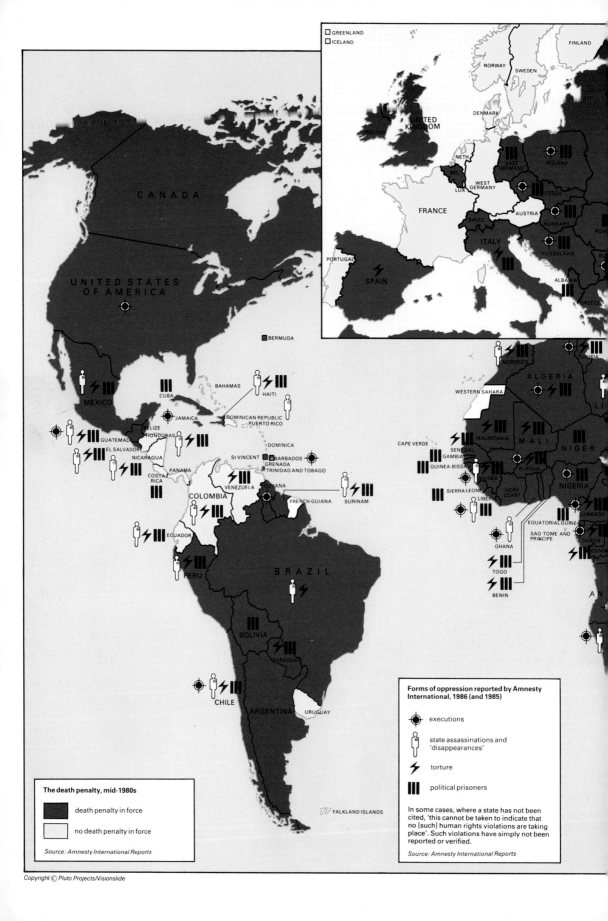

The death penalty, mid-1980s

death penalty in force

no death penalty in force

Source: Amnesty International Reports

Forms of oppression reported by Amnesty International, 1986 (and 1985)

executions

state assassinations and 'disappearances'

torture

political prisoners

In some cases, where a state has not been cited, 'this cannot be taken to indicate that no [such] human rights violations are taking place'. Such violations have simply not been reported or verified.

Source: Amnesty International Reports

All states are armed against their citizens. Many states use exceptional methods to terrorize them.

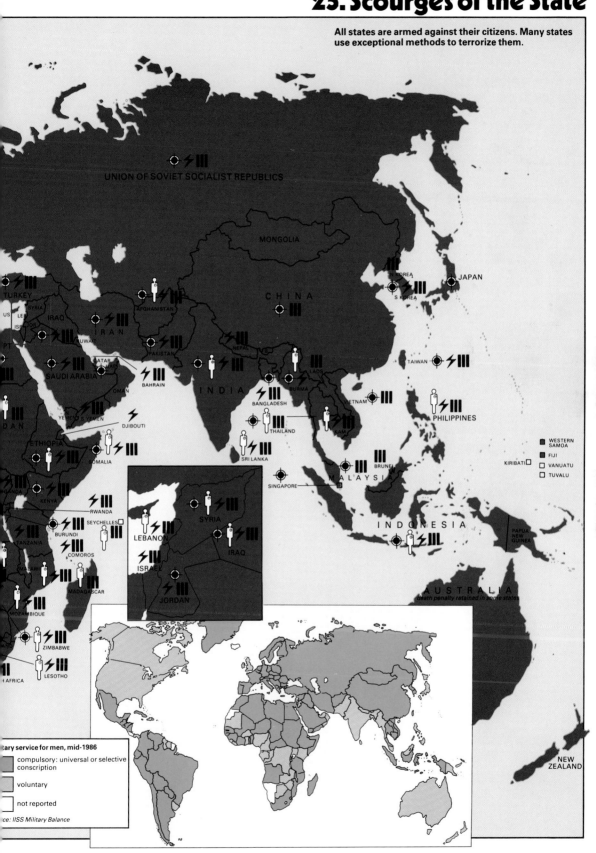

UNION OF SOVIET SOCIALIST REPUBLICS

MONGOLIA

CHINA

JAPAN

KOREA

S KOREA

TURKEY

US LEB

ISR JOR

PT

SYRIA

IRAQ

IRAN

KUWAIT

QATAR

SAUDI ARABIA

BAHRAIN

OMAN

AFGHANISTAN

PAKISTAN

NEPAL

INDIA

BANGLADESH

BURMA

TAIWAN

VIETNAM

LAOS

KAM...

PHILIPPINES

YEMEN S YEMEN

DJIBOUTI

ETHIOPIA

SOMALIA

THAILAND

SRI LANKA

BRUNEI

MALAYSIA

SINGAPORE

WESTERN SAMOA

FIJI

VANUATU

TUVALU

KIRIBATI

DAN

GANDA

KENYA

RWANDA

SEYCHELLES

BURUNDI

TANZANIA

COMOROS

MALAWI

MADAGASCAR

MOZAMBIQUE

ZIMBABWE

LESOTHO

H AFRICA

INDONESIA

PAPUA NEW GUINEA

AUSTRALIA
death penalty retained in some states

SYRIA

LEBANON

IRAQ

ISRAEL

JORDAN

NEW ZEALAND

...tary service for men, mid-1986

compulsory: universal or selective conscription

voluntary

not reported

ce: IISS Military Balance

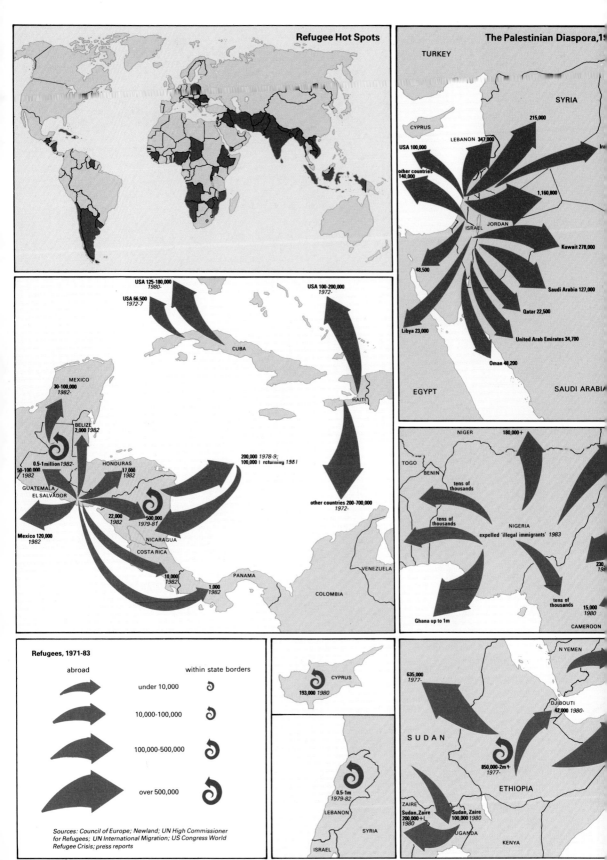

Refugee Hot Spots

The Palestinian Diaspora, 19

TURKEY

SYRIA

CYPRUS

215,000

LEBANON 347,000

USA 100,000

Ira

other countries
140,000

1,160,800

ISRAEL JORDAN

Kuwait 278,000

48,500

Saudi Arabia 127,000

Libya 23,000

Qatar 22,500

United Arab Emirates 34,700

Oman 48,200

EGYPT

SAUDI ARABIA

USA 125-180,000
1980-

USA 66,500
1972-7

USA 100-200,000
1972-

CUBA

MEXICO
30-100,000
1982-

BELIZE
2,000 1982

HAITI

0.5-1 million 1982-
50-100,000
1982

HONDURAS
17,000
1982

200,000 1978-9;
100,000 | returning 1981

GUATEMALA
EL SALVADOR

22,000
1982

500,000
1979-81

other countries 200-700,000
1972-

Mexico 120,000
1982

NICARAGUA

COSTA RICA

VENEZUELA

10,000
1982

PANAMA

1,000
1982

COLOMBIA

NIGER

180,000+

TOGO

BENIN

tens of
thousands

tens of
thousands

NIGERIA

expelled 'illegal immigrants' 1983

230,
198

tens of
thousands

15,000
1980

Ghana up to 1m

CAMEROON

Refugees, 1971-83

abroad

within state borders

under 10,000

10,000-100,000

100,000-500,000

over 500,000

*Sources: Council of Europe; Newland; UN High Commissioner
for Refugees; UN International Migration; US Congress World
Refugee Crisis; press reports*

CYPRUS

193,000 1980

N YEMEN

635,000
1977-

DJIBOUTI
42,000 1980-

SUDAN

850,000-2m+
1977-

0.5-1m
1979-82

ETHIOPIA

LEBANON

ZAIRE

SYRIA

Sudan, Zaire
200,000+L
1980

Sudan, Zaire
100,000 1980

ISRAEL

UGANDA

KENYA

Copyright © Pluto Projects/Visionslide

The world refugee population in the early 1980s was conservatively estimated at some 14 million people. About 200 private agencies operate assistance programmes.

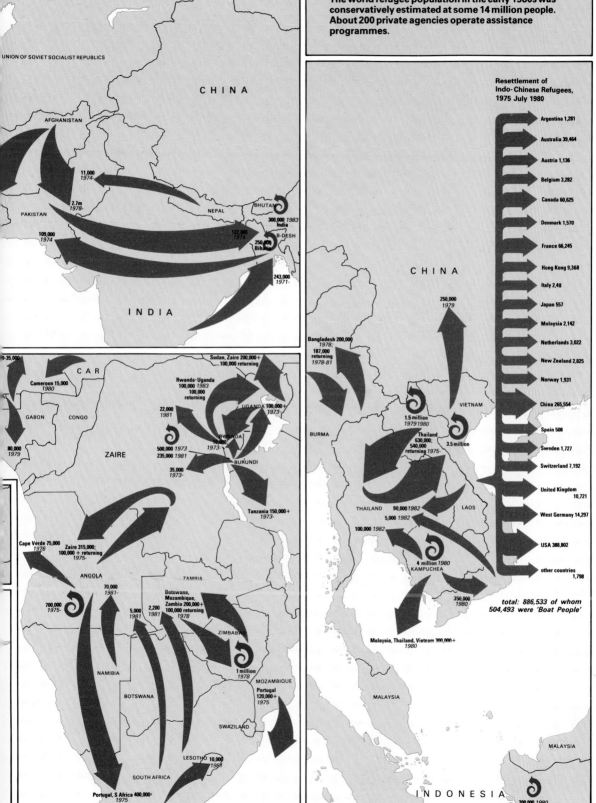

UNION OF SOVIET SOCIALIST REPUBLICS

CHINA

AFGHANISTAN

11,000
1974

2.7m
1978-

PAKISTAN

NEPAL

BHUTAN

300,000 1983
India
B-DESH

122,000
1974

250,000
Bihar

243,000
1971-

INDIA

109,000
1974

0-35,000

CAR

Cameroon 15,000
1980

GABON   CONGO

Sudan, Zaire 200,000+
100,000 returning

Rwanda-Uganda
100,000 1983
100,000
returning

22,000
1981

UGANDA 100,000+
1973-

80,000
1979

ZAIRE

RWANDA
10,000
1973-

500,000 1973
235,000 1981

BURUNDI

35,000
1973-

Tanzania 150,000+
1973-

Cape Verde 75,000
1976

Zaire 315,000;
100,000 + returning
1975-

ANGOLA

ZAMBIA

70,000
1981-

Botswana,
Mozambique,
Zambia 200,000+
100,000 returning
1978

700,000
1975-

5,000
1981

2,200
1981

ZIMBABWE

1 million
1978

NAMIBIA

MOZAMBIQUE

BOTSWANA

Portugal
120,000+
1975

SWAZILAND

LESOTHO 10,000
1981

SOUTH AFRICA

Portugal, S Africa 400,000+
1975

CHINA

250,000
1979

Bangladesh 200,000
1978;
187,000
returning
1978-81

VIETNAM

BURMA

1.5 million
1979 1980

3.5 million

Thailand
630,000;
540,000
returning 1975-

THAILAND   90,000 1982

5,000 1982

LAOS

100,000 1982

4 million 1980
KAMPUCHEA

350,000
1980

Malaysia, Thailand, Vietnam 300,000+
1980

MALAYSIA

MALAYSIA

INDONESIA

200,000 1980

Resettlement of
Indo- Chinese Refugees,
1975 July 1980

Argentina 1,281

Australia 39,464

Austria 1,136

Belgium 3,282

Canada 60,625

Denmark 1,570

France 66,245

Hong Kong 9,368

Italy 2,48

Japan 557

Malaysia 2,142

Netherlands 3,022

New Zealand 2,825

Norway 1,931

China 265,554

Spain 508

Sweden 1,727

Switzerland 7,192

United Kingdom
10,721

West Germany 14,297

USA 388,802

other countries
1,798

total: 886,533 of whom
504,493 were 'Boat People'

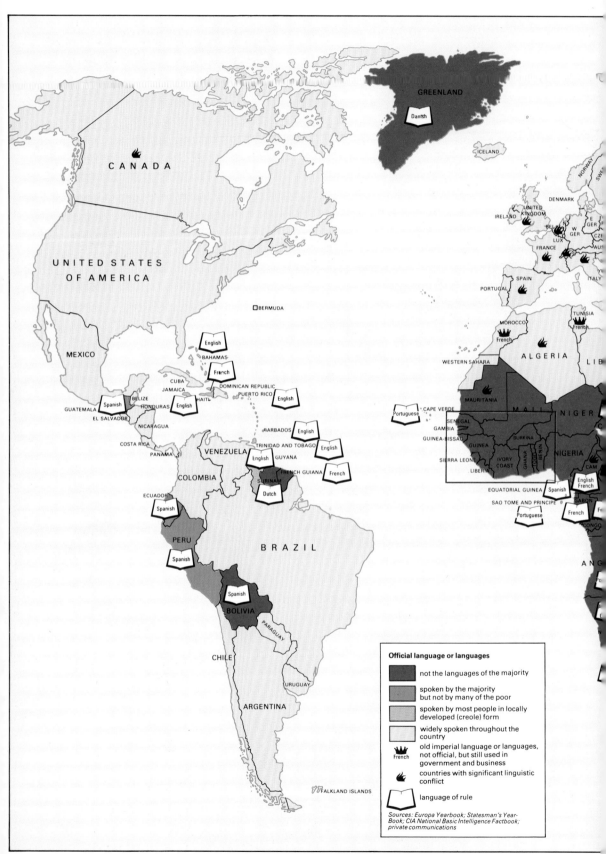

GREENLAND
Danish

ICELAND

CANADA

UNITED STATES
OF AMERICA

MEXICO

BERMUDA

English
BAHAMAS

French

CUBA
JAMAICA
GUATEMALA
BELIZE
HONDURAS
Spanish
EL SALVADOR
NICARAGUA
COSTA RICA
PANAMA

DOMINICAN REPUBLIC
PUERTO RICO
HAITI
English

English

BARBADOS
English

TRINIDAD AND TOBAGO
English

VENEZUELA
English GUYANA
COLOMBIA
SURINAM
FRENCH GUIANA
Dutch
French

ECUADOR
Spanish

PERU
Spanish

BRAZIL

Spanish
BOLIVIA

PARAGUAY

CHILE

URUGUAY

ARGENTINA

FALKLAND ISLANDS

NORWAY
SWE

DENMARK
IRELAND
UNITED
KINGDOM
E
GER
W
GER
CZE
BEL
LUX
FRANCE
AU

PORTUGAL
SPAIN
ITALY

TUNISIA
French

MOROCCO
French
ALGERIA
LIB

WESTERN SAHARA

CAPE VERDE
Portuguese
MAURITANIA
MALI
NIGER
SENEGAL
GAMBIA
BURKINA
GUINEA-BISSAU
GUINEA
NIGERIA
SIERRA LEONE
IVORY
COAST
GHANA
TOGO
BENIN
LIBERIA

EQUATORIAL GUINEA
Spanish
English
French
CAM

SAO TOME AND PRINCIPE
Portuguese
GABON
French
F
CONGO

ANG

Po

Official language or languages

not the languages of the majority

spoken by the majority
but not by many of the poor

spoken by most people in locally
developed (creole) form

widely spoken throughout the
country

old imperial language or languages,
not official, but still used in
government and business
French

countries with significant linguistic
conflict

language of rule

Sources: Europa Yearbook; Statesman's Year-
Book; CIA National Basic Intelligence Factbook;
private communications

A language of rule is one which is used by the governing classes, and which helps to secure their dominance. It is usually, but not always, designated an official language. And even where different languages spoken in a country are equally official, some are more equal than others.

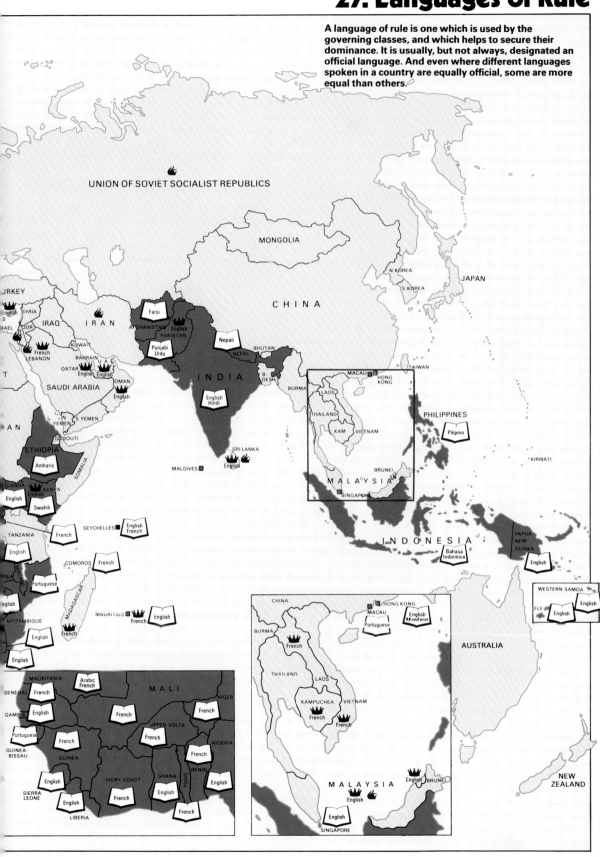

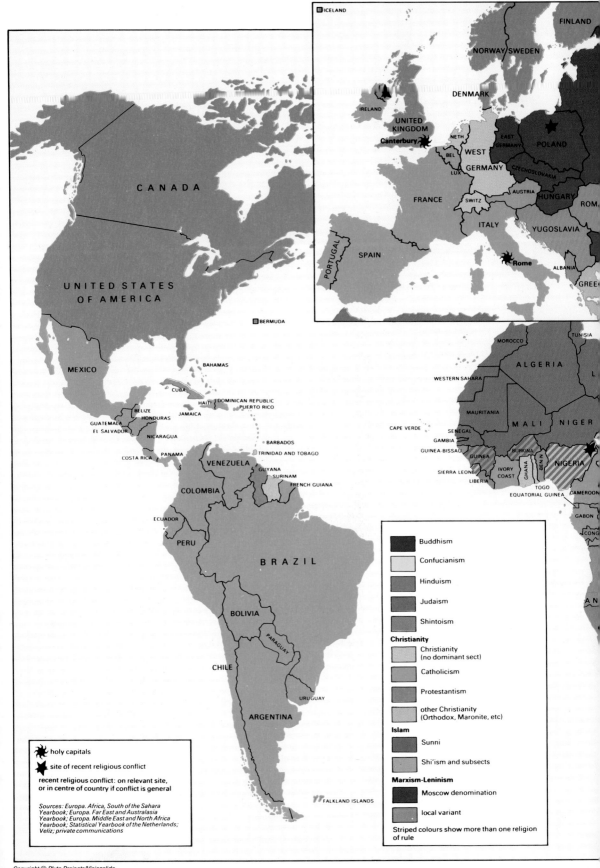

ICELAND

FINLAND

NORWAY SWEDEN

DENMARK

IRELAND

UNITED
KINGDOM

Canterbury

NETH.

BEL.

LUX.

WEST
GERMANY

EAST
GERMANY

POLAND

CZECHOSLOVAKIA

AUSTRIA

HUNGARY

ROM.

FRANCE

SWITZ.

ITALY

YUGOSLAVIA

GREE

PORTUGAL

SPAIN

Rome

ALBANIA

CANADA

UNITED STATES
OF AMERICA

BERMUDA

MEXICO

BAHAMAS

CUBA

HAITI

DOMINICAN REPUBLIC

PUERTO RICO

BELIZE

GUATEMALA

EL SALVADOR

HONDURAS

JAMAICA

NICARAGUA

BARBADOS

COSTA RICA

PANAMA

TRINIDAD AND TOBAGO

VENEZUELA

GUYANA

SURINAM

FRENCH GUIANA

COLOMBIA

ECUADOR

PERU

BRAZIL

BOLIVIA

PARAGUAY

CHILE

URUGUAY

ARGENTINA

FALKLAND ISLANDS

TUNISIA

MOROCCO

ALGERIA

L

WESTERN SAHARA

MAURITANIA

MALI

NIGER

CAPE VERDE

SENEGAL

GAMBIA

GUINEA-BISSAU

GUINEA

BURKINA

SIERRA LEONE

IVORY
COAST

GHANA

BENIN

NIGERIA

LIBERIA

TOGO

EQUATORIAL GUINEA

CAMEROON

GABON

CONG

AN

holy capitals

site of recent religious conflict

recent religious conflict: on relevant site,
or in centre of country if conflict is general

*Sources: Europa. Africa, South of the Sahara
Yearbook; Europa. Far East and Australasia
Yearbook; Europa. Middle East and North Africa
Yearbook; Statistical Yearbook of the Netherlands;
Veliz; private communications*

Buddhism

Confucianism

Hinduism

Judaism

Shintoism

Christianity

Christianity
(no dominant sect)

Catholicism

Protestantism

other Christianity
(Orthodox, Maronite, etc)

Islam

Sunni

Shi'ism and subsects

Marxism-Leninism

Moscow denomination

local variant

Striped colours show more than one religion
of rule

A religion of rule is one which is professed by the
governing classes and which sustains their solidarity.
Not surprisingly, religious conflict is intensifying.

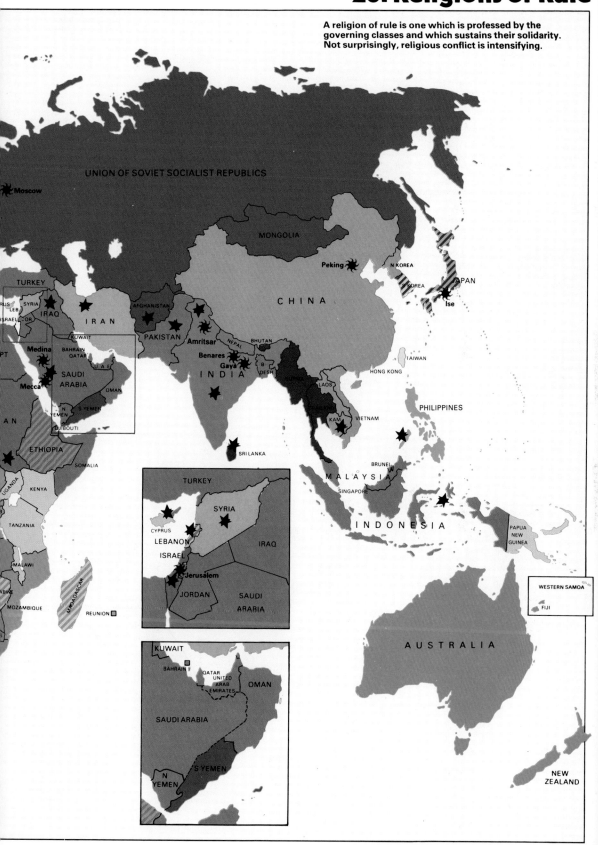

UNION OF SOVIET SOCIALIST REPUBLICS

Moscow

MONGOLIA

TURKEY

CYPRUS
LEB
SYRIA
ISRAEL JOR
IRAQ

IRAN

AFGHANISTAN

KUWAIT
BAHRAIN
QATAR
U.A.E
SAUDI
ARABIA
OMAN
N
YEMEN
S YEMEN

Medina

Mecca

PAKISTAN

Amritsar

Benares
Gaya

NEPAL

BHUTAN

B
DESH

INDIA

BURMA

LAOS

KAM

VIETNAM

SRI LANKA

Peking

N KOREA

KOREA

JAPAN

Ise

CHINA

TAIWAN

HONG KONG

PHILIPPINES

BRUNEI

MALAYSIA

SINGAPORE

INDONESIA

PAPUA
NEW
GUINEA

ETHIOPIA

SOMALIA

UGANDA

KENYA

TANZANIA

MALAWI

ZIMBABWE

MOZAMBIQUE

MADAGASCAR

REUNION

AN

PT

AUSTRALIA

NEW
ZEALAND

WESTERN SAMOA

FIJI

TURKEY

CYPRUS

SYRIA

LEBANON

ISRAEL

Jerusalem

JORDAN

IRAQ

SAUDI
ARABIA

KUWAIT

BAHRAIN

QATAR
UNITED
ARAB
EMIRATES

OMAN

SAUDI ARABIA

N
YEMEN

S YEMEN

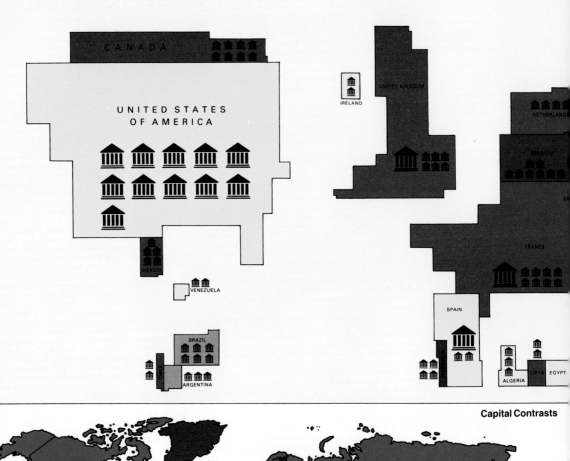

CANADA

UNITED STATES
OF AMERICA

MEXICO

VENEZUELA

BRAZIL

CHILE

ARGENTINA

IRELAND

UNITED KINGDOM

NETHERLANDS

BELGIUM

FRANCE

SPAIN

ALGERIA

LIBYA

EGYPT

Capital Contrasts

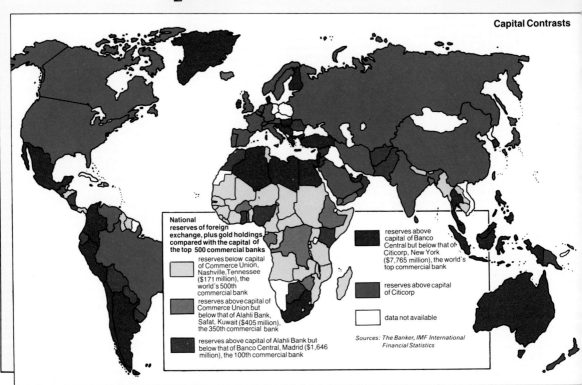

National reserves of foreign exchange, plus gold holdings, compared with the capital of the top 500 commercial banks

reserves below capital of Commerce Union, Nashville, Tennessee ($171 million), the world's 500th commercial bank

reserves above capital of Commerce Union but below that of Alahli Bank, Safat, Kuwait ($405 million), the 350th commercial bank

reserves above capital of Alahli Bank but below that of Banco Central, Madrid ($1,646 million), the 100th commercial bank

reserves above capital of Banco Central but below that of Citicorp, New York ($7,765 million), the world's top commercial bank

reserves above capital of Citicorp

data not available

Sources: The Banker, IMF International Financial Statistics

The total assets of the world's top 500 commercial banks were $9,250.5 billion in 1985, or more than two-thirds the Gross National Product of the whole world in 1984

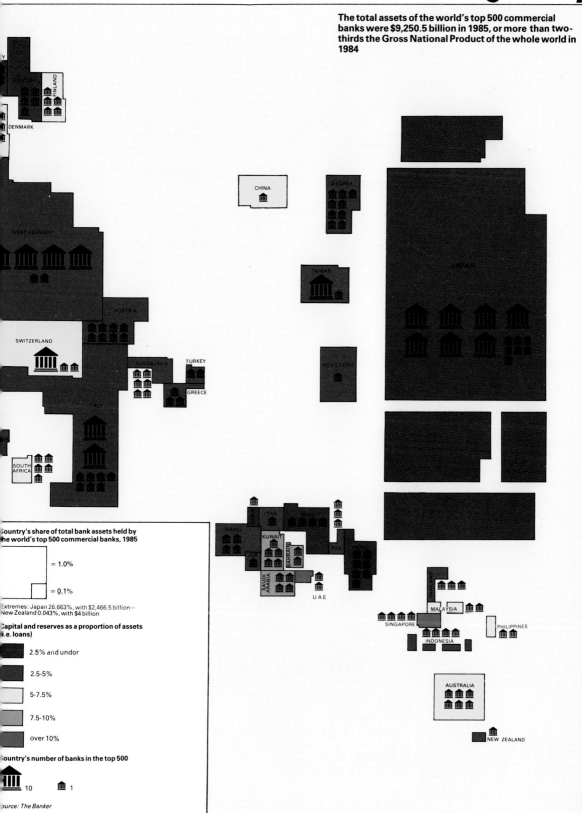

Country's share of total bank assets held by the world's top 500 commercial banks, 1985

= 1.0%

= 0,1%

Extremes: Japan 26.663%, with $2,466.5 billion – New Zealand 0.043%, with $4 billion

Capital and reserves as a proportion of assets (i.e. loans)

2.5% and under

2.5-5%

5-7.5%

7.5-10%

over 10%

Country's number of banks in the top 500

10   1

Source: The Banker

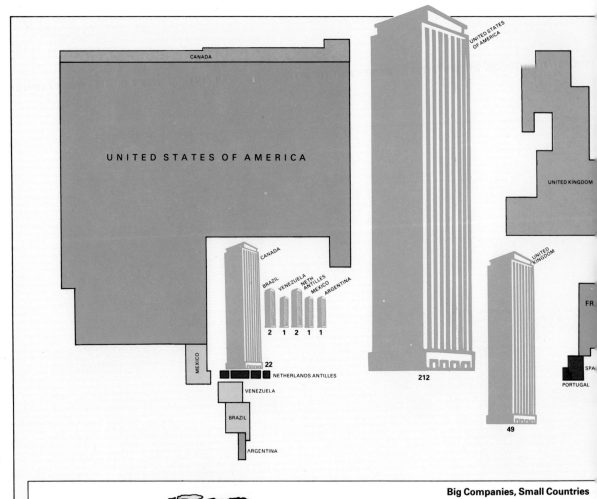

CANADA

UNITED STATES OF AMERICA

UNITED STATES OF AMERICA

UNITED KINGDOM

CANADA
BRAZIL
VENEZUELA
NETH. ANTILLES
MEXICO
ARGENTINA

2 1 2 1 1

22

NETHERLANDS ANTILLES

VENEZUELA

BRAZIL

ARGENTINA

MEXICO

212

UNITED KINGDOM

49

FR.

SPA

PORTUGAL

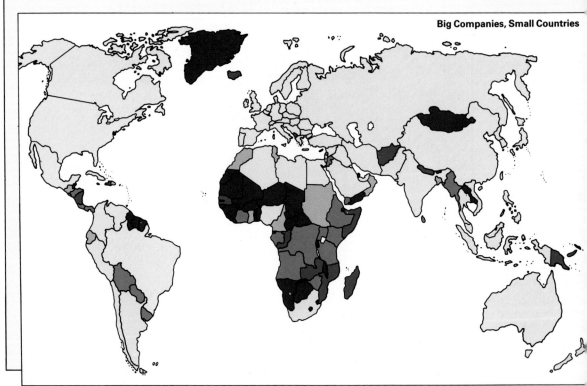

Big Companies, Small Countries

The world's top 500 industrial companies have sales roughly equivalent to nine-tenths of the US gross national product.

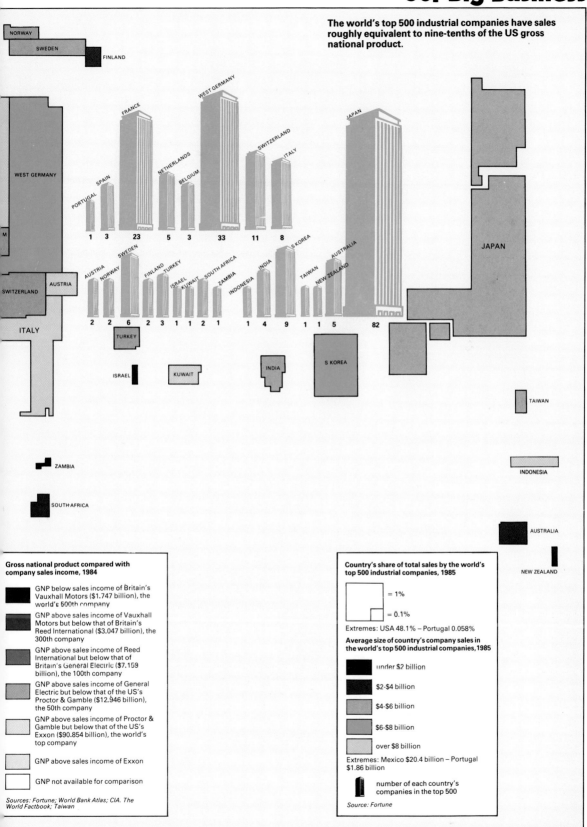

Gross national product compared with company sales income, 1984

- GNP below sales income of Britain's Vauxhall Motors ($1.747 billion), the world's 500th company
- GNP above sales income of Vauxhall Motors but below that of Britain's Reed International ($3.047 billion), the 300th company
- GNP above sales income of Reed International but below that of Britain's General Electric ($7.159 billion), the 100th company
- GNP above sales income of General Electric but below that of the US's Proctor & Gamble ($12.946 billion), the 50th company
- GNP above sales income of Proctor & Gamble but below that of the US's Exxon ($90.854 billion), the world's top company
- GNP above sales income of Exxon
- GNP not available for comparison

Sources: Fortune; World Bank Atlas; CIA. The World Factbook; Taiwan

Country's share of total sales by the world's top 500 industrial companies, 1985

- = 1%
- = 0.1%

Extremes: USA 48.1% – Portugal 0.058%

Average size of country's company sales in the world's top 500 industrial companies, 1985

- under $2 billion
- $2-$4 billion
- $4-$6 billion
- $6-$8 billion
- over $8 billion

Extremes: Mexico $20.4 billion – Portugal $1.86 billion

- number of each country's companies in the top 500

Source: Fortune

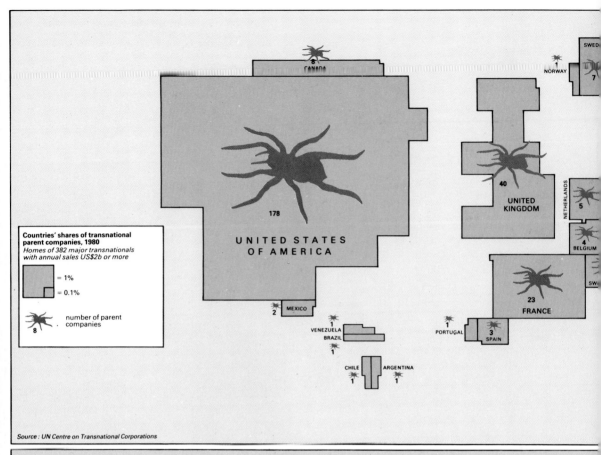

Countries' shares of transnational parent companies, 1980
Homes of 382 major transnationals with annual sales US$2b or more

◻ = 1%
◻ = 0.1%

🕷 number of parent companies
8

CANADA 8

UNITED STATES OF AMERICA 178

MEXICO 2

VENEZUELA 1
BRAZIL 1

CHILE 1 ARGENTINA 1

PORTUGAL 1 SPAIN 3

FRANCE 23

UNITED KINGDOM 40

NETHERLANDS 5

BELGIUM 4

NORWAY 1

SWED- 7

SW

Source : UN Centre on Transnational Corporations

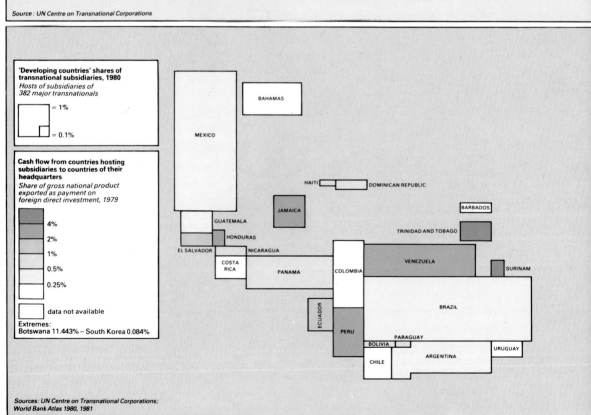

'Developing countries' shares of transnational subsidiaries, 1980
Hosts of subsidiaries of 382 major transnationals

◻ = 1%
◻ = 0.1%

Cash flow from countries hosting subsidiaries to countries of their headquarters
Share of gross national product exported as payment on foreign direct investment, 1979

4%
2%
1%
0.5%
0.25%

◻ data not available

Extremes:
Botswana 11.443% – South Korea 0.084%

MEXICO
BAHAMAS
HAITI DOMINICAN REPUBLIC
JAMAICA
BARBADOS
GUATEMALA
HONDURAS
EL SALVADOR NICARAGUA
COSTA RICA
PANAMA
COLOMBIA
TRINIDAD AND TOBAGO
VENEZUELA
SURINAM
ECUADOR
PERU
BRAZIL
PARAGUAY
BOLIVIA
CHILE
ARGENTINA
URUGUAY

Sources: UN Centre on Transnational Corporations;
World Bank Atlas 1980, 1981

Well over 90 per cent of major transnationals are sited in rich countries. One quarter of the top transnational companies raise more than half their sales income abroad; 8 per cent raise more than three-quarters of their income abroad; and 4 per cent more than nine-tenths.

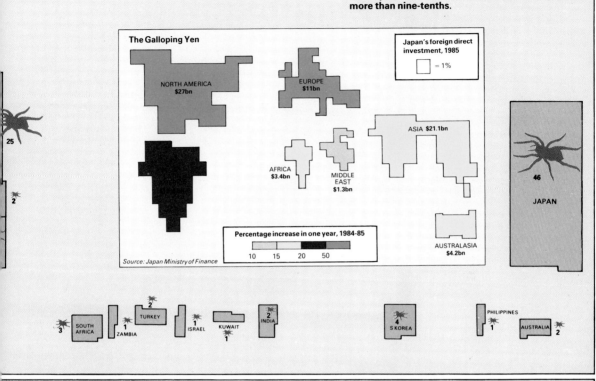

The Galloping Yen

Japan's foreign direct investment, 1985
☐ = 1%

NORTH AMERICA $27bn
EUROPE $11bn
ASIA $21.1bn
AFRICA $3.4bn
MIDDLE EAST $1.3bn
AUSTRALASIA $4.2bn
JAPAN 46

Percentage increase in one year, 1984-85
10 15 20 50

Source: Japan Ministry of Finance

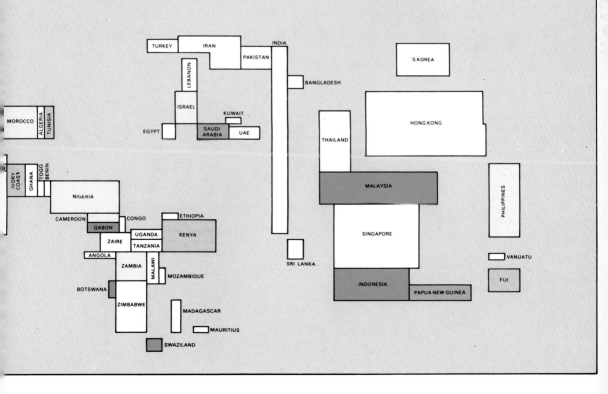

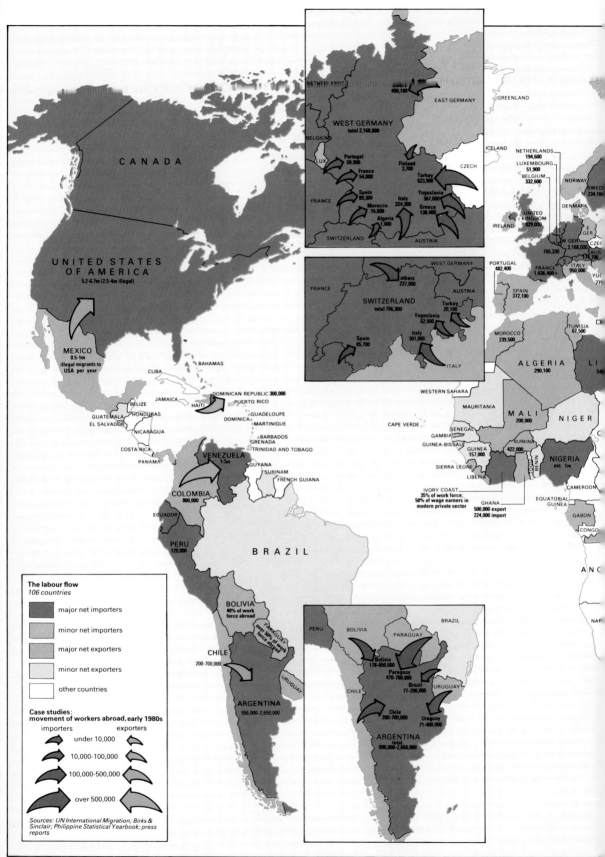

CANADA

UNITED STATES
OF AMERICA
5.2-6.7m (2.5-4m illegal)

MEXICO
0.5-1m
illegal migrants to
USA per year

BAHAMAS
CUBA
JAMAICA
HAITI
DOMINICAN REPUBLIC 300,000
PUERTO RICO
BELIZE
GUATEMALA
HONDURAS
EL SALVADOR
NICARAGUA
COSTA RICA
PANAMA
DOMINICA
GUADELOUPE
MARTINIQUE
BARBADOS
GRENADA
TRINIDAD AND TOBAGO
VENEZUELA
1.5m
GUYANA
SURINAM
FRENCH GUIANA
COLOMBIA
800,000
ECUADOR
PERU
120,000
BRAZIL
BOLIVIA
40% of work
force abroad
CHILE
200-700,000
URUGUAY
ARGENTINA
996,000-2,650,000

GREENLAND
ICELAND
IRELAND
UNITED
KINGDOM
929,000
NETHERLANDS
194,600
LUXEMBOURG
51,900
BELGIUM
332,600
NORWAY
SWED
234,10
DENMARK
W GER
2,168,000
706,300
CZEC
178,00
FRANCE
1,436,400+
ITALY
950,000
YU
77
PORTUGAL
482,400
SPAIN
372,100
MOROCCO
239,500
TUNISIA
67,500
ALGERIA
290,100
LI
5

WESTERN SAHARA
MAURITANIA
CAPE VERDE
SENEGAL
GAMBIA
GUINEA-BISSAU
GUINEA
157,000
SIERRA LEONE
LIBERIA
IVORY COAST
35% of work force;
50% of wage earners in
modern private sector
MALI
200,000
NIGER
BURKINA
422,000
TOGO
BENIN
NIGERIA
est. 1m
GHANA
500,000 export
224,000 import
CAMEROON
EQUATORIAL
GUINEA
GABON
CONGO
AN
NA

West Germany inset
NETHERLANDS
EAST GERMANY
WEST GERMANY
total 2,168,800
BELGIUM
LUX
Portugal
59,900
France
54,000
Spain
89,300
Morocco
16,600
Algeria
1,600
FRANCE
Finland
3,700
Turkey
623,900
Italy
324,200
Yugoslavia
367,000
Greece
138,400
CZECH
AUSTRIA
SWITZERLAND
490,100

Switzerland inset
FRANCE
others
237,000
WEST GERMANY
AUSTRIA
Turkey
20,100
Yugoslavia
62,500
Italy
301,000
Spain
85,700
SWITZERLAND
total 706,300
ITALY

Argentina inset
PERU
BOLIVIA
PARAGUAY
BRAZIL
PARAGUAY
over 50% of work
force abroad
Bolivia
178-650,000
Paraguay
470-700,000
Brazil
77-200,000
CHILE
Chile
200-700,000
Uruguay
71-400,000
URUGUAY
ARGENTINA
total
996,000-2,650,000

The labour flow
106 countries

- major net importers
- minor net importers
- major net exporters
- minor net exporters
- other countries

Case studies:
movement of workers abroad, early 1980s

importers | exporters
under 10,000
10,000-100,000
100,000-500,000
over 500,000

*Sources: UN International Migration; Birks &
Sinclair; Philippine Statistical Yearbook; press
reports*

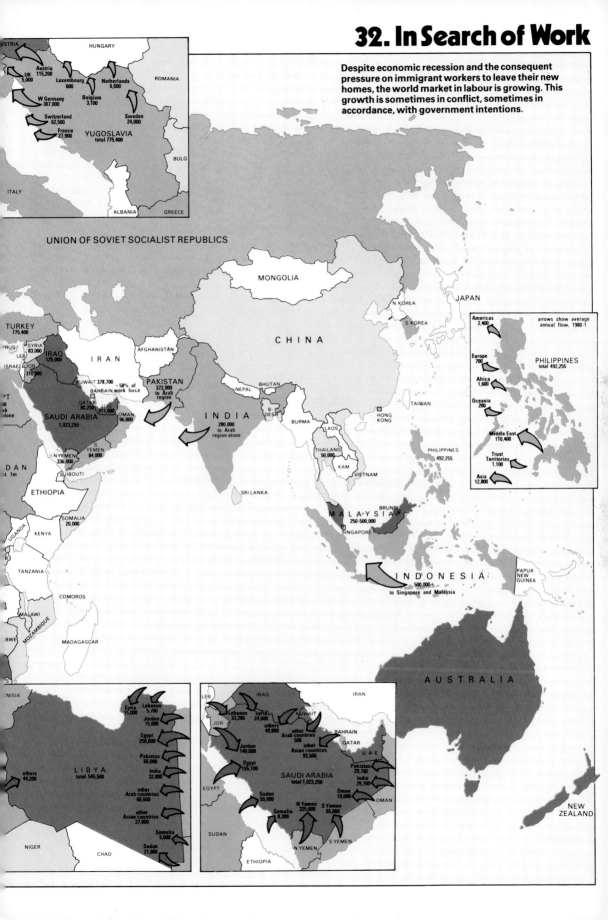

Despite economic recession and the consequent pressure on immigrant workers to leave their new homes, the world market in labour is growing. This growth is sometimes in conflict, sometimes in accordance, with government intentions.

Top-left inset (Europe / Yugoslavia)

HUNGARY
ROMANIA
AUSTRIA
Austria
115,200
UK
5,000
Luxembourg
600
Netherlands
6,600
W Germany
367,000
Belgium
3,100
Sweden
24,000
Switzerland
62,500
France
27,900
YUGOSLAVIA
total 775,400
ITALY
BULG
ALBANIA
GREECE

Main map labels

UNION OF SOVIET SOCIALIST REPUBLICS
MONGOLIA
CHINA
N KOREA
S KOREA
JAPAN
TURKEY
775,400
CYPRUS
LEB
SYRIA
83,000
ISRAEL
JOR
310,900
IRAQ
125,000
IRAN
AFGHANISTAN
PAKISTAN
372,000
to Arab
region
KUWAIT 378,700
+ 58% of
BAHRAIN work force
QATAR
80,250
UAE
411,000
OMAN
96,800
SAUDI ARABIA
1,023,250
NEPAL
BHUTAN
B-DESH
INDIA
280,000
to Arab
region alone
BURMA
TAIWAN
HONG KONG
LAOS
THAILAND
50,000
KAM
VIETNAM
PHILIPPINES
492,255
N YEMEN
336,000
S YEMEN
84,000
DAN
t. 1m
ETHIOPIA
SOMALIA
20,000
DJIBOUTI
UGANDA
KENYA
SRI LANKA
MALAYSIA
250-500,000
BRUNEI
SINGAPORE
TANZANIA
COMOROS
INDONESIA
500,000+
to Singapore and Malaysia
PAPUA
NEW
GUINEA
MALAWI
MOZAMBIQUE
MADAGASCAR
AUSTRALIA
NEW ZEALAND
NIGER
CHAD

Philippines inset

arrows show average
annual flow, 1980-1
Americas
2,400
Europe
700
Africa
1,600
Oceania
200
PHILIPPINES
total 492,255
Middle East
110,400
Trust
Territories
1,100
Asia
12,800

Libya inset

Syria
5,000
Lebanon
5,700
Jordan
15,000
Egypt
250,000
Pakistan
65,000
India
32,000
others
44,200
LIBYA
total 545,500
other
Arab countries
65,600
other
Asian countries
27,000
Somalia
5,000
Sudan
21,000
NIGER
CHAD

Saudi Arabia inset

LEB
IRAQ
IRAN
JOR
Lebanon
33,200
Syria
24,600
KUWAIT
others
49,800
other
Arab countries
500
BAHRAIN
QATAR
Jordan
140,000
other
Asian countries
93,500
UAE
Egypt
155,100
Pakistan
29,700
SAUDI ARABIA
total 1,023,250
India
29,700
Oman
10,000
OMAN
Sudan
55,600
EGYPT
N Yemen
325,000
S Yemen
65,000
Somalia
8,300
SUDAN
N YEMEN
S YEMEN
ETHIOPIA

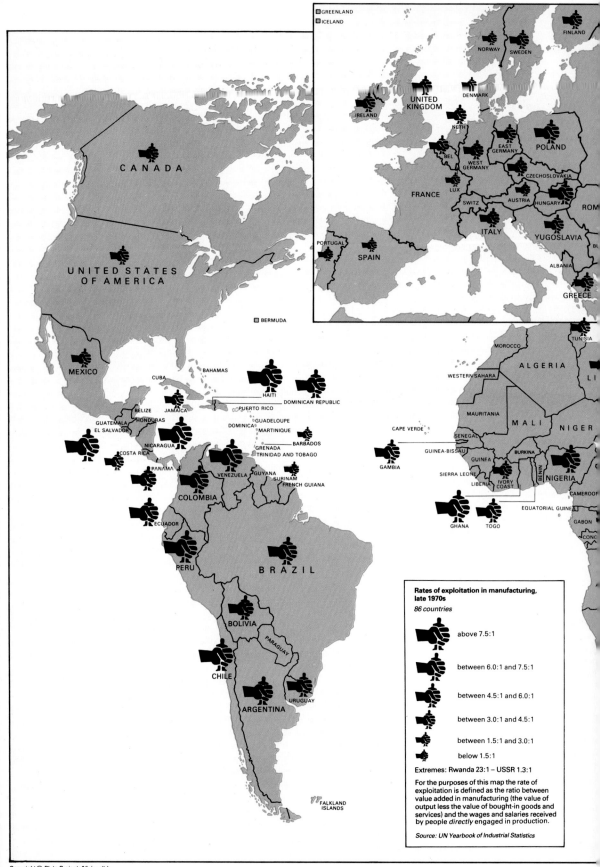

Rates of exploitation in manufacturing, late 1970s

86 countries

	above 7.5:1
	between 6.0:1 and 7.5:1
	between 4.5:1 and 6.0:1
	between 3.0:1 and 4.5:1
	between 1.5:1 and 3.0:1
	below 1.5:1

Extremes: Rwanda 23:1 – USSR 1.3:1

For the purposes of this map the rate of exploitation is defined as the ratio between value added in manufacturing (the value of output less the value of bought-in goods and services) and the wages and salaries received by people *directly* engaged in production.

Source: UN Yearbook of Industrial Statistics

Most people produce more than they earn – for the few who get more than they produce. The difference is measured by the rate of exploitation.
Oppression and exploitation are not the same. Some people are socially and politically oppressed more than they are exploited; of others the opposite is true.

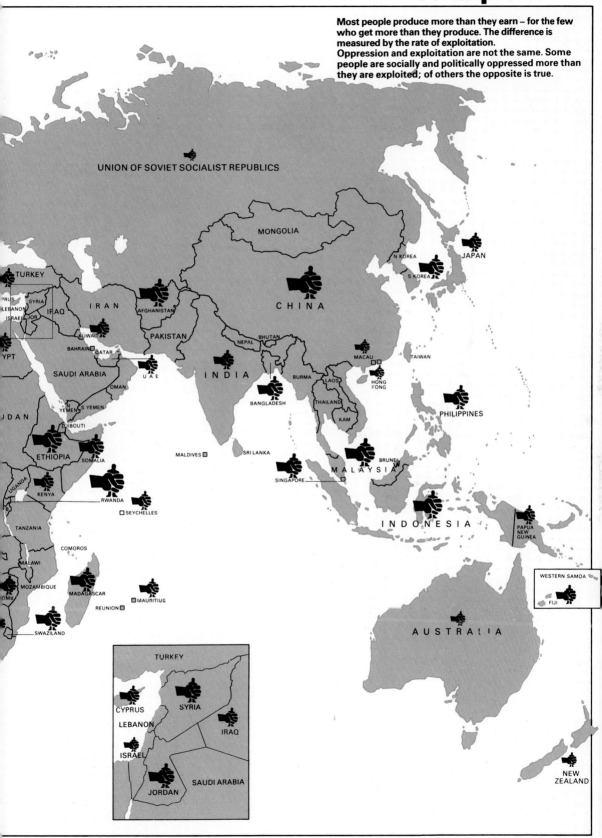

UNION OF SOVIET SOCIALIST REPUBLICS

MONGOLIA

N KOREA   JAPAN
S KOREA

TURKEY
CRUS   SYRIA
LEBANON   IRAN   CHINA
ISRAEL JOR   IRAQ   AFGHANISTAN
YPT   KUWAIT   PAKISTAN   NEPAL   BHUTAN
BAHRAIN   QATAR   MACAU   TAIWAN
SAUDI ARABIA   UAE   INDIA   BURMA   HONG KONG
OMAN   LAOS
N YEMEN S YEMEN   BANGLADESH   THAILAND   PHILIPPINES
JDAN   DJIBOUTI   KAM
ETHIOPIA   SOMALIA   MALDIVES   SRI LANKA
UGANDA   BRUNEI
KENYA   RWANDA   SINGAPORE   MALAYSIA
TANZANIA   SEYCHELLES   INDONESIA   PAPUA NEW GUINEA
COMOROS   WESTERN SAMOA
MALAWI   MOZAMBIQUE   MADAGASCAR   MAURITIUS   FIJI
ZIMB   REUNION   AUSTRALIA
SWAZILAND   NEW ZEALAND

TURKEY
CYPRUS   SYRIA
LEBANON   IRAQ
ISRAEL
JORDAN   SAUDI ARABIA

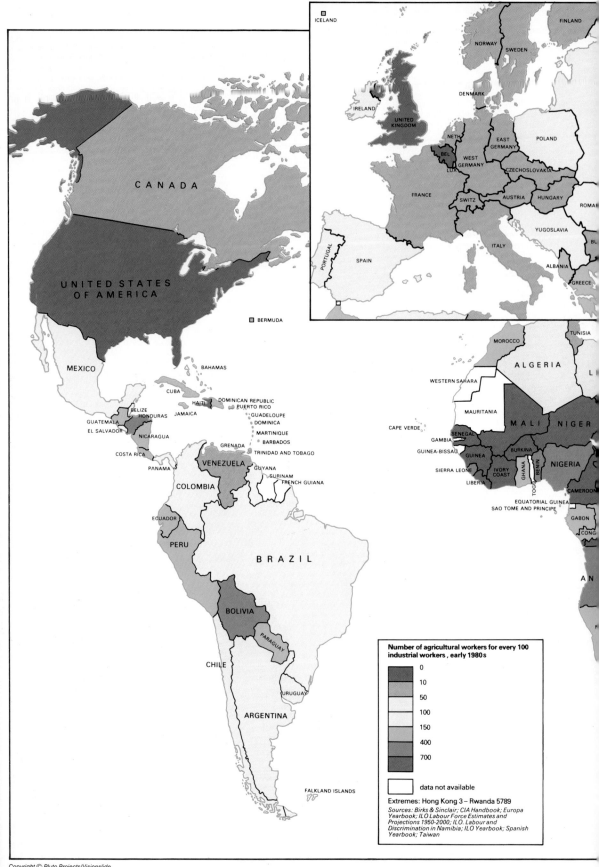

ICELAND

FINLAND

NORWAY
SWEDEN

IRELAND

DENMARK

UNITED
KINGDOM

NETH.

EAST
GERMANY
POLAND

BEL

WEST
GERMANY

LUX

CZECHOSLOVAKIA

FRANCE

SWITZ.
AUSTRIA
HUNGARY
ROMA

PORTUGAL
SPAIN

YUGOSLAVIA

ITALY
BU

ALBANIA

GREECE

CANADA

UNITED STATES
OF AMERICA

BERMUDA

MEXICO

BAHAMAS

CUBA

HAITI
JAMAICA
DOMINICAN REPUBLIC
PUERTO RICO

GUADELOUPE
DOMINICA

MARTINIQUE

BARBADOS

GRENADA

TRINIDAD AND TOBAGO

BELIZE
GUATEMALA
HONDURAS
EL SALVADOR
NICARAGUA
COSTA RICA
PANAMA

VENEZUELA
GUYANA
SURINAM
FRENCH GUIANA

COLOMBIA

ECUADOR

PERU

B R A Z I L

BOLIVIA

PARAGUAY

CHILE

URUGUAY

ARGENTINA

FALKLAND ISLANDS

MOROCCO

TUNISIA

ALGERIA

L

WESTERN SAHARA

CAPE VERDE

MAURITANIA

MALI

NIGER

SENEGAL

GAMBIA

GUINEA-BISSAU

GUINEA

BURKINA

BENIN

NIGERIA

SIERRA LEONE

IVORY
COAST

GHANA

TOGO

LIBERIA

CAMEROON

EQUATORIAL GUINEA
SAO TOME AND PRINCIPE

GABON

CONG

AN

**Number of agricultural workers for every 100
industrial workers , early 1980s**

0
10
50
100
150
400
700

data not available

Extremes: Hong Kong 3 – Rwanda 5789

*Sources: Birks & Sinclair; CIA Handbook; Europa
Yearbook; I.L.O Labour Force Estimates and
Projections 1950-2000; I.L.O. Labour and
Discrimination in Namibia; ILO Yearbook; Spanish
Yearbook; Taiwan*

The industrial age is more than two centuries old, but most workers in most countries still work on the land.

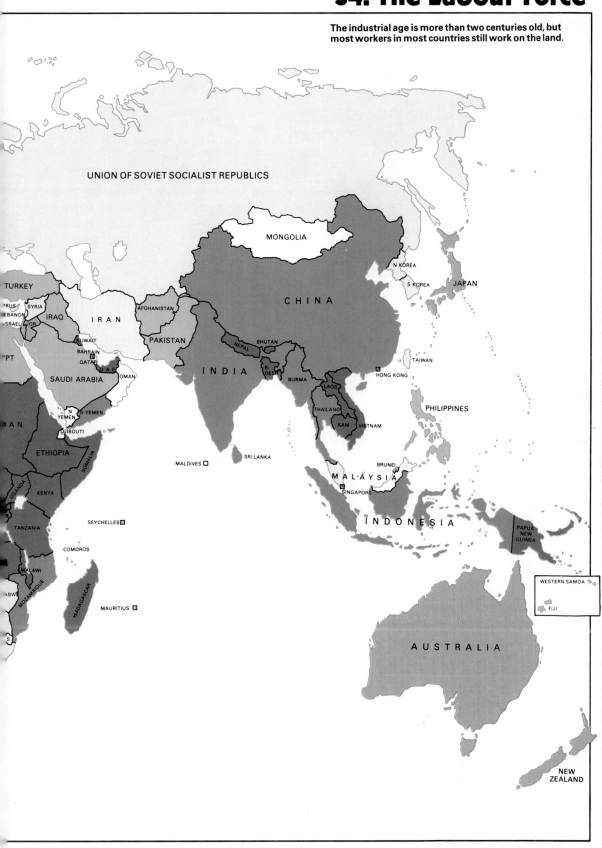

UNION OF SOVIET SOCIALIST REPUBLICS

MONGOLIA

N KOREA

S KOREA   JAPAN

TURKEY

PRUS   SYRIA
EBANON
SRAEL OR   IRAQ   IRAN

AFGHANISTAN

CHINA

PT

KUWAIT
BAHRAIN
QATAR
U A E   OMAN

PAKISTAN

NEPAL   BHUTAN

TAIWAN

SAUDI ARABIA

INDIA

B-
DESH   BURMA

HONG KONG

LAOS

N   S YEMEN
YEMEN

DJIBOUTI

THAILAND

PHILIPPINES

AN

ETHIOPIA

SOMALIA

MALDIVES ☐

SRI LANKA

KAM   VIETNAM

UGANDA

KENYA

SEYCHELLES ☐

BRUNEI

MALAYSIA

SINGAPORE

TANZANIA

COMOROS

INDONESIA

PAPUA
NEW
GUINEA

MALAWI

MADAGASCAR

MAURITIUS ☐

WESTERN SAMOA

FIJI

BWE
MOZAMBIQUE

AUSTRALIA

NEW
ZEALAND

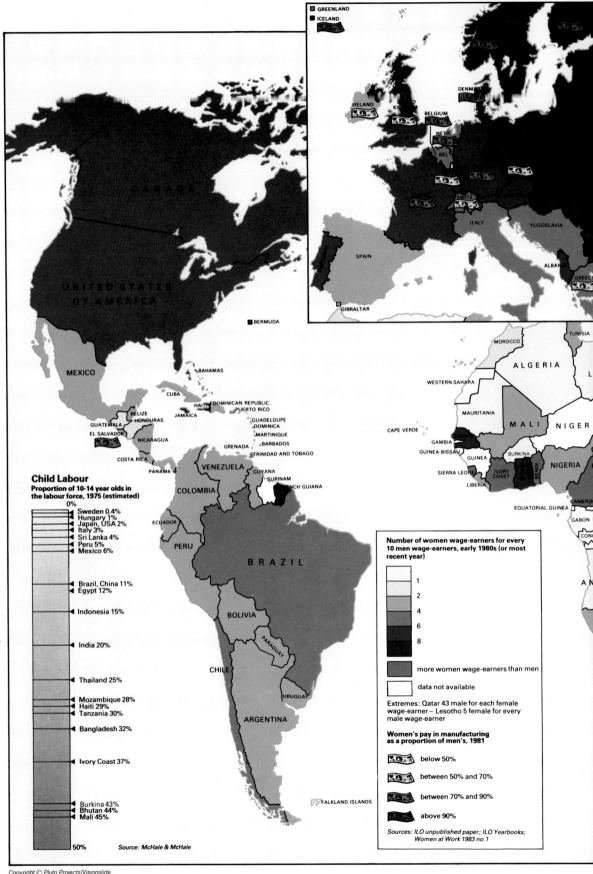

GREENLAND
ICELAND

GREENLAND

CANADA

UNITED STATES
OF AMERICA

■ BERMUDA

MEXICO

BAHAMAS

CUBA
HAITI DOMINICAN REPUBLIC.
PUERTO RICO
JAMAICA

BELIZE
GUATEMALA HONDURAS
EL SALVADOR
NICARAGUA
COSTA RICA
PANAMA

GUADELOUPE
DOMINICA
MARTINIQUE
BARBADOS
GRENADA
TRINIDAD AND TOBAGO

VENEZUELA
GUYANA
SURINAM
COLOMBIA
FRENCH GUIANA
ECUADOR

PERU

BRAZIL

BOLIVIA

PARAGUAY

CHILE

URUGUAY

ARGENTINA

FALKLAND ISLANDS

IRELAND
KINGDOM
BELGIUM
NETH
BEL
SWITZ
ITALY
SPAIN
PORTUGAL
GIBRALTAR

DENMARK

YUGOSLAVIA

ALBAN

GREECE

MOROCCO
TUNISIA

WESTERN SAHARA
ALGERIA
L

MAURITANIA
MALI
NIGER

CAPE VERDE
GAMBIA
BURKINA
GUINEA-BISSAU
GUINEA
NIGERIA
SIERRA LEONE
IVORY
BENIN
COAST
LIBERIA

EQUATORIAL GUINEA
CAMEROO

GABON

CONG

AN

Child Labour

**Proportion of 10-14 year olds in
the labour force, 1975 (estimated)**

0%

◄ Sweden 0.4%
◄ Hungary 1%
◄ Japan, USA 2%
◄ Italy 3%
◄ Sri Lanka 4%
◄ Peru 5%
◄ Mexico 6%

◄ Brazil, China 11%
◄ Egypt 12%

◄ Indonesia 15%

◄ India 20%

◄ Thailand 25%

◄ Mozambique 28%
◄ Haiti 29%
◄ Tanzania 30%

◄ Bangladesh 32%

◄ Ivory Coast 37%

◄ Burkina 43%
◄ Bhutan 44%
◄ Mali 45%

50%

Source: McHale & McHale

**Number of women wage-earners for every
10 men wage-earners, early 1980s (or most
recent year)**

1

2

4

6

8

more women wage-earners than men

data not available

Extremes: Qatar 43 male for each female
wage-earner – Lesotho 5 female for every
male wage-earner

**Women's pay in manufacturing
as a proportion of men's, 1981**

below 50%

between 50% and 70%

between 70% and 90%

above 90%

Sources: ILO unpublished paper; ILO Yearbooks;
Women at Work 1983 no.1

Men dominate paid labour and the higher rates of pay; women work longer hours and for much of their work are not paid at all.

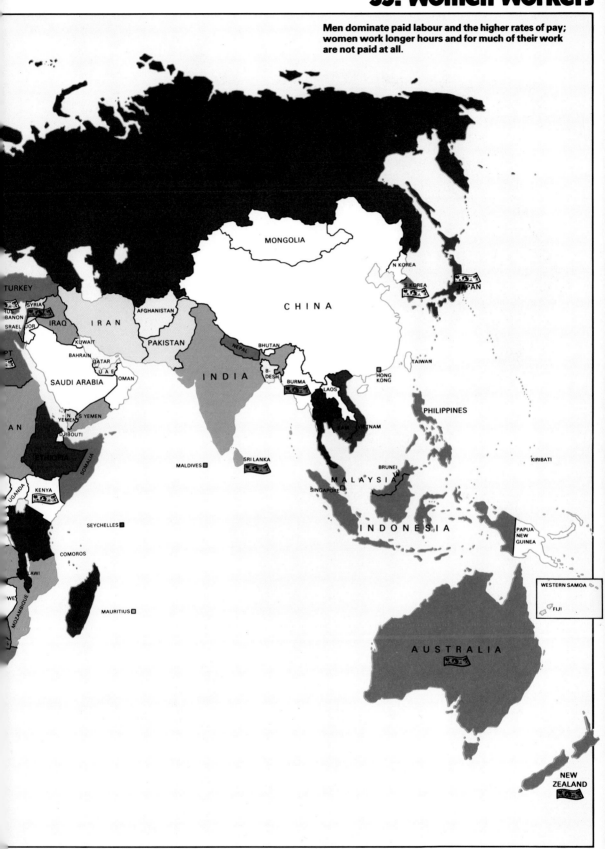

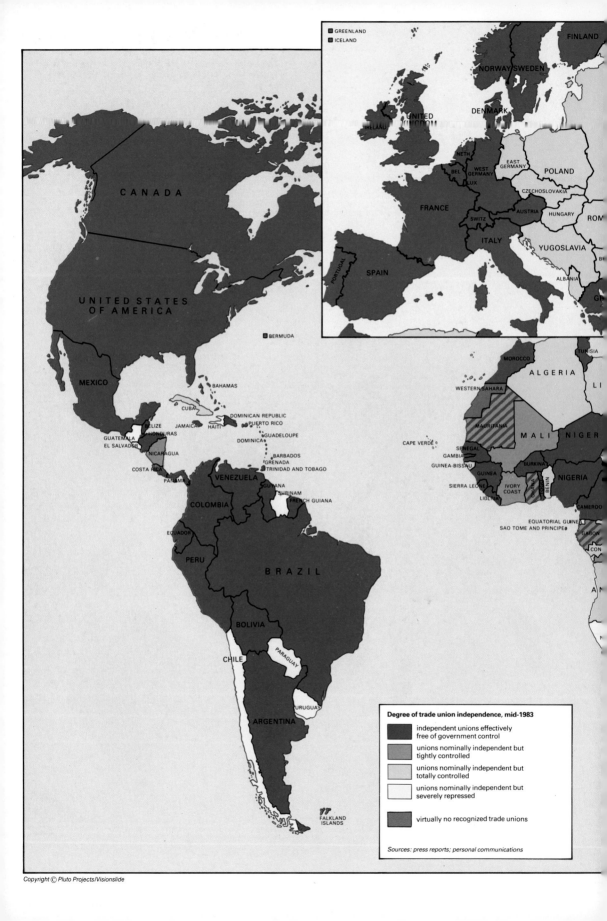

GREENLAND
ICELAND

FINLAND

NORWAY SWEDEN

DENMARK

NORWAY

UNITED KINGDOM

IRELAND

NETH

BEL

LUX

WEST GERMANY

EAST GERMANY

POLAND

CZECHOSLOVAKIA

FRANCE

SWITZ

AUSTRIA

HUNGARY

ITALY

YUGOSLAVIA

ROM

PORTUGAL

SPAIN

ALBANIA

GR

BE

CANADA

UNITED STATES
OF AMERICA

BERMUDA

MEXICO

BAHAMAS

CUBA

DOMINICAN REPUBLIC
PUERTO RICO

BELIZE

HONDURAS

JAMAICA   HAITI

GUADELOUPE

GUATEMALA

EL SALVADOR

NICARAGUA

DOMINICA

BARBADOS

COSTA RICA

PANAMA

GRENADA

TRINIDAD AND TOBAGO

VENEZUELA

GUYANA

SURINAM

COLOMBIA

FRENCH GUIANA

ECUADOR

PERU

BRAZIL

BOLIVIA

CHILE

PARAGUAY

URUGUAY

ARGENTINA

FALKLAND
ISLANDS

MOROCCO

TUNISIA

ALGERIA

LI

WESTERN SAHARA

CAPE VERDE

MAURITANIA

MALI

NIGER

SENEGAL

GAMBIA

BURKINA

GUINEA-BISSAU

GUINEA

NIGERIA

SIERRA LEONE

IVORY
COAST

GHANA

TOGO

BENIN

CAMEROO

LIBERIA

EQUATORIAL GUINEA

SAO TOME AND PRINCIPE

GABON

CON

AN

Degree of trade union independence, mid-1983

independent unions effectively
free of government control

unions nominally independent but
tightly controlled

unions nominally independent but
totally controlled

unions nominally independent but
severely repressed

virtually no recognized trade unions

Sources: press reports; personal communications

The essential conflict for authority between the state
and its alternatives runs through trade unionism and the
trade unions.

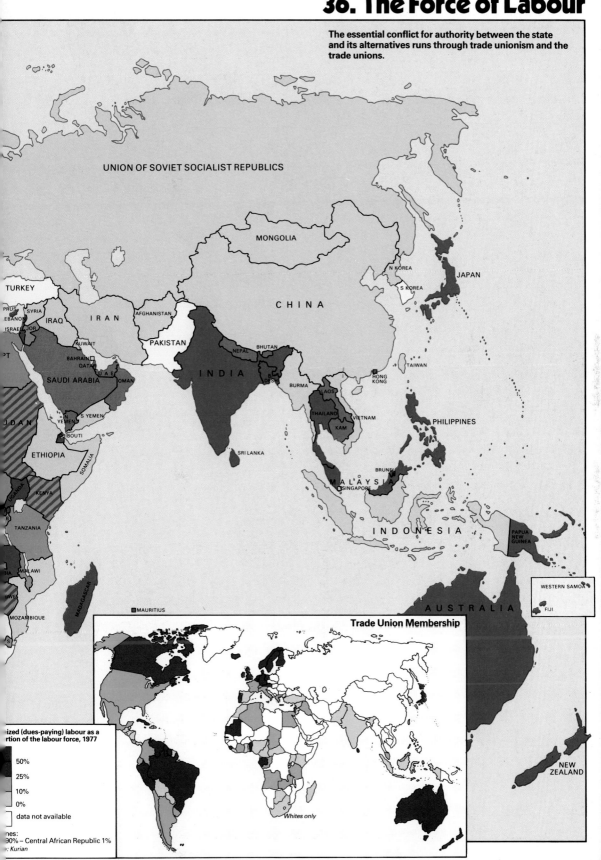

UNION OF SOVIET SOCIALIST REPUBLICS

TURKEY

PRUS
SYRIA
EBANON
ISRAEL JOR
PT

IRAQ

IRAN

AFGHANISTAN

KUWAIT

BAHRAIN
QATAR

SAUDI ARABIA

UAE

OMAN

JDAN

N
YEMEN

S YEMEN

DJIBOUTI

ETHIOPIA

SOMALIA

UGANDA

KENYA

TANZANIA

MALAWI

MOZAMBIQUE

MADAGASCAR

MAURITIUS

PAKISTAN

NEPAL

BHUTAN

INDIA

B
DESH

BURMA

SRI LANKA

MONGOLIA

CHINA

N KOREA

S KOREA

JAPAN

TAIWAN

HONG
KONG

LAOS

THAILAND

KAM

VIETNAM

PHILIPPINES

BRUNEI

MALAYSIA

SINGAPORE

INDONESIA

PAPUA
NEW
GUINEA

AUSTRALIA

WESTERN SAMOA

FIJI

NEW
ZEALAND

Trade Union Membership

ized (dues-paying) labour as a
rtion of the labour force, 1977

50%

25%

10%

0%

data not available

Whites only

nes:
90% – Central African Republic 1%
: Kurian

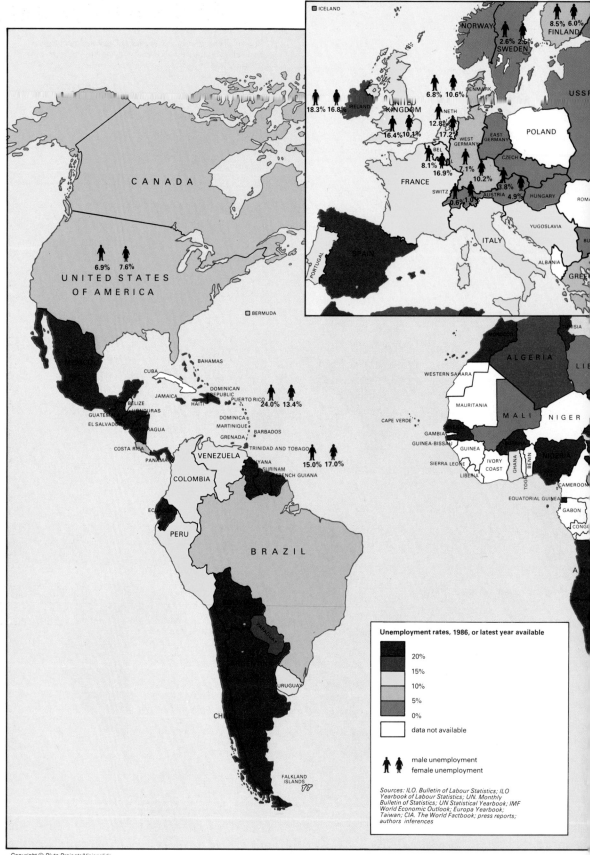

ICELAND

NORWAY
2.6% 2.5%
SWEDEN

8.5% 6.0%
FINLAND

USSR

6.8% 10.6%
DENMARK

18.3% 16.8%
IRELAND

UNITED
KINGDOM

16.4% 10.1%

NETH
12.8%

17.2%

WEST
GERMANY
7.1%

EAST
GERMANY

POLAND

BEL
8.1%

L
16.9%

FRANCE

SWITZ
0.6% 1.0%

10.2%

AUSTRIA
4.9%

CZECH

3.8%
HUNGARY

ROMA

YUGOSLAVIA

BU

PORTUGAL

SPAIN

ITALY

ALBANIA

GREE

BERMUDA

CANADA

UNITED STATES
OF AMERICA
6.9% 7.6%

MEXICO

BAHAMAS

CUBA

JAMAICA

BELIZE
GUATEMALA HONDURAS
EL SALVADOR
NICARAGUA
COSTA RICA
PANAMA

DOMINICAN
REPUBLIC
HAITI PUERTO RICO
24.0% 13.4%

DOMINICA
MARTINIQUE
GRENADA
BARBADOS
TRINIDAD AND TOBAGO
15.0% 17.0%

VENEZUELA

COLOMBIA

GUYANA
SURINAM
FRENCH GUIANA

ECU

PERU

BRAZIL

PARAGUAY

URUGUAY

CHI

FALKLAND
ISLANDS

WESTERN SAHARA

MOROCCO

ALGERIA

TUNISIA

LIB

MAURITANIA

MALI

NIGER

CAPE VERDE

GAMBIA
GUINEA-BISSAU
GUINEA
SIERRA LEONE
LIBERIA

SENEGAL

IVORY
COAST

GHANA

TOGO
BENIN

NIGERIA

CAMEROON

EQUATORIAL GUINEA

GABON

CONGO

A

Unemployment rates, 1986, or latest year available

20%
15%
10%
5%
0%

data not available

male unemployment
female unemployment

Sources: ILO. Bulletin of Labour Statistics; ILO
Yearbook of Labour Statistics; UN. Monthly
Bulletin of Statistics; UN Statistical Yearbook; IMF
World Economic Outlook; Europa Yearbook;
Taiwan; CIA. The World Factbook; press reports;
authors inferences

Unemployment is a matter of political semantics rather than of economic or social statistics. In the Philippines the unemployment figures exclude anyone who has had at least one hour of paid employment in the previous three months. In most countries they have no relevance to most of the population, who live on the land.

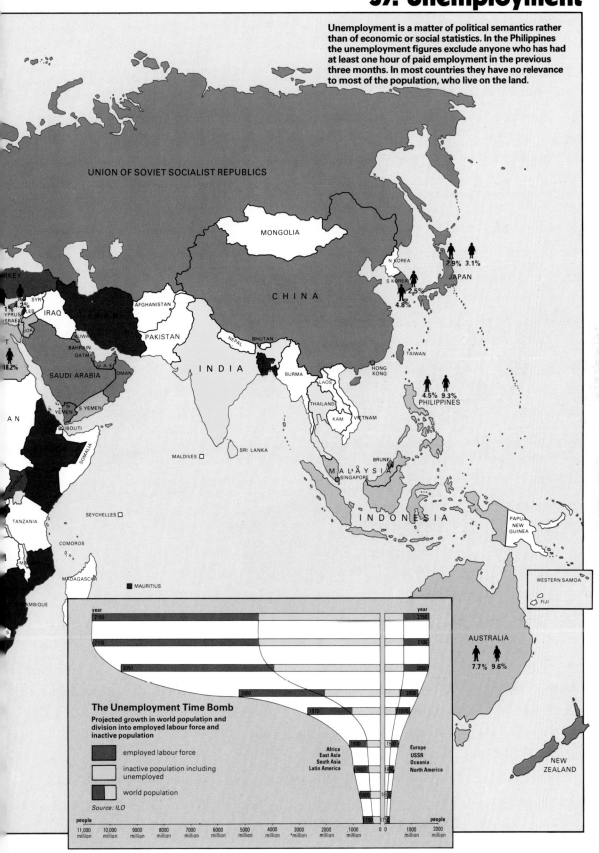

UNION OF SOVIET SOCIALIST REPUBLICS

MONGOLIA

CHINA

N KOREA   7.9% 3.1%

S KOREA 2.5%   JAPAN
         4.8%

TKEY

SYR
4.2%
CYPRUS
ISRAEL
IRAQ

AFGHANISTAN

JOR

KUWAIT
BAHRAIN
QATAR
18.2%   U.A.E

SAUDI ARABIA   OMAN

YEMEN   S YEMEN

DJIBOUTI

PAKISTAN

NEPAL BHUTAN

INDIA   BURMA

SOMALIA

TANZANIA

SEYCHELLES ☐

COMOROS

MADAGASCAR

MAURITIUS

MALDIVES ☐

SRI LANKA

LAOS

THAILAND

KAM VIETNAM

TAIWAN

HONG KONG

4.5% 9.3%
PHILIPPINES

BRUNEI

MALAYSIA
SINGAPORE

INDONESIA

PAPUA NEW GUINEA

WESTERN SAMOA

FIJI

AUSTRALIA

7.7% 9.6%

NEW ZEALAND

The Unemployment Time Bomb

Projected growth in world population and division into employed labour force and inactive population

year 2150
year 2100
year 2050
year 2000
year 1970
year 1900
1850
1800
1750

Africa
East Asia
South Asia
Latin America

Europe
USSR
Oceania
North America

■ employed labour force

☐ inactive population including unemployed

◩ world population

Source: ILO

people
11,000 million 10,000 million 9000 million 8000 million 7000 million 6000 million 5000 million 4000 million 3000 million 2000 million 1000 million 0

people
0 1000 million 2000 million

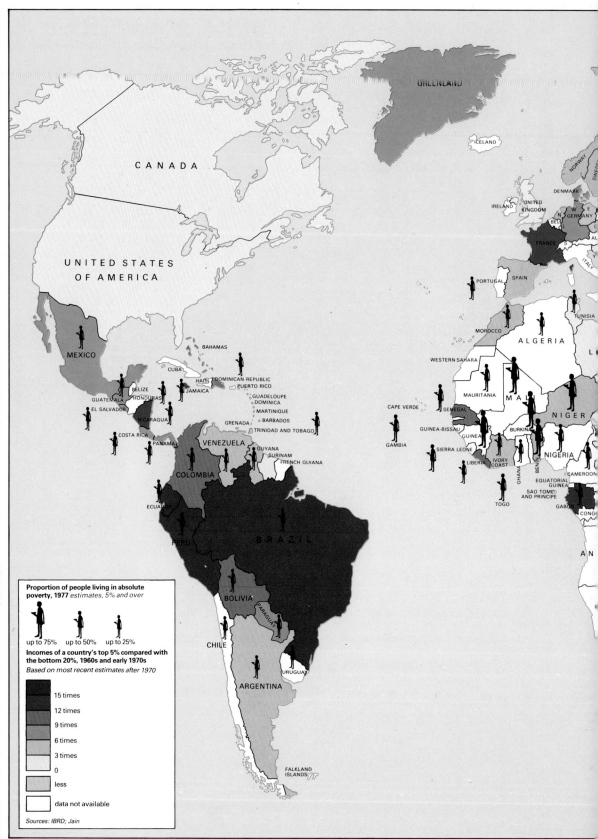

Proportion of people living in absolute
poverty, 1977 *estimates, 5% and over*

up to 75%   up to 50%   up to 25%

**Incomes of a country's top 5% compared with
the bottom 20%, 1960s and early 1970s**
Based on most recent estimates after 1970

15 times

12 times

9 times

6 times

3 times

0

less

data not available

Sources: IBRD; Jain

38. Rich and Poor People

It is the world order that makes rich and poor states, and rich and poor people within each of them. It is said that the poor will inherit the earth. But meanwhile the rich are in profitable possession.

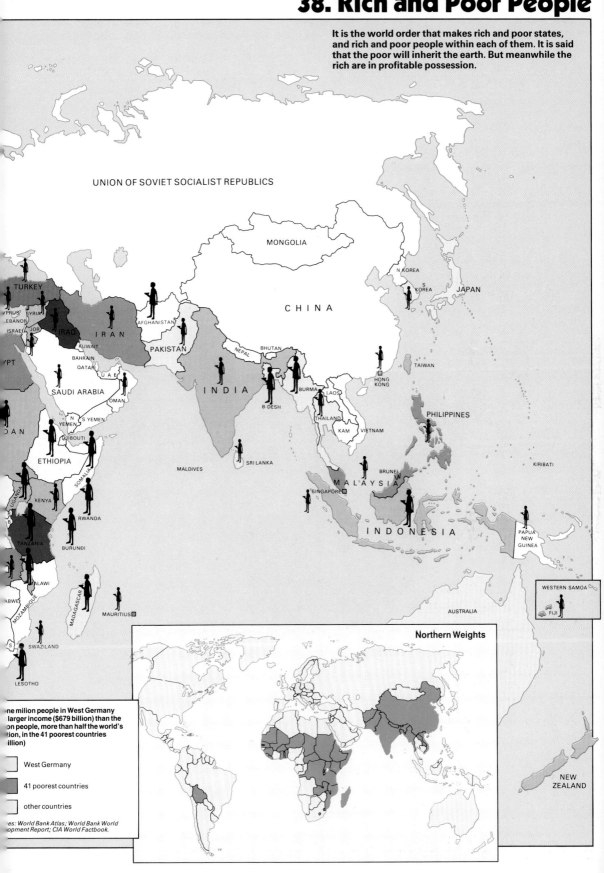

Northern Weights

ne milion people in West Germany
larger income ($679 billion) than the
on people, more than half the world's
tion, in the 41 poorest countries
illion)

- West Germany
- 41 poorest countries
- other countries

es: World Bank Atlas; World Bank World
opment Report; CIA World Factbook.

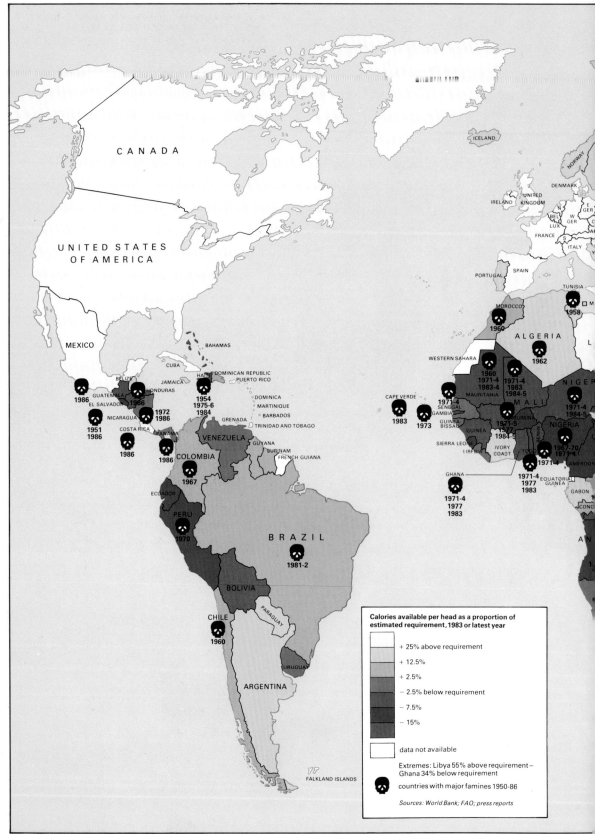

CANADA

UNITED STATES
OF AMERICA

ICELAND

NORWAY

DENMARK

IRELAND UNITED
KINGDOM

N GER
BEL W GER
LUX
FRANCE

PORTUGAL SPAIN

ITALY

MEXICO

BAHAMAS

CUBA

BELIZE DOMINICAN REPUBLIC
JAMAICA HAITI PUERTO RICO
GUATEMALA HONDURAS
EL SALVADOR
1986 NICARAGUA
**1951
1986**
COSTA RICA
1986 PANAMA
1986

**1954
1975-6
1984**

DOMINICA
MARTINIQUE
BARBADOS
GRENADA
TRINIDAD AND TOBAGO

**1972
1986**

VENEZUELA

GUYANA
SURINAM
FRENCH GUIANA

COLOMBIA
1967

ECUADOR

PERU
1970

B R A Z I L

1981-2

BOLIVIA

PARAGUAY

CHILE
1960

URUGUAY

ARGENTINA

FALKLAND ISLANDS

TUNISIA
M
1958

MOROCCO
1960

ALGERIA
1962

L

WESTERN SAHARA

**1960
1971-4
1983-4**

**1971-4
1983
1984-5**

N I G E R

MAURITANIA

M A L I

**1971-4
1984-5**

CAPE VERDE

SENEGAL
GAMBIA
1983 **1973**
GUINEA
BISSAU

1971-4

**1971-5
1977
1984-5**

NIGERIA

SIERRA LEONE

LIBERIA

GUINEA

IVORY
COAST

BENIN

**1967-70
1971-4**

CAMEROON

TOGO
1971-4

**1971-4
1977
1983**

GHANA
**1971-4
1977
1983**

EQUATORIAL
GUINEA

GABON

CONGO

A N

**Calories available per head as a proportion of
estimated requirement, 1983 or latest year**

+ 25% above requirement

+ 12.5%

+ 2.5%

– 2.5% below requirement

– 7.5%

– 15%

data not available

Extremes: Libya 55% above requirement –
Ghana 34% below requirement

countries with major famines 1950-86

Sources: World Bank; FAO; press reports

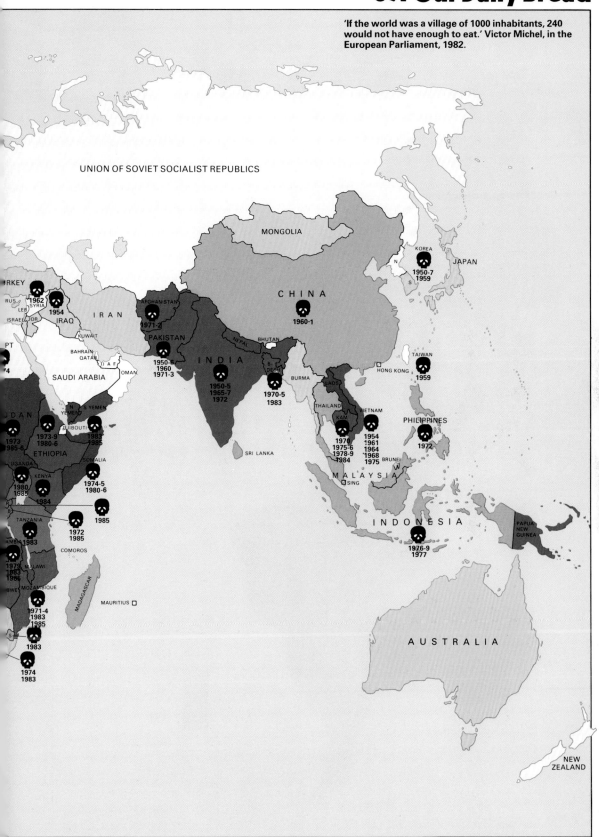

'If the world was a village of 1000 inhabitants, 240 would not have enough to eat.' Victor Michel, in the European Parliament, 1982.

UNION OF SOVIET SOCIALIST REPUBLICS

MONGOLIA

CHINA
1960-1

KOREA
1950-7
1959

JAPAN

RKEY
1962
SYRIA 1954
IRAQ
ISRAEL JOR
LEB
RUS
KUWAIT
IRAN
AFGHANISTAN
1971-2
PAKISTAN
1950-6
1960
1971-3

NEPAL
BHUTAN
INDIA
1950-5
1965-7
1972

B DESH
1970-5
1983

BURMA
LAOS
THAILAND
KAM
1970
1975-6
1978-9
1984
VIETNAM
1954
1961
1964
1968
1975

PHILIPPINES
1972

TAIWAN
1959
HONG KONG

BAHRAIN
QATAR
U A E
SAUDI ARABIA
OMAN

PT
4

N S YEMEN
YEMEN
1983
1985
DJIBOUTI

SRI LANKA

BRUNEI

MALAYSIA
SING

DAN
1973
1985-6
1973-9
1980-6
ETHIOPIA
SOMALIA
1974-5
1980-6

UGANDA
1980
1985
KENYA
1984
1972
1985
1985

TANZANIA
1983
COMOROS

INDONESIA
1976-9
1977

PAPUA
NEW
GUINEA

1979
1983
1986
MALAWI
MADAGASCAR
MAURITIUS

MOZAMBIQUE
1971-4
1983
1985
S
1983

BWE

1974
1983

AUSTRALIA

NEW
ZEALAND

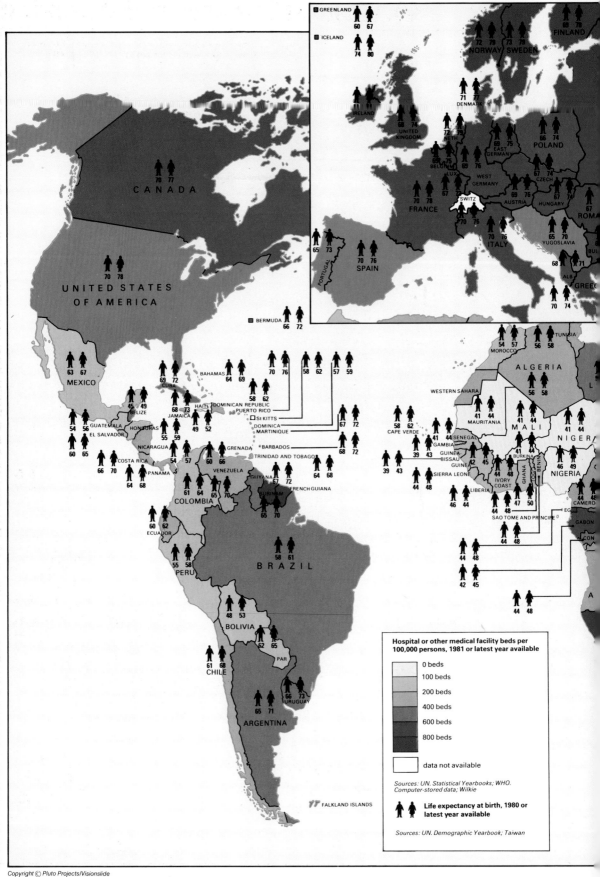

GREENLAND 60 67
ICELAND 74 80
FINLAND 69 78
NORWAY 72 79 SWEDEN 73 79
IRELAND
DENMARK 71
UNITED KINGDOM 69
NETH 72 75
EAST GERMANY 75 POLAND 66 74
BELGIUM 69 75
LUX
WEST GERMANY 69 76
CZECH 67 74
AUSTRIA 69 76
HUNGARY 66 74
FRANCE 70 78
SWITZ 70 76
ITALY 70 76
YUGOSLAVIA 65 70
ALB 68 71
ROMA 67
GREE 70 74
BUL

CANADA 70 77

UNITED STATES OF AMERICA 70 78

BERMUDA 66 72

PORTUGAL 65 73
SPAIN 70 76

MEXICO 63 67

BELIZE 45 49
GUATEMALA 54 56
EL SALVADOR 60 65
HONDURAS
NICARAGUA 54
COSTA RICA 66 70
PANAMA 64 68
CUBA 69 72
JAMAICA 68 73
HAITI 55 59
DOMINICAN REPUBLIC 49 52
PUERTO RICO 58 62
St KITTS 67 72
DOMINICA
MARTINIQUE 68 72
GRENADA
BARBADOS
TRINIDAD AND TOBAGO 64 68

BAHAMAS 64 69
70 76
58 62
57 59

COLOMBIA 61 64
VENEZUELA 65 70
GUYANA 67 72
SURINAM 65 70
FRENCH GUIANA

ECUADOR 60 62

PERU 55 58

BRAZIL 58 61

BOLIVIA 48 53
62 65
PAR

CHILE 61 68

URUGUAY 66 73

ARGENTINA 65 71

FALKLAND ISLANDS

MOROCCO 54 57
TUNISIA 56 58
ALGERIA 56 58
WESTERN SAHARA
MAURITANIA 41 44
CAPE VERDE 58 62
SENEGAL 41 44
GAMBIA 39 43
GUINEA-BISSAU 42 45
GUINEA
SIERRA LEONE 44 48
LIBERIA 46 44
MALI 41 44
NIGER 41 44
BURKINA 46 49
IVORY COAST 44 48
GHANA 47 50
TOGO
BENIN
NIGERIA
CAMER 44 48
SAO TOME AND PRINCIPE 44 48
GABON
EG
CON 42 45
44 48
A

Hospital or other medical facility beds per 100,000 persons, 1981 or latest year available

0 beds
100 beds
200 beds
400 beds
600 beds
800 beds

data not available

Sources: UN. Statistical Yearbooks; WHO. Computer-stored data; Wilkie

Life expectancy at birth, 1980 or latest year available

Sources: UN. Demographic Yearbook; Taiwan

'The days of our years are three-score years and ten' –
if you happen to be European or North American.

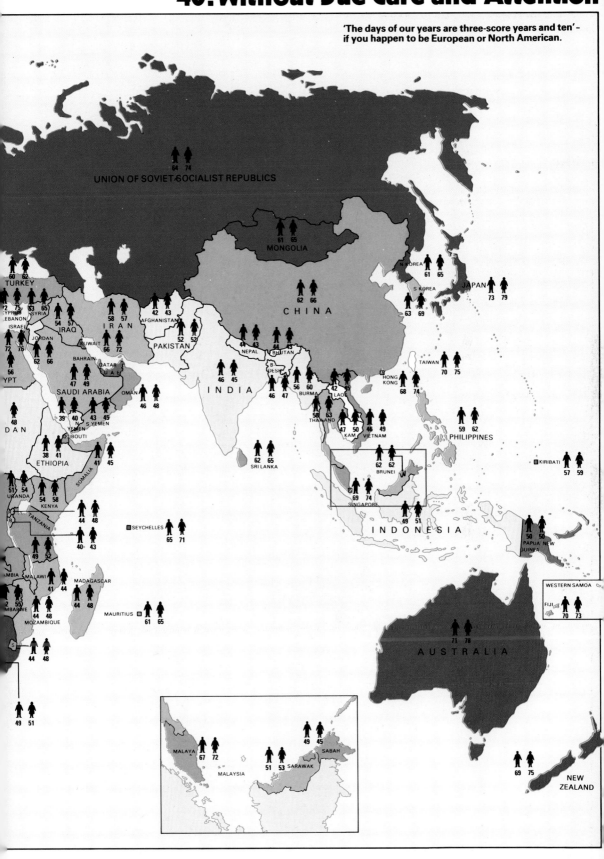

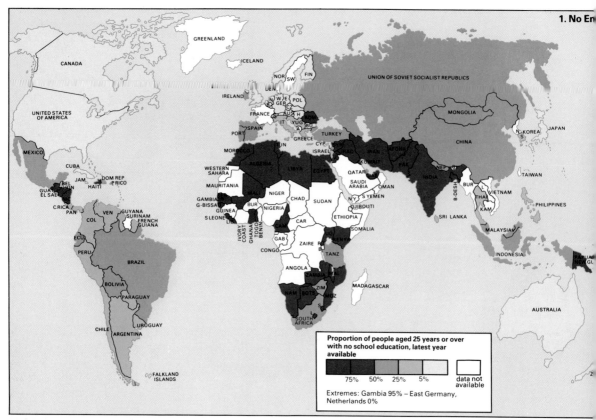

**Proportion of people aged 25 years or over
with no school education, latest year
available**

75% 50% 25% 5% data not available

Extremes: Gambia 95% – East Germany,
Netherlands 0%

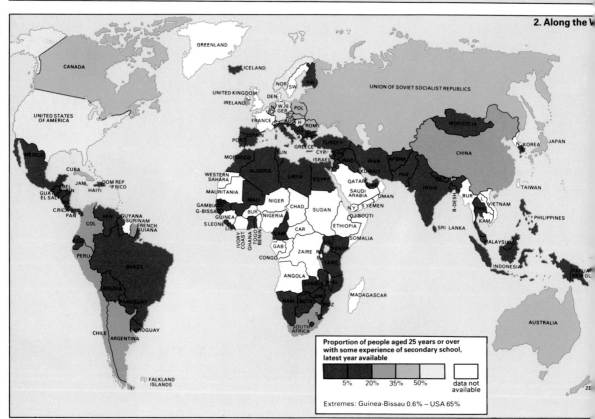

**Proportion of people aged 25 years or over
with some experience of secondary school,
latest year available**

5% 20% 35% 50% data not available

Extremes: Guinea-Bissau 0.6% – USA 65%

41. The Right to Learn

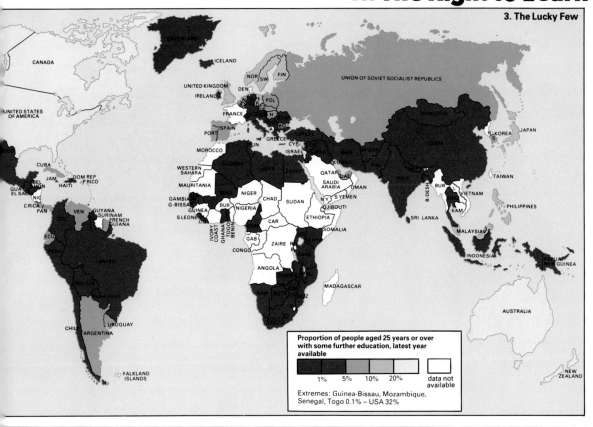

Proportion of people aged 25 years or over with some further education, latest year available

1%   5%   10%   20%   data not available

Extremes: Guinea-Bissau, Mozambique, Senegal, Togo 0.1% – USA 32%

4. Not Even a Beginning

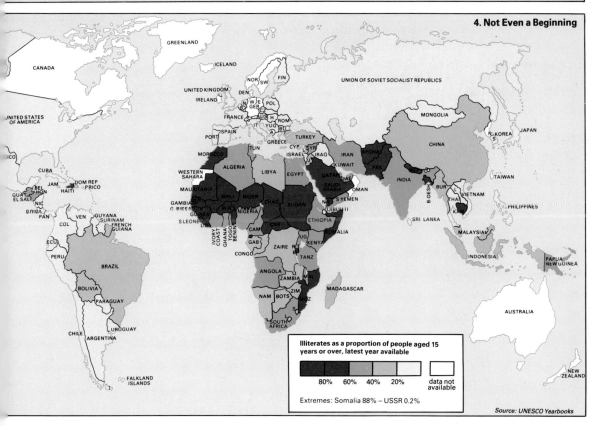

Illiterates as a proportion of people aged 15 years or over, latest year available

80%   60%   40%   20%   data not available

Extremes: Somalia 88% – USSR 0.2%

Source: UNESCO Yearbooks

ICELAND GREENLAND

NORWAY SWEDEN FINLAND

DENMARK

IRELAND

UNITED KINGDOM

BELGIUM NETH EAST GERMANY POLAND

LUX WEST GERMANY CZECHOSLOVAKIA

FRANCE SWITZ AUS HUNGARY ROMA

ITALY YUGOSLAVIA BU

PORTUGAL SPAIN ALBANIA

GREECE

GIBRALTAR

CANADA

UNITED STATES OF AMERICA

BERMUDA

MEXICO

BAHAMAS

CUBA DOMINICAN REPUBLIC PUERTO RICO

HAITI GUADELOUPE DOMINICA

BELIZE MARTINIQUE

GUATEMALA HONDURAS JAMAICA GRENADA BARBADOS

EL SALVADOR TRINIDAD AND TOBAGO

NICARAGUA PANAMA

COSTA RICA VENEZUELA GUYANA FRENCH GUIANA

COLOMBIA SURINAM

ECUADOR

PERU BRAZIL

BOLIVIA

CHILE PARAGUAY

URUGUAY

ARGENTINA

FALKLAND ISLANDS

MOROCCO TUNISIA

ALGERIA LI

WESTERN SAHARA

MAURITANIA MALI NIGER

CAPE VERDE SENEGAL

GAMBIA GUINEA-BISSAU BURKINA

GUINEA NIGERIA

SIERRA LEONE IVORY COAST GHANA BENIN

LIBERIA TOGO CAMEROO

EQUATORIAL GUINEA

SAO TOME AND PRINCIPE GABON

CONGO AN

Domestic letters received and foreign letters received/sent* per inhabitant, 1984 or latest year available

- 0
- 5
- 10
- 20
- 50
- 150

data not available

Extremes: Chad 0.11 – USA 308

Source: Universal Postal Union

Radio receivers per 1000 inhabitants, 1982 or latest year available

above 750

251–750

51–250

50 and below

Extremes: Bangladesh, Bhutan 8 – USA 2,133

Source: US Statistical Yearbook

Often it is poverty that imprisons people in their place; sometimes it is policy.

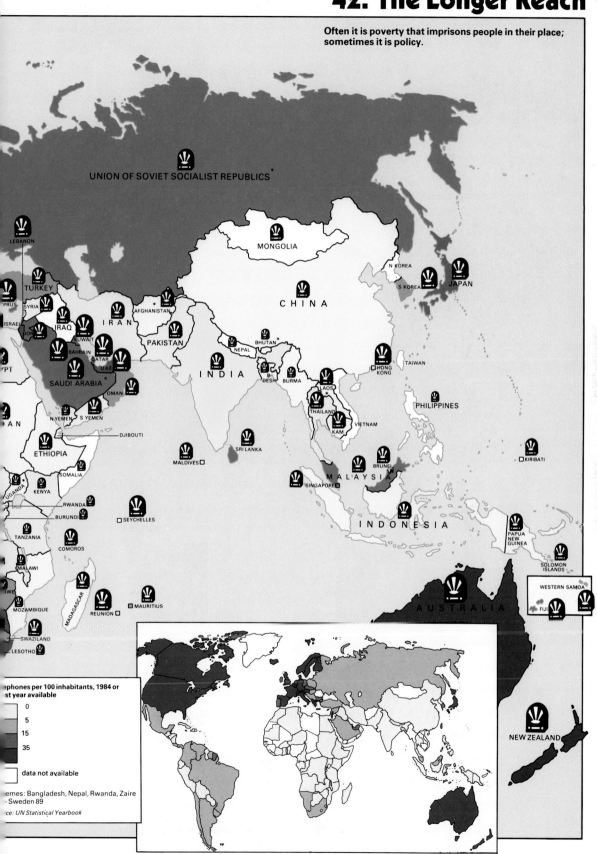

UNION OF SOVIET SOCIALIST REPUBLICS *

LEBANON

TURKEY

CYPRUS
SYRIA
ISRAEL

MONGOLIA

N KOREA
S KOREA

JAPAN

AFGHANISTAN *

IRAQ
KUWAIT
IRAN

PAKISTAN

C H I N A

TAIWAN

BAHRAIN
QATAR
UAE *
SAUDI ARABIA

OMAN

NEPAL
BHUTAN *

I N D I A

B.
DESH BURMA

HONG
KONG

LAOS
THAILAND

PHILIPPINES

N.YEMEN
S YEMEN

DJIBOUTI

ETHIOPIA

SOMALIA

SRI LANKA

MALDIVES

KAM

VIETNAM

KIRIBATI

UGANDA *
KENYA

RWANDA
BURUNDI

SEYCHELLES

MALAYSIA
SINGAPORE

BRUNEI

TANZANIA

COMOROS

I N D O N E S I A

PAPUA
NEW
GUINEA

MALAWI

MADAGASCAR

REUNION

MAURITIUS

SOLOMON
ISLANDS

MOZAMBIQUE

SWAZILAND

LESOTHO

A U S T R A L I A

WESTERN SAMOA

FIJI

ephones per 100 inhabitants, 1984 or
st year available

0
5
15
35

data not available

emes: Bangladesh, Nepal, Rwanda, Zaire
- Sweden 89

ce: *UN Statistical Yearbook*

NEW ZEALAND

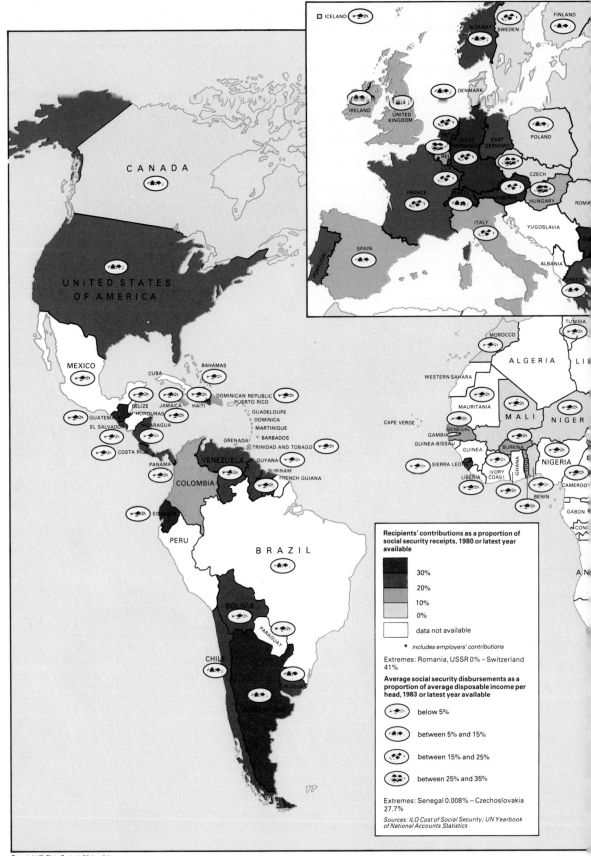

ICELAND

Recipients' contributions as a proportion of social security receipts, 1980 or latest year available

- 30%
- 20%
- 10%
- 0%
- data not available

* *includes employers' contributions*

Extremes: Romania, USSR 0% – Switzerland 41%

Average social security disbursements as a proportion of average disposable income per head, 1983 or latest year available

- below 5%
- between 5% and 15%
- between 15% and 25%
- between 25% and 35%

Extremes: Senegal 0.008% – Czechoslovakia 27.7%

Sources: ILO Cost of Social Security; UN Yearbook of National Accounts Statistics

In general, the richer the government, the more it intrudes, even with its 'benevolence', in the life of the individual citizen.

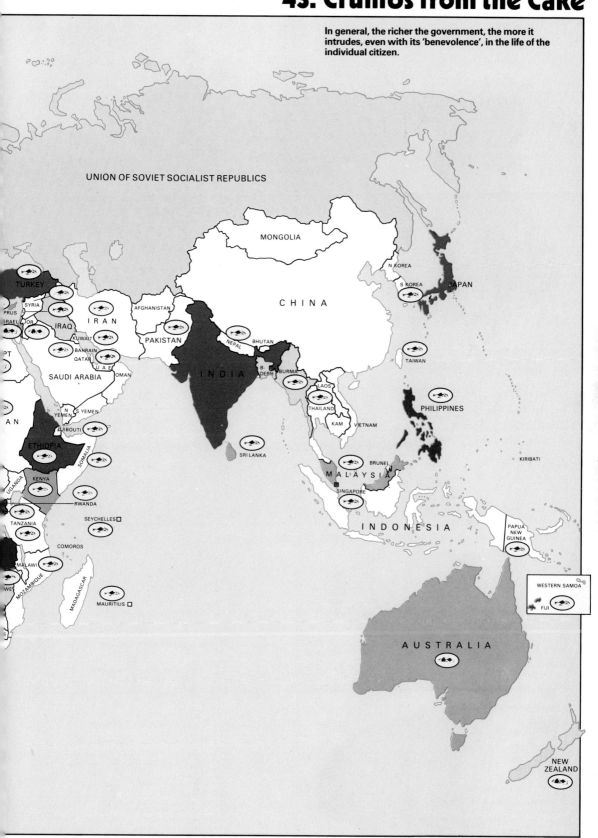

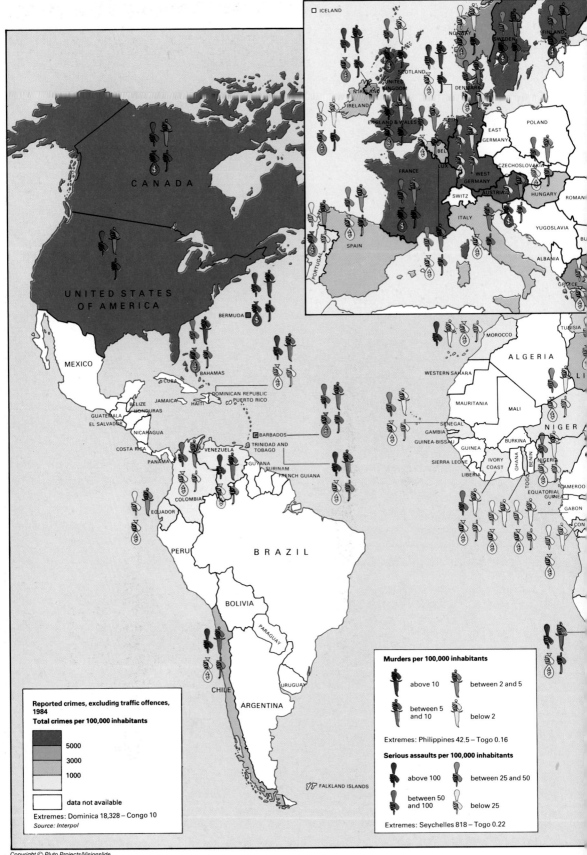

□ ICELAND

ICELAND
NORWAY
SWEDEN
FINLAND
SCOTLAND
UNITED KINGDOM
DENMARK
IRELAND
ENGLAND & WALES
EAST GERMANY
POLAND
BEL
LUX
CZECHOSLOVAKIA
FRANCE
WEST GERMANY
SWITZ
AUSTRIA
HUNGARY
ROMAN
ITALY
YUGOSLAVIA
BU
SPAIN
ALBANIA
PORTUGAL
GREECE

CANADA

UNITED STATES
OF AMERICA

MEXICO

BERMUDA

CUBA
BAHAMAS
JAMAICA
DOMINICAN REPUBLIC
HAITI
PUERTO RICO
BELIZE
HONDURAS
GUATEMALA
EL SALVADOR
NICARAGUA
BARBADOS
COSTA RICA
TRINIDAD AND
TOBAGO
PANAMA
VENEZUELA
GUYANA
SURINAM
FRENCH GUIANA
COLOMBIA
ECUADOR

PERU

BRAZIL

BOLIVIA

PARAGUAY

CHILE

URUGUAY

ARGENTINA

FALKLAND ISLANDS

MOROCCO
TUNISIA
WESTERN SAHARA
ALGERIA
LI
MAURITANIA
MALI
NIGER
SENEGAL
GAMBIA
BURKINA
GUINEA-BISSAU
GUINEA
IVORY
COAST
GHANA
BENIN
NIGERIA
SIERRA LEONE
LIBERIA
TOGO
CAMEROO
EQUATORIAL
GUINEA
GABON
CON

**Reported crimes, excluding traffic offences,
1984**

Total crimes per 100,000 inhabitants

5000

3000

1000

data not available

Extremes: Dominica 18,328 – Congo 10

Source: Interpol

Murders per 100,000 inhabitants

above 10   between 2 and 5

between 5
and 10   below 2

Extremes: Philippines 42.5 – Togo 0.16

Serious assaults per 100,000 inhabitants

above 100   between 25 and 50

between 50
and 100   below 25

Extremes: Seychelles 818 – Togo 0.22

Not all crimes are similarly defined; not all similarly defined crimes are reported; not all reported crimes are recorded; and not all recorded crimes are communicated.

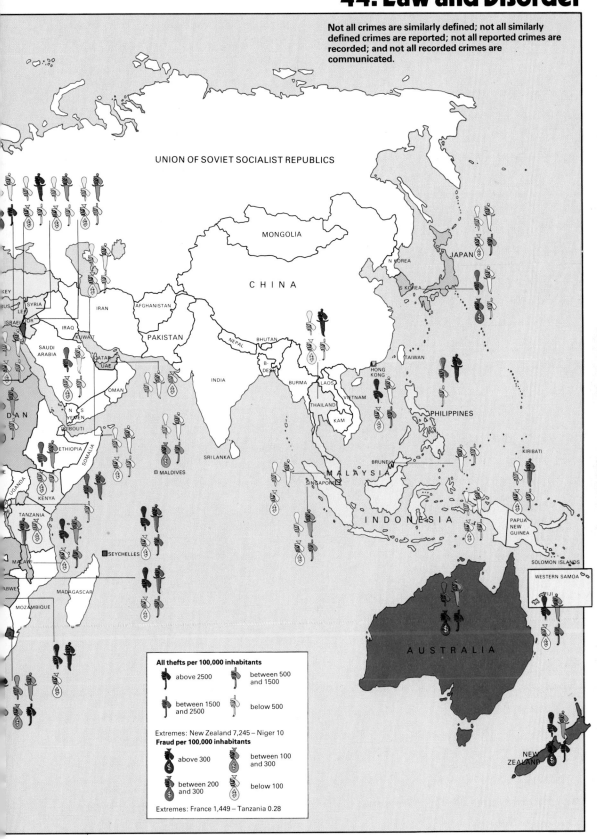

UNION OF SOVIET SOCIALIST REPUBLICS

MONGOLIA

CHINA

N KOREA
S KOREA
JAPAN

TURKEY
CYPRUS
SYRIA
LEB
ISRAEL JOR
IRAN
AFGHANISTAN
IRAQ
KUWAIT
PAKISTAN
NEPAL
BHUTAN
B-DESH
TAIWAN
HONG KONG
SAUDI ARABIA
QATAR
UAE
OMAN
INDIA
BURMA
LAOS
VIETNAM
THAILAND
KAM
PHILIPPINES
N S YEMEN
DJIBOUTI
SRI LANKA
MALDIVES
MALAYSIA
BRUNEI
SINGAPORE
SUDAN
ETHIOPIA
SOMALIA
KENYA
UGANDA
TANZANIA
SEYCHELLES
INDONESIA
KIRIBATI
PAPUA NEW GUINEA
SOLOMON ISLANDS
MALAWI
ZIMBABWE
MADAGASCAR
MOZAMBIQUE

WESTERN SAMOA
FIJI

AUSTRALIA

NEW ZEALAND

All thefts per 100,000 inhabitants

above 2500

between 500 and 1500

between 1500 and 2500

below 500

Extremes: New Zealand 7,245 – Niger 10

Fraud per 100,000 inhabitants

above 300

between 100 and 300

between 200 and 300

below 100

Extremes: France 1,449 – Tanzania 0.28

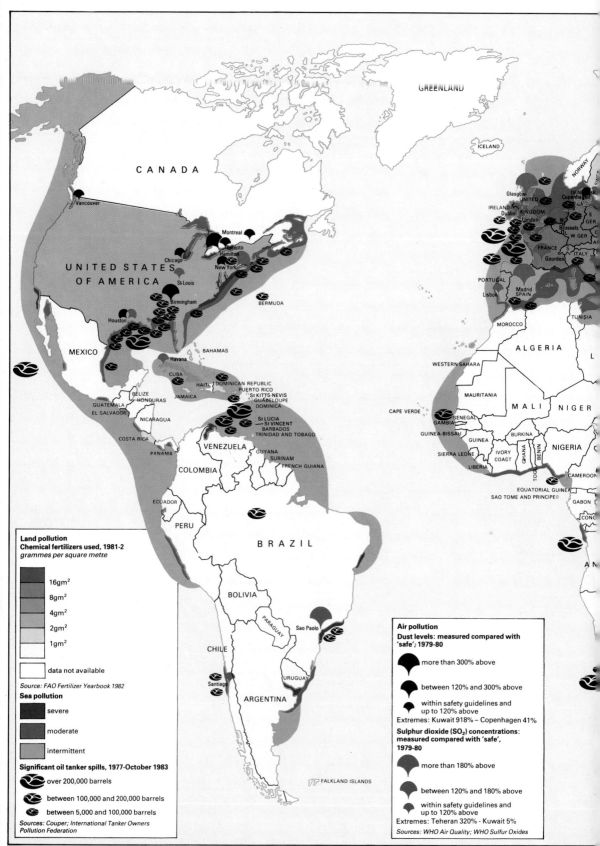

Land pollution
Chemical fertilizers used, 1981-2
grammes per square metre

- 16gm²
- 8gm²
- 4gm²
- 2gm²
- 1gm²
- data not available

Source: FAO Fertilizer Yearbook 1982

Sea pollution

- severe
- moderate
- intermittent

Significant oil tanker spills, 1977-October 1983

- over 200,000 barrels
- between 100,000 and 200,000 barrels
- between 5,000 and 100,000 barrels

Sources: Couper; International Tanker Owners Pollution Federation

Air pollution
Dust levels: measured compared with 'safe', 1979-80

- more than 300% above
- between 120% and 300% above
- within safety guidelines and up to 120% above

Extremes: Kuwait 918% – Copenhagen 41%

Sulphur dioxide (SO₂) concentrations: measured compared with 'safe', 1979-80

- more than 180% above
- between 120% and 180% above
- within safety guidelines and up to 120% above

Extremes: Teheran 320% - Kuwait 5%

Sources: WHO Air Quality; WHO Sulfur Oxides

Pollution is the measure of our failure to organize for a larger human presence in the biosphere.

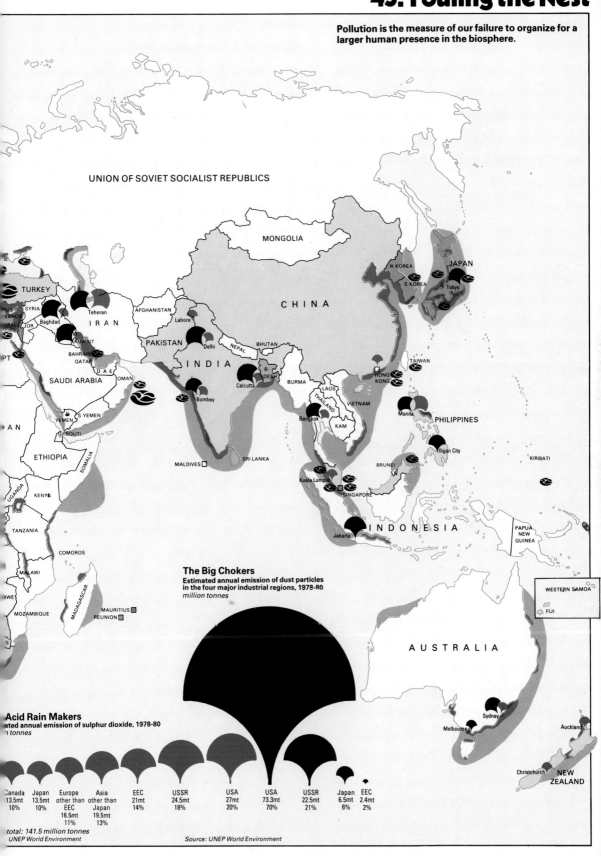

UNION OF SOVIET SOCIALIST REPUBLICS

MONGOLIA

CHINA

TURKEY

IRAN

Teheran

AFGHANISTAN

Baghdad

KUWAIT

BAHRAIN

QATAR

U.A.E

SAUDI ARABIA

OMAN

YEMEN

S YEMEN

DJIBOUTI

ETHIOPIA

SOMALIA

UGANDA

KENYA

TANZANIA

COMOROS

MALAWI

MADAGASCAR

MOZAMBIQUE

MAURITIUS

REUNION

PAKISTAN

Lahore

Delhi

NEPAL

BHUTAN

INDIA

Calcutta

B-DESH

BURMA

Bombay

MALDIVES

SRI LANKA

LAOS

THAILAND

VIETNAM

Bangkok

KAM

N KOREA

S KOREA

JAPAN

Tokyo

TAIWAN

HONG KONG

Manila

PHILIPPINES

Iligan City

KIRIBATI

BRUNEI

Kuala Lumpur

SINGAPORE

INDONESIA

Jakarta

PAPUA NEW GUINEA

WESTERN SAMOA

FIJI

The Big Chokers
Estimated annual emission of dust particles in the four major industrial regions, 1978-80
million tonnes

AUSTRALIA

Sydney

Melbourne

Auckland

Christchurch

NEW ZEALAND

Acid Rain Makers
ated annual emission of sulphur dioxide, 1978-80
n tonnes

| Canada 13.5mt 10% | Japan 13.5mt 10% | Europe other than EEC 16.5mt 11% | Asia other than Japan 19.5mt 13% | EEC 21mt 14% | USSR 24.5mt 18% | USA 27mt 20% | USA 73.3mt 70% | USSR 22.5mt 21% | Japan 6.5mt 6% | EEC 2.4mt 2% |

total: 141.5 million tonnes
UNEP World Environment

Source: UNEP World Environment

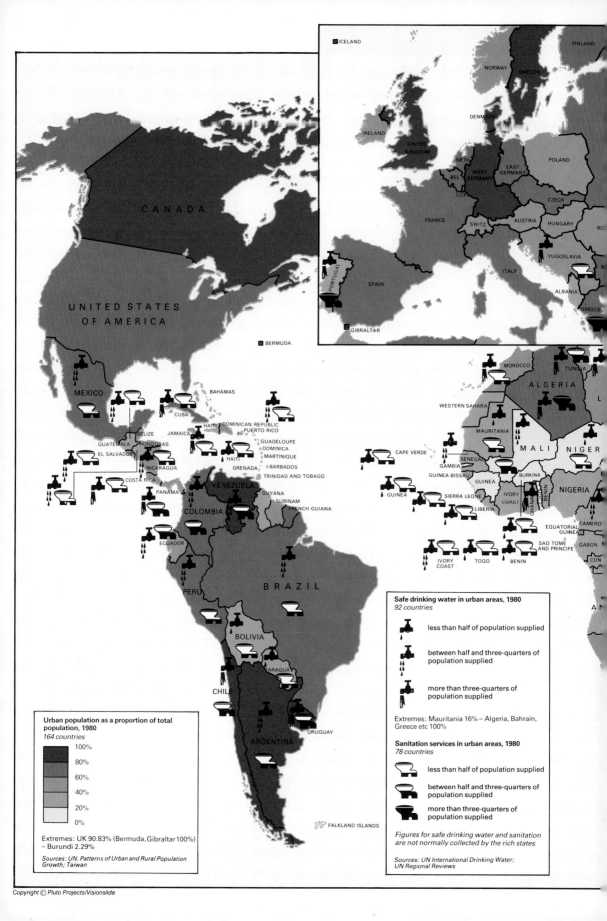

ICELAND

FINLAND

NORWAY
SWEDEN

DENMARK

IRELAND

UNITED
KINGDOM

NETH
WEST
GERMANY

EAST
GERMANY

POLAND

BEL
LUX

CZECH

FRANCE
SWITZ

AUSTRIA

HUNGARY

RO

ITALY

YUGOSLAVIA

PORTUGAL

SPAIN

ALBANIA

GREECE

GIBRALTAR

CANADA

UNITED STATES
OF AMERICA

BERMUDA

MEXICO

BAHAMAS

CUBA

BELIZE

JAMAICA

HAITI

DOMINICAN REPUBLIC
PUERTO RICO

GUATEMALA

HONDURAS

GUADELOUPE
DOMINICA
MARTINIQUE

EL SALVADOR

NICARAGUA

HAITI

COSTA RICA

GRENADA

BARBADOS

PANAMA

TRINIDAD AND TOBAGO

VENEZUELA

GUYANA

SURINAM

COLOMBIA

FRENCH GUIANA

ECUADOR

BRAZIL

PERU

BOLIVIA

PARAGUAY

CHILE

URUGUAY

ARGENTINA

FALKLAND ISLANDS

MOROCCO

TUNISIA

ALGERIA

L

WESTERN SAHARA

MAURITANIA

MALI

NIGER

CAPE VERDE

SENEGAL

GAMBIA

BURKINA

NIGERIA

GUINEA-BISSAU

GUINEA

BENIN

GUINEA

SIERRA LEONE

IVORY
COAST

GHANA

LIBERIA

EQUATORIAL
GUINEA

CAMERO

SAO TOME
AND PRINCIPE

GABON

IVORY
COAST

TOGO

BENIN

CON

A

N

Urban population as a proportion of total population, 1980
164 countries

- 100%
- 80%
- 60%
- 40%
- 20%
- 0%

Extremes: UK 90.83% (Bermuda, Gibraltar 100%) – Burundi 2.29%

Sources: UN. Patterns of Urban and Rural Population Growth; Taiwan

Safe drinking water in urban areas, 1980
92 countries

less than half of population supplied

between half and three-quarters of population supplied

more than three-quarters of population supplied

Extremes: Mauritania 16% – Algeria, Bahrain, Greece etc 100%

Sanitation services in urban areas, 1980
78 countries

less than half of population supplied

between half and three-quarters of population supplied

more than three-quarters of population supplied

Figures for safe drinking water and sanitation are not normally collected by the rich states

Sources: UN International Drinking Water; UN Regional Reviews

Two out of every five people live in cities and their number is growing faster, by a quarter, than the total population.

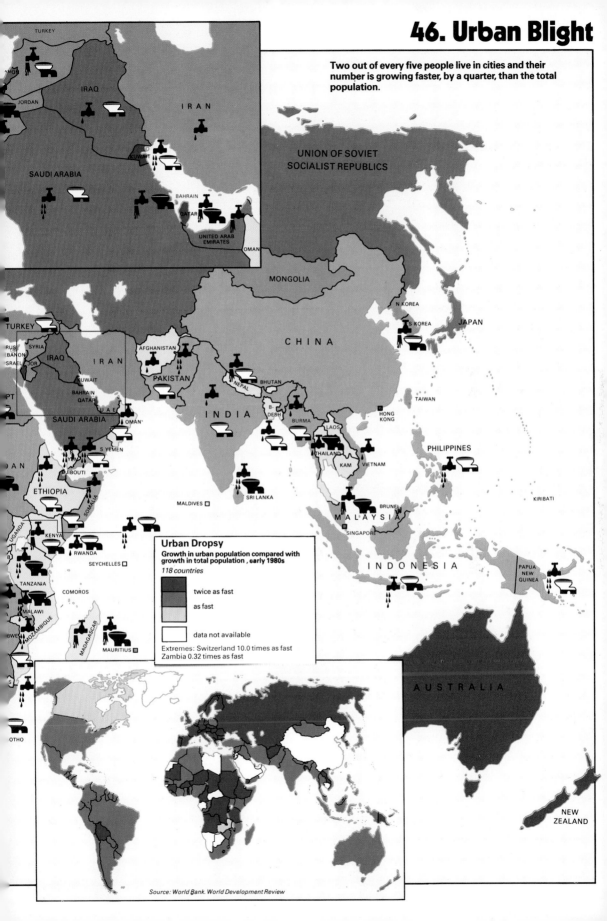

TURKEY
IRAQ
JORDAN
IRAN
SAUDI ARABIA
KUWAIT
BAHRAIN
QATAR
UNITED ARAB EMIRATES
OMAN

UNION OF SOVIET SOCIALIST REPUBLICS

MONGOLIA

TURKEY
RUS
SYRIA
BANON
SRAEL
JOR
IRAQ
IRAN
AFGHANISTAN
PAKISTAN
SAUDI ARABIA
KUWAIT
BAHRAIN
QATAR
U A E
OMAN
S YEMEN
DJIBOUTI
ETHIOPIA
SOMALIA
NEPAL
BHUTAN
INDIA
B-DESH
BURMA
LAOS
THAILAND
KAM
VIETNAM
N KOREA
S KOREA
JAPAN
CHINA
TAIWAN
HONG KONG
MALDIVES
SRI LANKA
PHILIPPINES
KIRIBATI
MALAYSIA
BRUNEI
SINGAPORE
INDONESIA
PAPUA NEW GUINEA

UGANDA
KENYA
RWANDA
SEYCHELLES
TANZANIA
COMOROS
MALAWI
MOZAMBIQUE
BWE
MADAGASCAR
MAURITIUS
OTHO

Urban Dropsy
Growth in urban population compared with growth in total population , early 1980s
118 countries

twice as fast

as fast

data not available

Extremes: Switzerland 10.0 times as fast
Zambia 0.32 times as fast

A U S T R A L I A

NEW ZEALAND

Source: World Bank. World Development Review

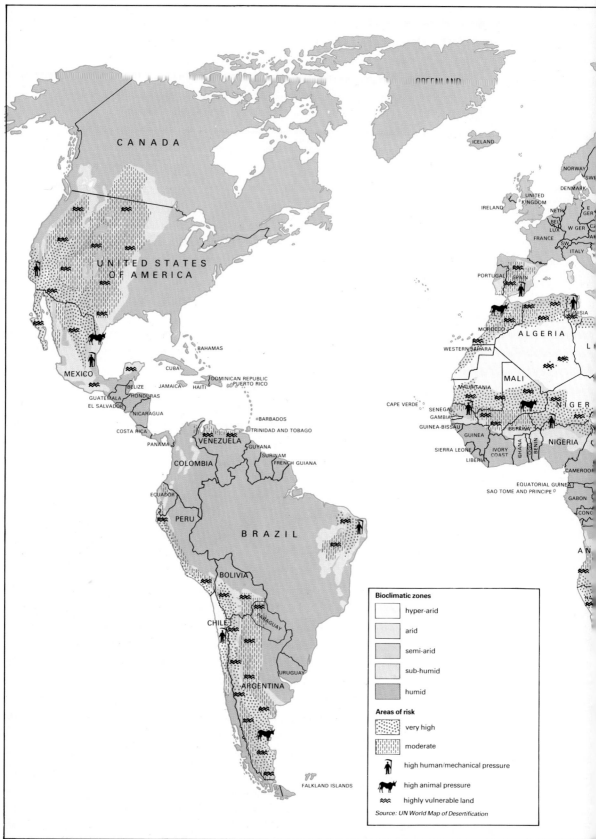

Bioclimatic zones

	hyper-arid
	arid
	semi-arid
	sub-humid
	humid

Areas of risk

	very high
	moderate
	high human/mechanical pressure
	high animal pressure
	highly vulnerable land

Source: UN World Map of Desertification

People create the very deserts that threaten their survival.

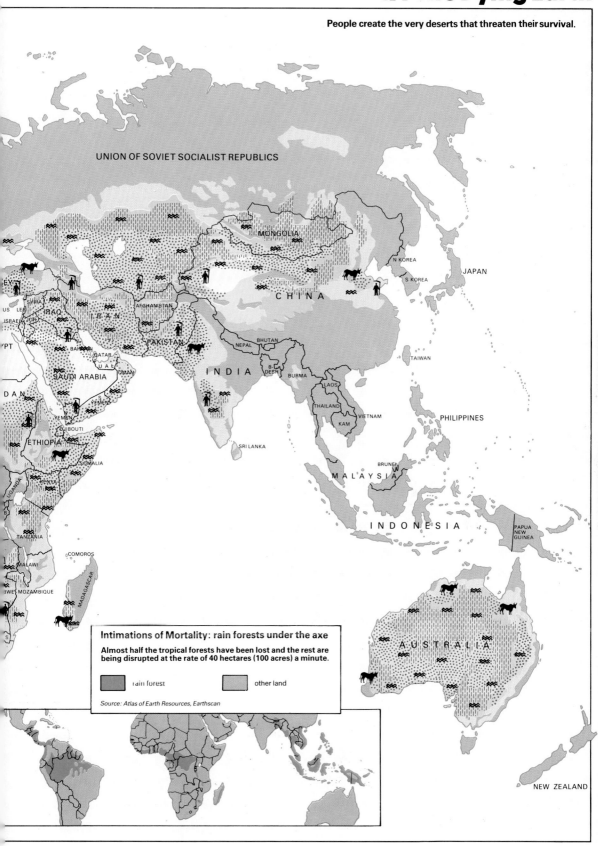

UNION OF SOVIET SOCIALIST REPUBLICS

MONGOLIA

N KOREA

S KOREA

JAPAN

CHINA

EY

SYRIA

US LEB

ISRAEL JOR

IRAQ

IRAN

AFGHANISTAN

PT

BAH

QATAR

U.A.E

OMAN

SAUDI ARABIA

PAKISTAN

NEPAL

BHUTAN

TAIWAN

INDIA

B.G.
DESH

BURMA

DAN

S
YEMEN

YEMEN

DJIBOUTI

LAOS

THAILAND

VIETNAM

PHILIPPINES

KAM

ETHIOPIA

SOMALIA

SRI LANKA

UGANDA

KENYA

BRUNEI

B

MALAYSIA

TANZANIA

COMOROS

INDONESIA

PAPUA
NEW
GUINEA

MALAWI

MADAGASCAR

BWE MOZAMBIQUE

Intimations of Mortality: rain forests under the axe

Almost half the tropical forests have been lost and the rest are being disrupted at the rate of 40 hectares (100 acres) a minute.

rain forest   other land

Source: Atlas of Earth Resources, Earthscan

AUSTRALIA

NEW ZEALAND

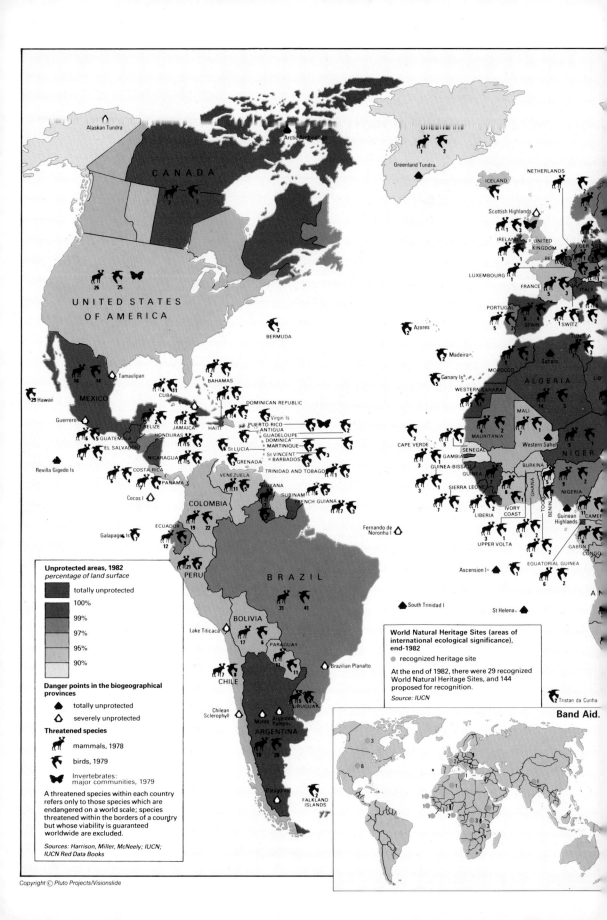

Unprotected areas, 1982
percentage of land surface

totally unprotected
- 100%
- 99%
- 97%
- 95%
- 90%

Danger points in the biogeographical provinces

▲ totally unprotected

△ severely unprotected

Threatened species

🐾 mammals, 1978

🦅 birds, 1979

🦋 Invertebrates: major communities, 1979

A threatened species within each country refers only to those species which are endangered on a world scale; species threatened within the borders of a country but whose viability is guaranteed worldwide are excluded.

Sources: Harrison, Miller, McNeely; IUCN; IUCN Red Data Books

World Natural Heritage Sites (areas of international ecological significance), end-1982

● recognized heritage site

At the end of 1982, there were 29 recognized World Natural Heritage Sites, and 144 proposed for recognition.

Source: IUCN

Band Aid.

Alaskan Tundra
Arctic Archipelago
Greenland Tundra
CANADA
ICELAND
NETHERLANDS
Scottish Highlands
IRELAND
UNITED KINGDOM
LUXEMBOURG
FRANCE
PORTUGAL
SPAIN
SWITZ
ITALY
UNITED STATES OF AMERICA
BERMUDA
Azores
Madeira
Canary Is
WESTERN SAHARA
MOROCCO
ALGERIA
MALI
MAURITANIA
CAPE VERDE
SENEGAL
Western Sahel
NIGER
GAMBIA
GUINEA-BISSAU
BURKINA
GUINEA
NIGERIA
SIERRA LEONE
IVORY COAST
GHANA
TOGO
BENIN
LIBERIA
Guinean Highlands
CAMER
Tamaulipan
BAHAMAS
CUBA
DOMINICAN REPUBLIC
MEXICO
Hawaii
Guerrero
BELIZE
JAMAICA
HAITI
PUERTO RICO
Virgin Is
ANTIGUA
GUADELOUPE
DOMINICA
MARTINIQUE
St LUCIA
St VINCENT
BARBADOS
GRENADA
GUATEMALA
EL SALVADOR
HONDURAS
NICARAGUA
TRINIDAD AND TOBAGO
Revilla Gigedo Is
COSTA RICA
PANAMA
VENEZUELA
GUYANA
SURINAM
FRENCH GUIANA
Cocos I
COLOMBIA
Fernando de Noronha I
CAPE VERDE
UPPER VOLTA
EQUATORIAL GUINEA
GABON
CONGO
Galapagos Is
ECUADOR
Ascension I
PERU
BRAZIL
South Trinidad I
St Helena
BOLIVIA
Lake Titicaca
PARAGUAY
Brazilian Planalto
CHILE
Chilean Sclerophyll
Monte
Argentinian Pampas
URUGUAY
Tristan da Cunha
ARGENTINA
Patagonia
FALKLAND ISLANDS

48. Protection and Extinction

Some 2611 protected areas covering nearly 4 million square kilometres have been established in 124 countries, but a thousand species of mammals and birds are currently in danger of elimination.

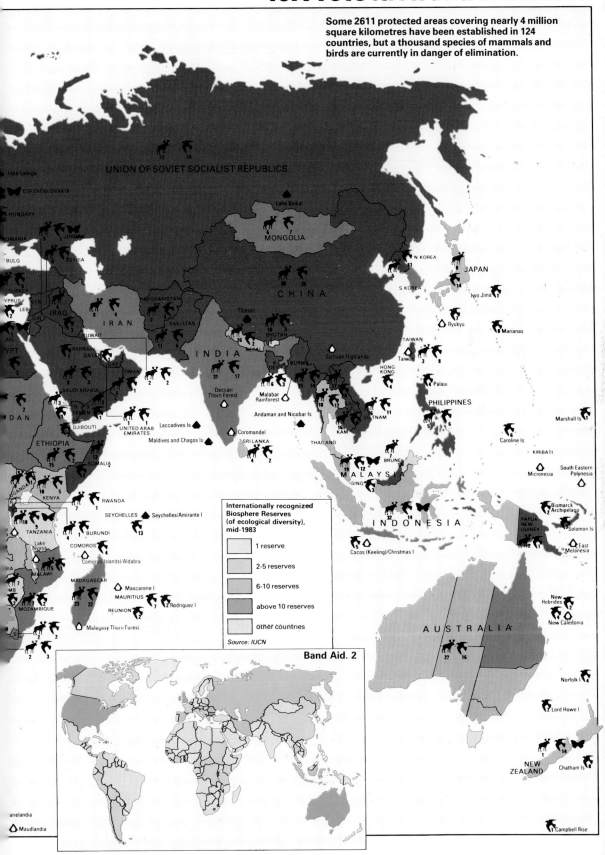

Internationally recognized Biosphere Reserves (of ecological diversity), mid-1983

- 1 reserve
- 2-5 reserves
- 6-10 reserves
- above 10 reserves
- other countries

Source: IUCN

Band Aid. 2

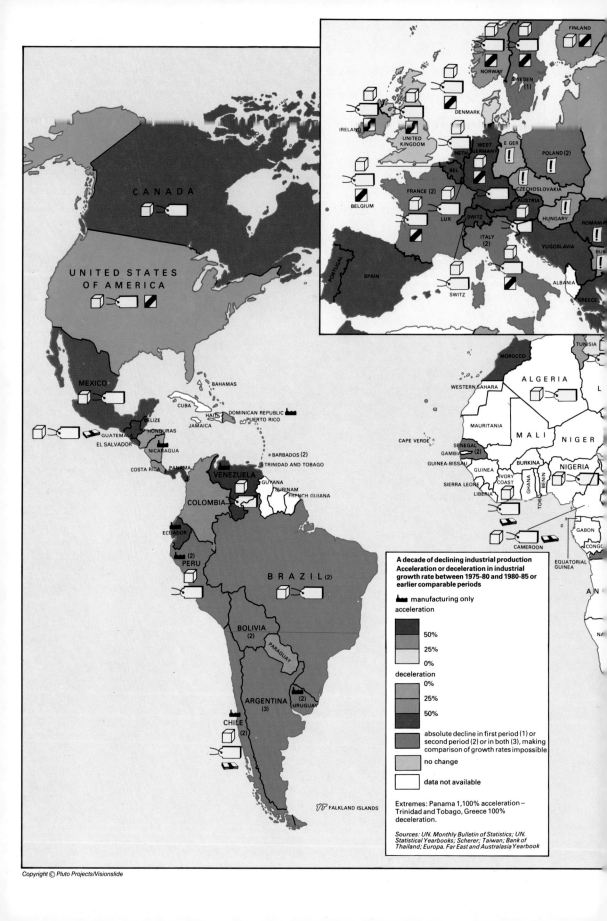

A decade of declining industrial production
Acceleration or deceleration in industrial
growth rate between 1975-80 and 1980-85 or
earlier comparable periods

manufacturing only

acceleration

50%
25%
0%

deceleration

0%
25%
50%

absolute decline in first period (1) or
second period (2) or in both (3), making
comparison of growth rates impossible

no change

data not available

Extremes: Panama 1,100% acceleration –
Trinidad and Tobago, Greece 100%
deceleration.

*Sources: UN. Monthly Bulletin of Statistics; UN.
Statistical Yearbooks; Scherer; Taiwan; Bank of
Thailand; Europa. Far East and Australasia Yearbook*

Decline in industrial growth has promoted the development of devices to discourage or prevent imports.

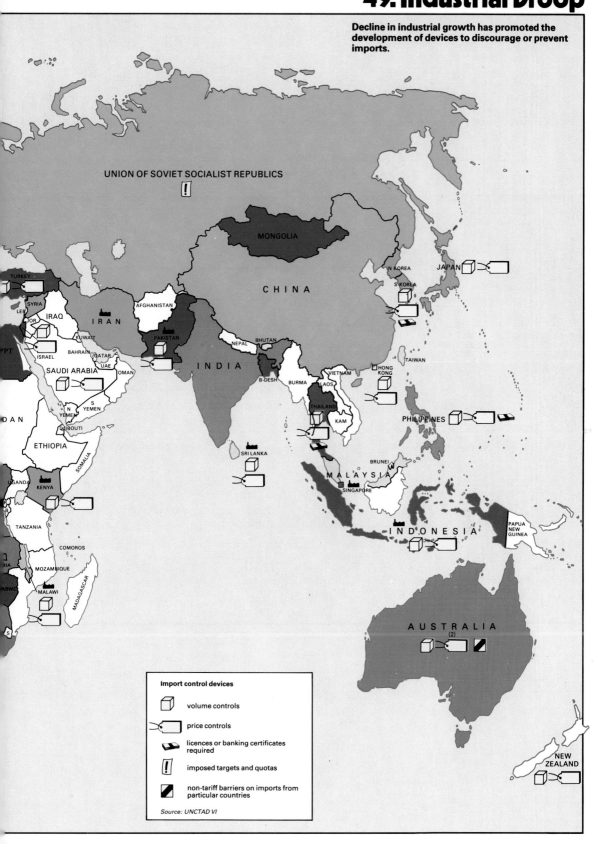

Import control devices

◻ volume controls

◻ price controls

◻ licences or banking certificates required

❗ imposed targets and quotas

◢ non-tariff barriers on imports from particular countries

Source: UNCTAD VI

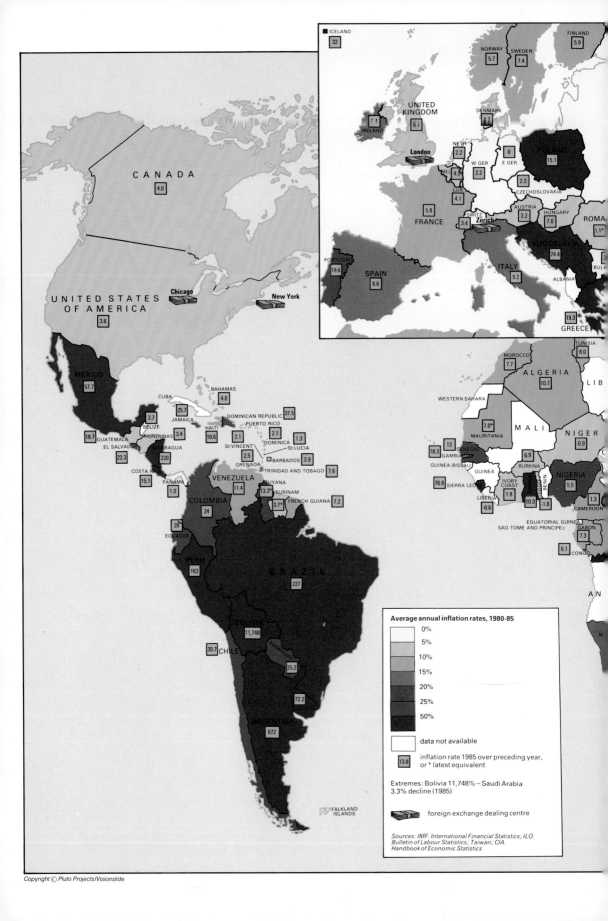

Average annual inflation rates, 1980-85

- 0%
- 5%
- 10%
- 15%
- 20%
- 25%
- 50%

data not available

[13.8] inflation rate 1985 over preceding year, or * latest equivalent

Extremes: Bolivia 11,748% – Saudi Arabia 3.3% decline (1985)

foreign exchange dealing centre

Sources: IMF. International Financial Statistics; ILO. Bulletin of Labour Statistics; Taiwan; CIA. Handbook of Economic Statistics

Copyright © Pluto Projects/Visionslide

50. The Paper Chase

While the countries of the rich West have been
gradually reducing their inflation rates, overall inflation
in the world has been rising: from 12.2 per cent in 1982
to 13.8 per cent in 1985, and correspondingly more so
in the poor South, from an annual 28.3 per cent in 1982
to 48.9 per cent in 1985.

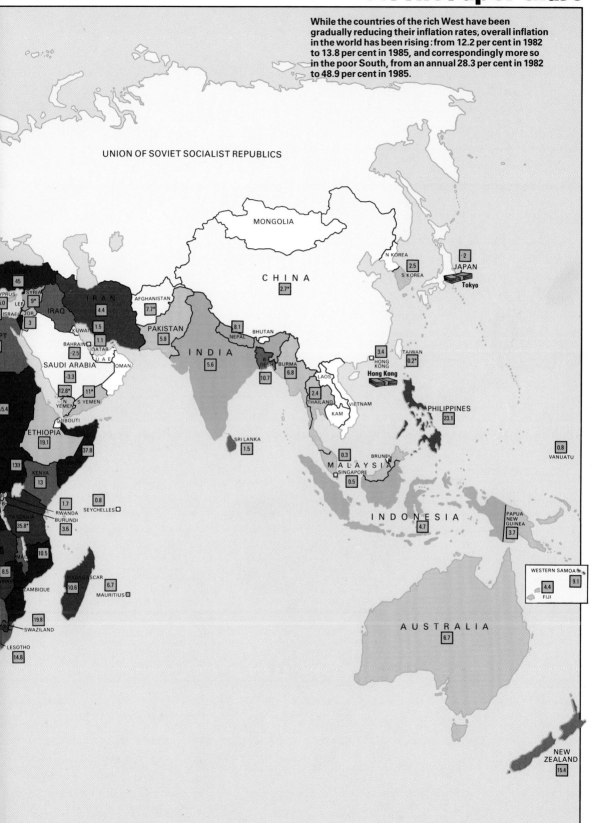

UNION OF SOVIET SOCIALIST REPUBLICS

MONGOLIA

CHINA
2.7*

N KOREA
S KOREA 2.5

JAPAN ·2
Tokyo

45

YPRUS
5.0 LEB
ISRAEL JOR 3
PT

SYRIA 9*

IRAN 4.4

AFGHANISTAN 7.7*

KUWAIT 1.5

BAHRAIN -2.5
QATAR 1.1
U.A.E

OMAN

PAKISTAN 5.8

NEPAL

BHUTAN 8.1

INDIA 5.6

B-LA
DESH 10.7
BURMA 6.8

LAOS

TAIWAN 0.2*

HONG 3.4
KONG
Hong Kong

SAUDI ARABIA -3.3

12.8* 11*
N S YEMEN
YEMEN

DJIBOUTI

THAILAND 2.4

KAM

VIETNAM

PHILIPPINES 23.1

.5.4

ETHIOPIA 19.1

37.8

SRI LANKA 1.5

MALAYSIA
SINGAPORE 0.5

0.3

BRUNEI

0.8
VANUATU

133

KENYA 13

1.7
RWANDA
BURUNDI 3.6

0.8
SEYCHELLES

INDONESIA 4.7

PAPUA
NEW
GUINEA 3.7

TANZANIA 35.8*

10.5

MAL

8.5
WI
ZAMBIQUE

MADAGASCAR 10.6

6.7
MAURITIUS

WESTERN SAMOA 9.1

4.4
FIJI

AUSTRALIA 6.7

19.8
SWAZILAND

LESOTHO 14.8

NEW
ZEALAND 15.4

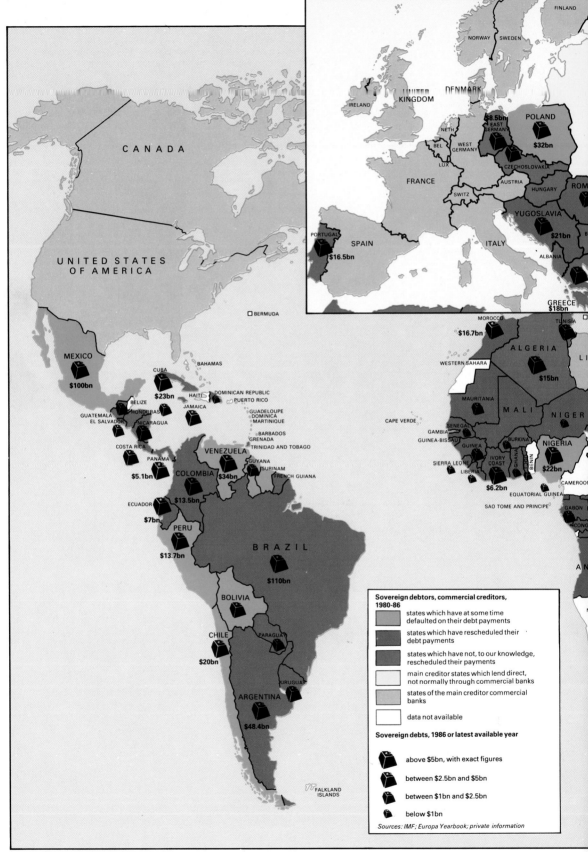

Sovereign debtors, commercial creditors, 1980-86

states which have at some time defaulted on their debt payments

states which have rescheduled their debt payments

states which have not, to our knowledge, rescheduled their payments

main creditor states which lend direct, not normally through commercial banks

states of the main creditor commercial banks

data not available

Sovereign debts, 1986 or latest available year

above $5bn, with exact figures

between $2.5bn and $5bn

between $1bn and $2.5bn

below $1bn

Sources: IMF; Europa Yearbook; private information

CANADA

UNITED STATES OF AMERICA

BERMUDA

MEXICO
$100bn

CUBA
$23bn

BAHAMAS

BELIZE
GUATEMALA
EL SALVADOR
HONDURAS
NICARAGUA
COSTA RICA
PANAMA
$5.1bn

HAITI
DOMINICAN REPUBLIC
PUERTO RICO
JAMAICA

GUADELOUPE
DOMINICA
MARTINIQUE
BARBADOS
GRENADA
TRINIDAD AND TOBAGO

VENEZUELA
$34bn

COLOMBIA
$13.5bn

GUYANA
SURINAM
FRENCH GUIANA

ECUADOR
$7bn

PERU
$13.7bn

BRAZIL
$110bn

BOLIVIA

CHILE
$20bn

PARAGUAY

URUGUAY

ARGENTINA
$48.4bn

FALKLAND ISLANDS

FINLAND

NORWAY SWEDEN

IRELAND
UNITED KINGDOM
DENMARK

NETH
BEL
LUX
WEST GERMANY
EAST GERMANY
$8.5bn
POLAND
$32bn
CZECHOSLOVAKIA

FRANCE
SWITZ
AUSTRIA
HUNGARY
ROMA
YUGOSLAVIA
$21bn
BL

PORTUGAL
$16.5bn
SPAIN
ITALY
ALBANIA

GREECE
$18bn

MOROCCO
$16.7bn
TUNISIA

ALGERIA
$15bn
LI

WESTERN SAHARA

MAURITANIA
MALI
NIGER

CAPE VERDE

SENEGAL
GAMBIA
GUINEA-BISSAU
GUINEA
SIERRA LEONE
$6.2bn
LIBERIA
IVORY COAST
BURKINA
GHANA
BENIN
NIGERIA
$22bn
CAMEROON
EQUATORIAL GUINEA
SAO TOME AND PRINCIPE
GABON
CONG
AN

Copyright © Pluto Projects/Visionslide

States can, and do, go broke. But their insolvency is disguised to avoid, if only by postponement, the problem for their creditor banks.

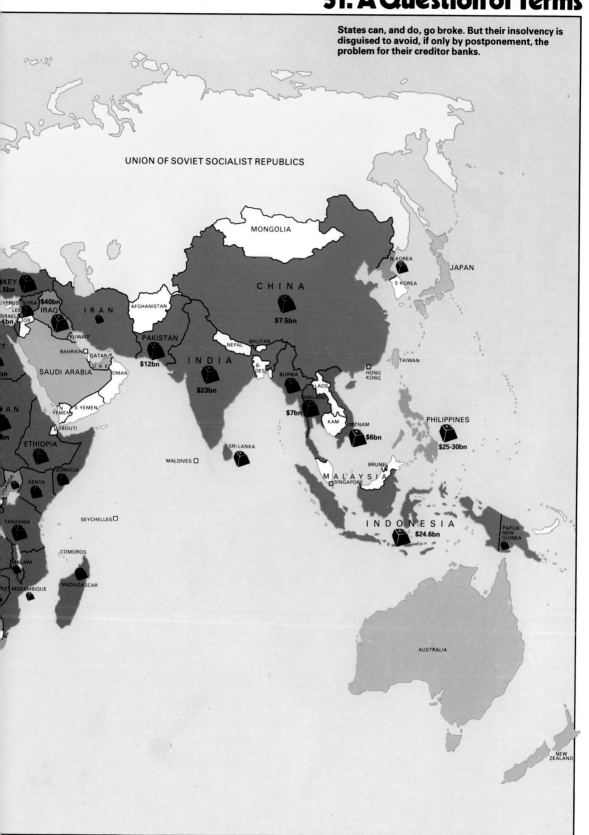

UNION OF SOVIET SOCIALIST REPUBLICS

MONGOLIA

N.KOREA

JAPAN

S KOREA

CHINA

$7.5bn

KEY
.5bn

CYPRUS SYRIA $40bn
LEB
ISRAEL IRAQ
JOR
4bn

IRAN

AFGHANISTAN

KUWAIT

PAKISTAN

$12bn

BAHRAIN QATAR
U A E
OMAN

SAUDI ARABIA

NEPAL BHUTAN

INDIA

$23bn

B-
DESH

BURMA

LAOS

THAILAND

$7bn

TAIWAN

HONG
KONG

N
YEMEN S YEMEN

DJIBOUTI

ETHIOPIA

SOMALIA

UGANDA KENYA

SRI LANKA

MALDIVES

KAM VIETNAM

$6bn

PHILIPPINES

$25-30bn

bn

TANZANIA

SEYCHELLES

BRUNEI

MALAYSIA

SINGAPORE

MALAWI

COMOROS

INDONESIA $24.6bn

PAPUA
NEW
GUINEA

VES MOZAMBIQUE

MADAGASCAR

AUSTRALIA

NEW
ZEALAND

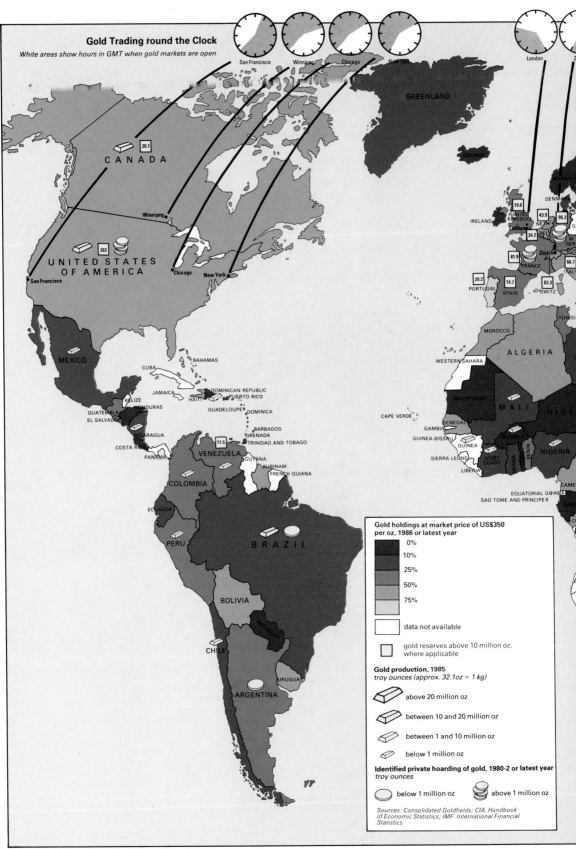

Gold Trading round the Clock

White areas show hours in GMT when gold markets are open

San Francisco   Winnipeg   Chicago   New York   London   Zür

GREENLAND

CANADA

20.1

UNITED STATES
OF AMERICA

263

San Francisco

Winnipeg

Chicago   New York

ICELAND

NORWAY   SW

DENMAR

IRELAND

19.0
UNITED
KINGDOM
London

NETH   43.9   95.2
BEL   E
GER

34.2

81.9   Zürich   W
GER
FRANCE   AUS
66.7
ITALY

20.2
PORTUGAL   14.7
SPAIN   83.3
SWITZ

TUNISIA

MOROCCO

WESTERN SAHARA

ALGERIA   L

MEXICO

BAHAMAS

CUBA

JAMAICA   HAITI   DOMINICAN REPUBLIC
PUERTO RICO

BELIZE
GUATEMALA
EL SALVADOR   HONDURAS   GUADELOUPE   DOMINICA

NICARAGUA
COSTA RICA
PANAMA   BARBADOS
GRENADA
TRINIDAD AND TOBAGO

VENEZUELA   11.5

GUYANA
SURINAM
FRENCH GUIANA

COLOMBIA

ECUADOR

PERU

BRAZIL

BOLIVIA

CHILE

PARAGUAY

URUGUAY

ARGENTINA

CAPE VERDE

MAURITANIA

MALI   NIGER

SENEGAL
GAMBIA
GUINEA-BISSAU
GUINEA
SIERRA LEONE
LIBERIA   IVORY
COAST   BURKINA   BENIN   NIGERIA

GHANA

CAMERO

EQUATORIAL GUINEA
SAO TOME AND PRINCIPE 0

GABO

CON

A

**Gold holdings at market price of US$350
per oz, 1986 or latest year**

- 0%
- 10%
- 25%
- 50%
- 75%

data not available

gold reserves above 10 million oz,
where applicable

Gold production, 1985
troy ounces (approx. 32.1oz = 1 kg)

above 20 million oz

between 10 and 20 million oz

between 1 and 10 million oz

below 1 million oz

Identified private hoarding of gold, 1980-2 or latest year
troy ounces

below 1 million oz   above 1 million oz

*Sources: Consolidated Goldfields; CIA. Handbook
of Economic Statistics; IMF. International Financial
Statistics*

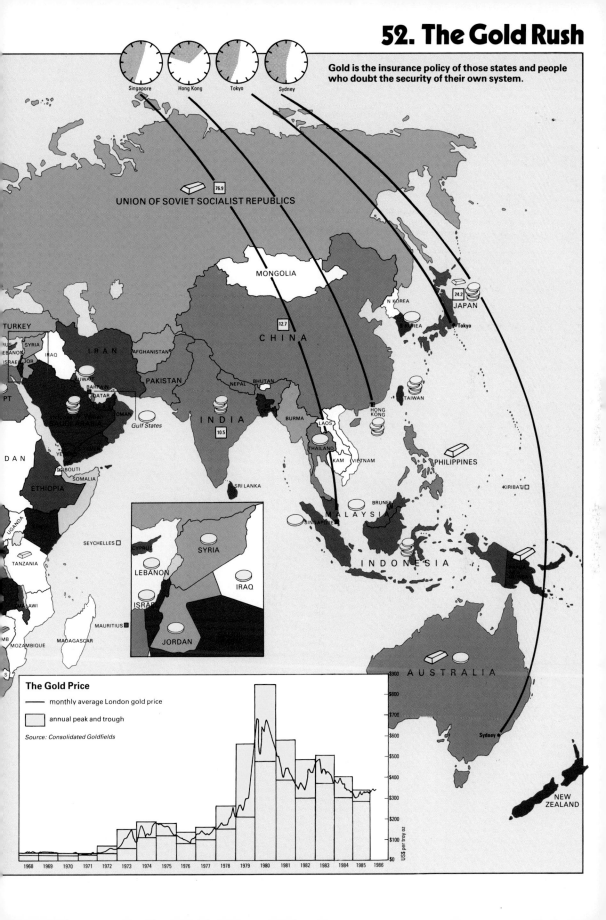

52. The Gold Rush

Gold is the insurance policy of those states and people who doubt the security of their own system.

Singapore   Hong Kong   Tokyo   Sydney

UNION OF SOVIET SOCIALIST REPUBLICS   76.9

MONGOLIA

CHINA   12.7

N KOREA
S KOREA

JAPAN   24.2
Tokyo

TURKEY
SYRIA
LEBANON   IRAQ
ISRAEL   JOR
PT

IRAN   AFGHANISTAN

PAKISTAN

NEPAL   BHUTAN

INDIA   10.5

BURMA

TAIWAN

HONG KONG

LAOS

THAILAND

KAM   VIETNAM

PHILIPPINES

KIRIBATI

KUWAIT
BAHRAIN
QATAR
OMAN
SAUDI ARABIA
Gulf States

DAN

YEMEN

DJIBOUTI
SOMALIA

ETHIOPIA

SRI LANKA

UGANDA

SEYCHELLES

TANZANIA

MALAWI

MAURITIUS

MB
MOZAMBIQUE   MADAGASCAR

S

BRUNEI

MALAYSIA
SINGAPORE

INDONESIA

AUSTRALIA

Sydney

NEW
ZEALAND

CYPRUS   SYRIA

LEBANON

ISRAEL   IRAQ

JORDAN

The Gold Price

—— monthly average London gold price

☐ annual peak and trough

Source: Consolidated Goldfields

US$ per troy oz

$900
$800
$700
$600
$500
$400
$300
$200
$100
$0

1968 1969 1970 1971 1972 1973 1974 1975 1976 1977 1978 1979 1980 1981 1982 1983 1984 1985 1986

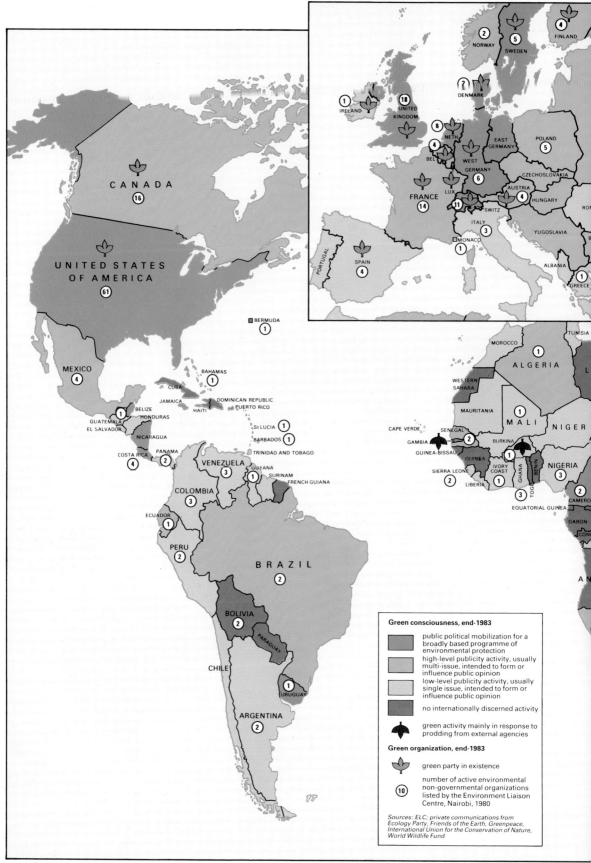

CANADA
(16)

UNITED STATES
OF AMERICA
(61)

MEXICO
(4)

BAHAMAS
(1)

CUBA
JAMAICA
HAITI
DOMINICAN REPUBLIC
PUERTO RICO

BELIZE
GUATEMALA
EL SALVADOR
HONDURAS
NICARAGUA
COSTA RICA (4)
PANAMA (2)

BERMUDA
(1)

St LUCIA (1)
BARBADOS (1)
TRINIDAD AND TOBAGO

VENEZUELA
(3)
GUYANA
SURINAM
FRENCH GUIANA

COLOMBIA
(3)

ECUADOR
(1)

PERU
(2)

BRAZIL
(2)

BOLIVIA
(2)

PARAGUAY

CHILE

URUGUAY (1)

ARGENTINA
(2)

NORWAY (2)
SWEDEN (5)
FINLAND (4)

IRELAND (1)
UNITED KINGDOM (18)
DENMARK (2)
NETH (8)
BEL (4)
WEST GERMANY (6)
LUX (2)
EAST GERMANY
POLAND (5)
CZECHOSLOVAKIA
AUSTRIA (4)
HUNGARY
SWITZ (11)
FRANCE (14)
ITALY (3)
MONACO (1)
PORTUGAL
SPAIN (4)
YUGOSLAVIA
ALBANIA
GREECE
ROM

TUNISIA
MOROCCO
ALGERIA (1)
WESTERN SAHARA
MAURITANIA
MALI (1)
NIGER
L

CAPE VERDE
SENEGAL (2)
GAMBIA
GUINEA-BISSAU
GUINEA
SIERRA LEONE (2)
LIBERIA
IVORY COAST (1)
GHANA (3)
TOGO
BENIN
BURKINA
NIGERIA (3)
EQUATORIAL GUINEA
CAMERO (2)
GABON
CON
AN

Green consciousness, end-1983

public political mobilization for a broadly based programme of environmental protection

high-level publicity activity, usually multi-issue, intended to form or influence public opinion

low-level publicity activity, usually single issue, intended to form or influence public opinion

no internationally discerned activity

green activity mainly in response to prodding from external agencies

Green organization, end-1983

green party in existence

(10) number of active environmental non-governmental organizations listed by the Environment Liaison Centre, Nairobi, 1980

Sources: ELC; private communications from Ecology Party, Friends of the Earth, Greenpeace, International Union for the Conservation of Nature, World Wildlife Fund

Public sensitivity to environmental issues is rising,
particularly in the rich countries. As it grows, the green
movement divides into two broad streams: separatists
who wish to protect nature for a lucky few, and
integrationists who wish to promote a benign
relationship between the social and natural orders.

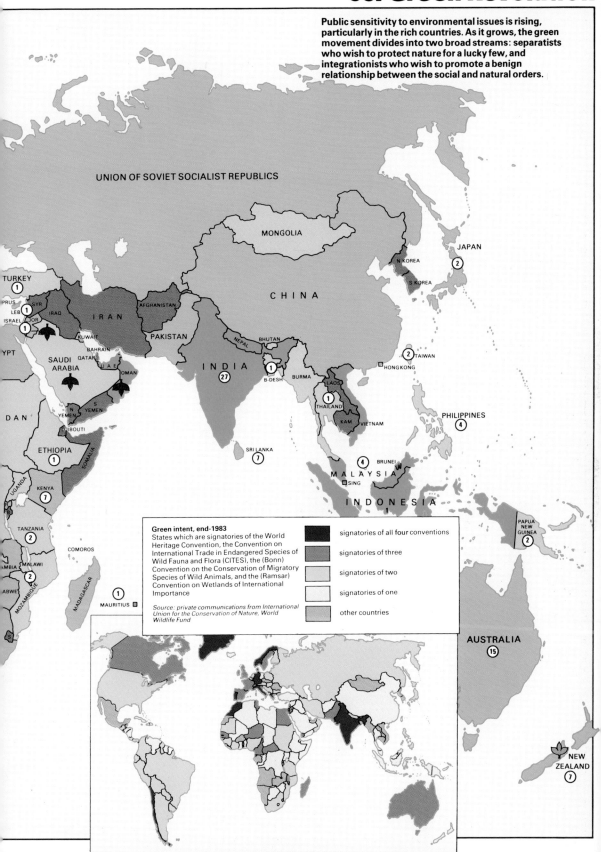

UNION OF SOVIET SOCIALIST REPUBLICS

MONGOLIA

JAPAN
②

N KOREA

S KOREA

CHINA

TURKEY
①

PRUS
LEB
SYR
ISRAEL
JOR
①
IRAQ
IRAN
AFGHANISTAN

KUWAIT
PAKISTAN
NEPAL
BHUTAN

BAHRAIN
QATAR
U A E
I N D I A
②
②
TAIWAN
HONGKONG

YPT
SAUDI
ARABIA
OMAN
㉗
B-DESH
BURMA

PHILIPPINES
④

DAN
N
YEMEN
S
YEMEN
LAOS
①
THAILAND

DJIBOUTI
SRI LANKA
⑦
KAM
VIETNAM

ETHIOPIA
①

UGANDA
KENYA
⑦
④
BRUNEI
M A L A Y S I A
□ SING

TANZANIA
②
COMOROS
I N D O N E S I A
1

PAPUA
NEW
GUINEA
②

MBIA
MALAWI
②

Green intent, end-1983
States which are signatories of the World
Heritage Convention, the Convention on
International Trade in Endangered Species of
Wild Fauna and Flora (CITES), the (Bonn)
Convention on the Conservation of Migratory
Species of Wild Animals, and the (Ramsar)
Convention on Wetlands of International
Importance

*Source: private communications from International
Union for the Conservation of Nature, World
Wildlife Fund*

ABWE
MADAGASCAR
①
MAURITIUS □

signatories of all **four** conventions

signatories of three

signatories of two

signatories of one

other countries

AUSTRALIA
⑮

NEW
ZEALAND
⑦

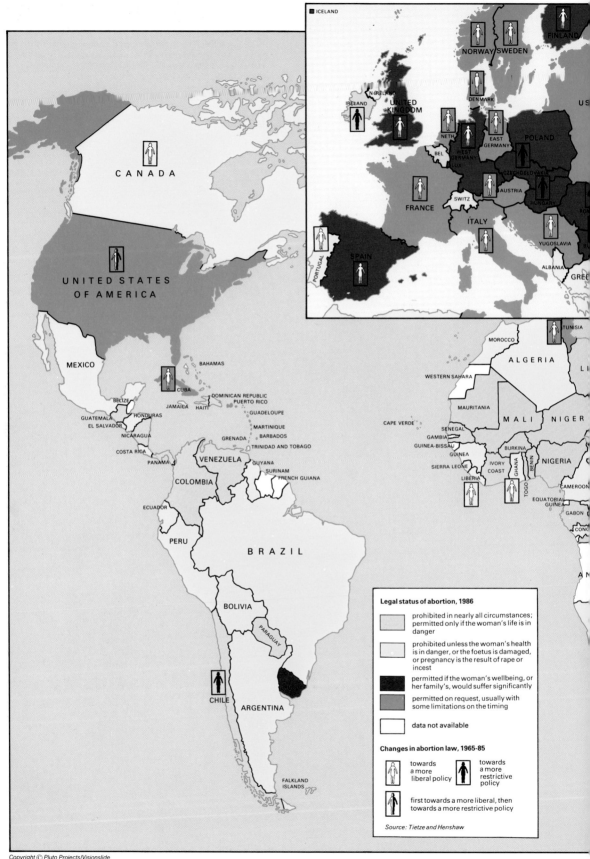

Legal status of abortion, 1986

prohibited in nearly all circumstances; permitted only if the woman's life is in danger

prohibited unless the woman's health is in danger, or the foetus is damaged, or pregnancy is the result of rape or incest

permitted if the woman's wellbeing, or her family's, would suffer significantly

permitted on request, usually with some limitations on the timing

data not available

Changes in abortion law, 1965-85

towards a more liberal policy

towards a more restrictive policy

first towards a more liberal, then towards a more restrictive policy

Source: Tietze and Henshaw

Nowhere are women fully equal to men. What little progress has been made is under constant threat in a male-dominated world. Women's control over reproduction is a case in point.

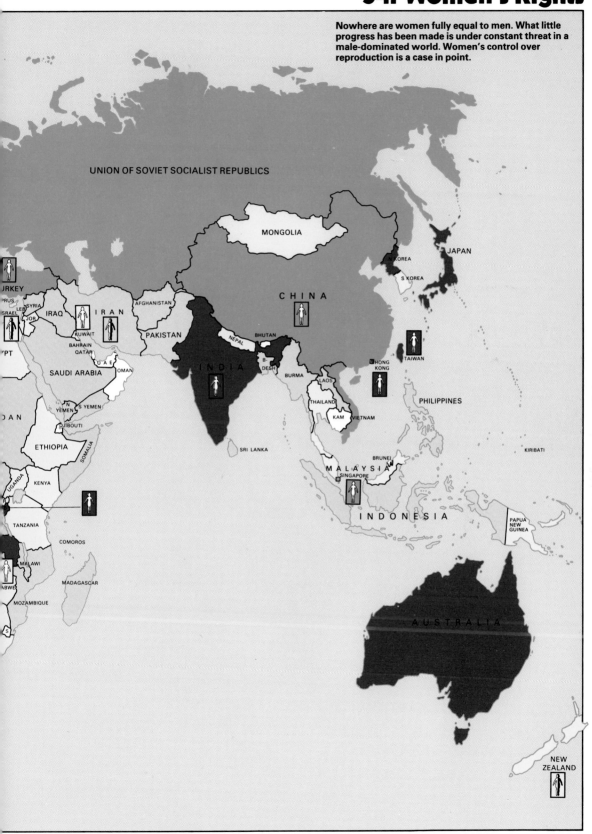

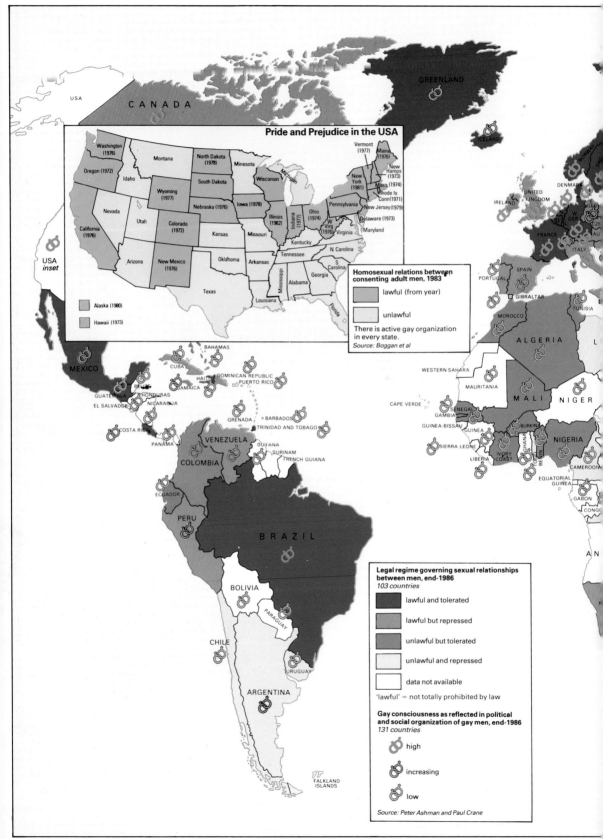

Pride and Prejudice in the USA

Washington (1976)
Oregon (1972)
Montana
North Dakota (1978)
Minnesota
Vermont (1977)
Maine (1976)
Idaho
South Dakota
Wisconsin
Michigan
New Hamps (1973)
New York (1981)
Mass. (1974)
Rhode Is Conn(1971)
Wyoming (1977)
Nebraska (1976)
Iowa (1978)
Nevada
Utah
Colorado (1972)
Illinois (1962)
Indiana (1977)
Ohio (1974)
Pennsylvania
New Jersey(1979)
Delaware (1973)
California (1976)
Kansas
Missouri
Virg (1976)
Virginia
Maryland
Kentucky
Arizona
New Mexico (1976)
Oklahoma
Arkansas
Tennessee
N Carolina
S Carolina
Texas
Mississippi
Alabama
Georgia
Louisiana
Florida

Alaska (1980)
Hawaii (1973)

Homosexual relations between consenting adult men, 1983

lawful (from year)

unlawful

There is active gay organization in every state.

Source: Boggan et al

Legal regime governing sexual relationships between men, end-1986
103 countries

lawful and tolerated

lawful but repressed

unlawful but tolerated

unlawful and repressed

data not available

'lawful' = not totally prohibited by law

Gay consciousness as reflected in political and social organization of gay men, end-1986
131 countries

high

increasing

low

Source: Peter Ashman and Paul Crane

Entrenched public attitudes, whether enshrined in the law or not, make it physically perilous to be gay in most states, and socially precarious in almost all.

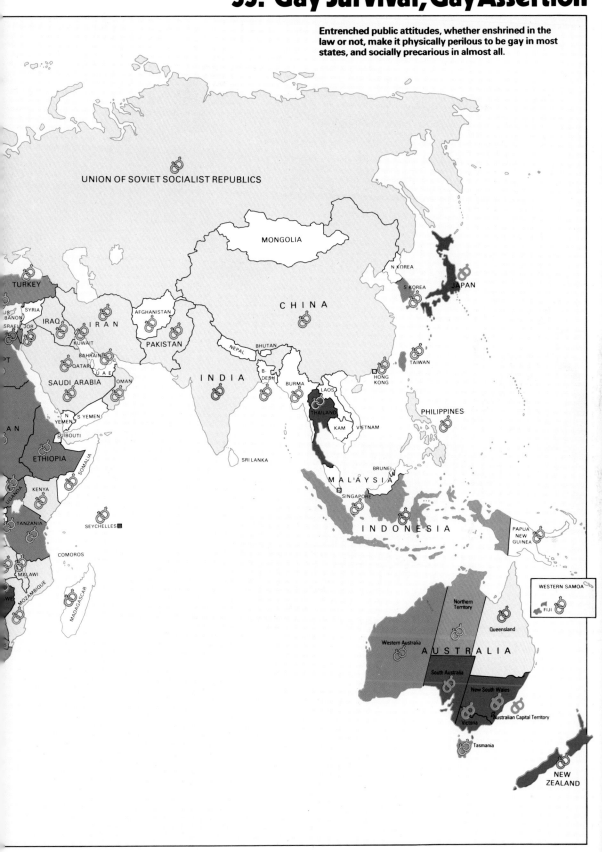

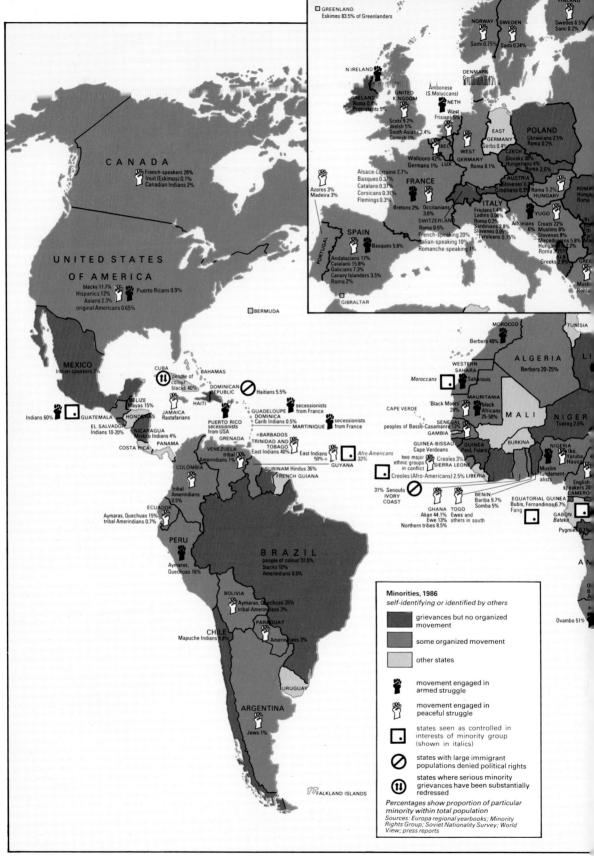

GREENLAND
Eskimos 83.5% of Greenlanders

FINLAND
Swedes 6.5%
Sami 0.2%

NORWAY
Sami 0.75%

SWEDEN
Sami 0.24%

N IRELAND

DENMARK
Germans 11%

POLAND
Ukrainians 2.5%
Roma 0.2%

IRELAND
Roma 0.6%
Protestants 5%

UNITED
KINGDOM

NETH
West
Frisians 5%

Ambonese
(S.Moluccans)

EAST
GERMANY
Sorbs 0.4%

CZECH
Slovaks 30%
Hungarians 4%
Roma 2.6%

Scots 9.2%
Welsh 5%
South Asians 2.4%
Cornish 1%

BEL

WEST
GERMANY
Roma 0.1%

AUSTRIA
Slovenes 0.2%
Croatians 0.3%

HUNGARY

ROMA
Hunga
Roma

Walloons 42%
Germans 1%

LUX

Azores 3%
Madeira 3%

Alsace-Lorraine 2.7%
Basques 0.37%
Catalans 0.37%
Corsicans 0.37%
Flemings 0.3%

FRANCE

ITALY
Friulians 1.4%
Ladins 0.06%
Roma 0.2%
Sardinians 2.8%
Slovenes 0.05%
Tyroleans 0.75%

YUGO
Albanians
6%
Croats 22%
Muslims 8%
Slovenes 8%
Macedonians 5.8%
Hungarians 2.2%
Roma 0.9%

BL
Eth
Ma

Bretons 2%
Occitanians
3.6%

SWITZERLAND
Roma 0.5%
French-speaking 20%
Italian-speaking 10%
Romanche-speaking 1%

ALB
Greeks 2.9%

GREE

PORTUGAL

SPAIN
Basques 5.6%

Andalucians 17%
Catalans 15.8%
Galicians 7.3%
Canary Islanders 3.5%
Roma 2%

Musli
Roma

GIBRALTAR

CANADA
French-speakers 28%
Inuit (Eskimos) 0.1%
Canadian Indians 2%

BERMUDA

MOROCCO
Berbers 40%

TUNISIA

UNITED STATES
OF AMERICA
blacks 11.7%
Hispanics 12%
Asians 2.3%
original Americans 0.65%

WESTERN
SAHARA

ALGERIA
Berbers 20-25%

LI

Moroccans

Saharouis

MEXICO
Indian-speakers 7%

CUBA
people of
colour
blacks 40%

BAHAMAS

DOMINICAN
REPUBLIC

Haitians 5.5%

CAPE VERDE

'Black Moors'
28%

MAURITANIA
black
Africans
25-50%

MALI

NIGER

BELIZE
Mayas 15%

HAITI

JAMAICA
Rastafarians

GUADELOUPE
DOMINICA
Carib Indians 0.5%

secessionists
from France

SENEGAL
Peul, Fulani

Tuareg 2.5%

Indians 60%

GUATEMALA

EL SALVADOR
Indians 10-20%

NICARAGUA
Miskito Indians 4%

HONDURAS

PUERTO RICO
secessionists
from USA

MARTINIQUE

secessionists
from France

GAMBIA

GUINEA-BISSAU
Cape Verdeans

GUINEA
Peul, Fulani

NIGERIA
Ibo,
Yoruba,
Hausa

Muslim
fundament-
alists

COSTA RICA

PANAMA

GRENADA

BARBADOS
TRINIDAD AND
TOBAGO
East Indians 40%

East Indians
50%+

Afro-Americans
33%

two major
ethnic groups
in conflict

Creoles 3%

BURKINA

English-
speakers 20
CAMERO

COLOMBIA

VENEZUELA
tribal
Amerindians 1%

GUYANA

SIERRA LEONE

Creoles (Afro-Americans) 2.5% LIBERIA

EQUATORIAL GUINEA
Bubis, Fernandinos 6.7%
Fang

GABON
Bateka

SURINAM Hindus 36%
FRENCH GUIANA

31% Senoufo
IVORY
COAST

BENIN
Bariba 9.7%
Somba 5%

tribal
Amerindians
0.5%

ECUADOR
Aymaras, Quechuas 15%
tribal Amerindians 0.7%

GHANA
Akan 44.1%
Ewe 13%
Northern tribes 8.5%

TOGO
Ewes and
others in south

Pygmies 0.1%

AN

PERU
Aymaras,
Quechuas 16%

BRAZIL
people of colour 37.5%
blacks 10%
Amerindians 0.5%

O
B
A

BOLIVIA
Aymaras, Quechuas 35%
tribal Amerindians 2%

Ovambo 51%

CHILE
Mapuche Indians 4.8%

PARAGUAY
Amerindians 3%

ARGENTINA
Jews 1%

URUGUAY

FALKLAND ISLANDS

Minorities, 1986

self-identifying or identified by others

grievances but no organized
movement

some organized movement

other states

movement engaged in
armed struggle

movement engaged in
peaceful struggle

states seen as controlled in
interests of minority group
(shown in italics)

states with large immigrant
populations denied political rights

states where serious minority
grievances have been substantially
redressed

*Percentages show proportion of particular
minority within total population*

Sources: Europa regional yearbooks; Minority
Rights Group; Soviet Nationality Survey; World
View; press reports

'Civilization is to be judged by its treatment of minorities.' Mahatma Gandhi.

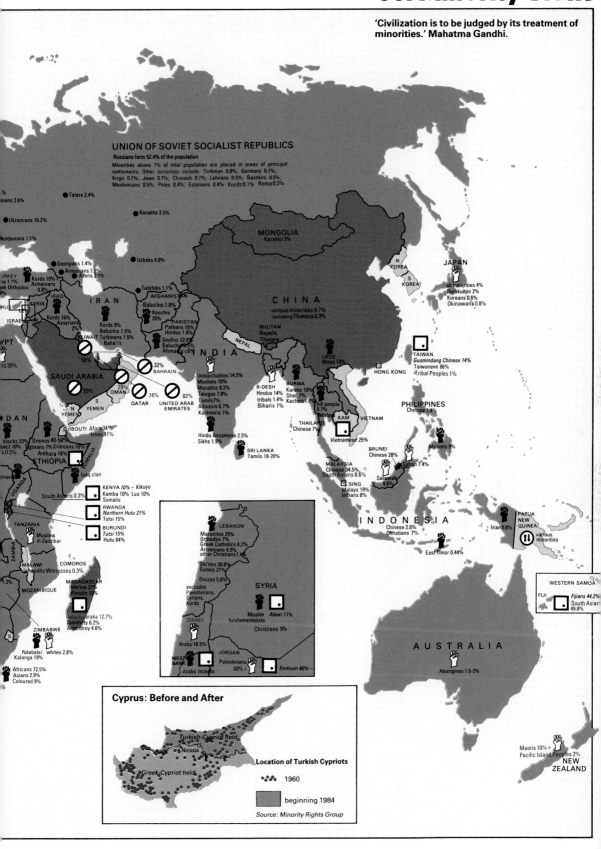

UNION OF SOVIET SOCIALIST REPUBLICS

Russians form 52.4% of the population

Minorities above 1% of total population are placed in areas of principal settlements. Other minorities include: Turkmen 0.8%; Germans 0.7%; Kirgiz 0.7%; Jews 0.7%; Chuvash 0.7%; Latvians 0.5%; Bashkirs 0.5%; Mordvinians 0.5%; Poles 0.4%; Estonians 0.4%; Kurds 0.1%; Roma 0.2%

...ians 3.6%

Tatars 2.4%

Kazakhs 2.5%

Ukrainians 16.2%

Moldavians 1.1%

Uzbeks 4.8%

Georgians 1.4%
Armenians 1.6%
Azeris 2.1%

URKEY
...ia 1.1%
ek Orthodox
0.8%

Kurds 10% +
Armenians
0.8%

Tadzhiks 1.1%

MONGOLIA
Kazakhs 5%

N
KOREA

S
KOREA

JAPAN
all minorities 4%
Burakumin 2%
Koreans 0.6%
Okinawans 0.8%

RUS
SYRIA
ISRAEL
IRAQ

I R A N

Kurds 16%
Assyrians
2%

Kurds 9%
Baluchis 1.5%
Turkmens 1.5%
Baha'is

AFGHANISTAN
Baluchis 1.8%
Koochis
20%

PAKISTAN
Pathans 15%
Hindus 1.6%
Sindhis 22.6%
Baluchis 3.5%
Ahmadis c6%

BHUTAN
Nepalis,
Tibetans

CHINA
various minorities 6.7%
including Tibetans 0.3%

TAIWAN
Guomindang Chinese 14%
Taiwanese 86%
Tribal Peoples 1%

KUWAIT
58%

SAUDI ARABIA

29%

N
YEMEN

32%
BAHRAIN

29%
OMAN

74%
QATAR

82%
**UNITED ARAB
EMIRATES**

S
YEMEN

I N D I A
Untouchables 14.5%
Muslims 10%
Marathis 9.2%
Telugus 7.8%
Tamils 7%
Adivasis 6.7%
Kashmiris 0.1%

NEPAL

B-DESH
Hindus 14%
tribals 1.4%
Biharis 1%

BURMA
Karens 10%
Shan 7%
Kachins 1.8%

LAOS
Meos 10%

hill people
0.7%

HONG KONG

PHILIPPINES
Chinese 1.4%

DAN

DJIBOUTI Afars 31%
Issas 31%

blacks 33% Oromos 40-50%
sect 10% greans 7% Eritreans 10%
s 0.5% Amhara 18%
ETHIOPIA

SOMALIA

Hindu Assamese 2.5%
Sikhs 1.9%

SRI LANKA
Tamils 18-20%

THAILAND
Chinese 7%

Malays **KAM**

VIETNAM

Vietnamese 25%

BRUNEI
Chinese 28%

Muslims 9%

UGANDA

Isaq clan

KENYA *10% + Kikuyu*
Kamba 10% Luo 10%
Somalis

South Asians 0.3%

MALAYSIA
Chinese 34.5%,
South Asians 8.6%

Sabah 7.4%

SING
Malays 19%
Indians 8%

Sarawak
8.6%

I N D O N E S I A
Chinese 2.6%
Christians 7%

Irian 0.8%

**PAPUA
NEW
GUINEA**
various
minorities

TANZANIA

Muslims
in Zanzibar

RWANDA
Northern Hutu 21%
Tutsi 15%

BURUNDI
Tutsi 15%
Hutu 84%

East Timor 0.44%

ZAMBIA

MALAWI
Jehovahs Witnesses 0.3%

COMOROS

..2%

MOZAMBIQUE

MADAGASCAR
Merina 22%
Betsilio 10%

Betsimisaraka 12.7%
Tsimihety 6.2%
Antandroy 4.6%

LEBANON
Maronites 25%
Orthodox 7%
Greek Catholics 4.2%
Armenians 4.9%
other Christians 1.4%

Shi'ites 30.8%
Sunnis 21%
Druzes 5.6%

excludes
Palestinians,
Syrians,
Kurds

SYRIA

Muslim
fundamentalists

Alawi 11%

Christians 9%

ISRAEL

Arabs 16.5%

JORDAN
Palestinians
60% +

Bedouin 40% –

WESTERN SAMOA

FIJI

Fijians 44.2%
South Asians
49.8%

ZIMBABWE

Ndebele/ whites 2.8%
Kalanga 19%

Africans 72.5%
Asians 2.9%
Coloured 9%

WEST
BANK

Arabs *Israelis*

A U S T R A L I A

Aborigines 1.5-2%

Maoris 10% +
Pacific Island Peoples 2%
**NEW
ZEALAND**

Cyprus: Before and After

Turkish-Cypriot held

Nicosia

Greek-Cypriot held

Location of Turkish Cypriots

•••• 1960

beginning 1984

Source: Minority Rights Group

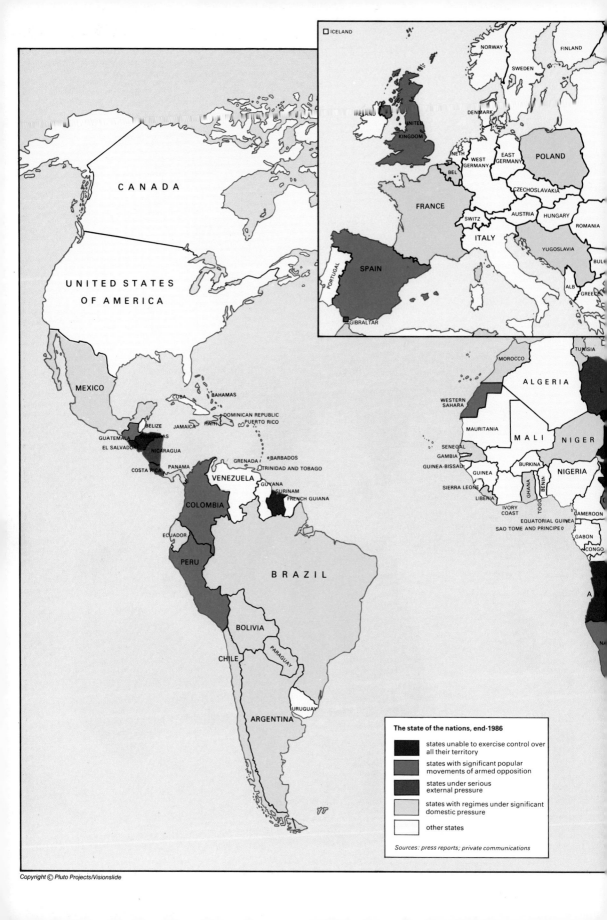

The state of the nations, end-1986

- states unable to exercise control over all their territory
- states with significant popular movements of armed opposition
- states under serious external pressure
- states with regimes under significant domestic pressure
- other states

Sources: press reports; private communications

The state has in its time been an instrument for the extension of personal liberty and for much material progress. It has also been an instrument of personal oppression, collective violence and economic waste. These destructive aspects of the state, which have come crucially to exceed the constructive ones, are inciting popular revulsion and some opposition.

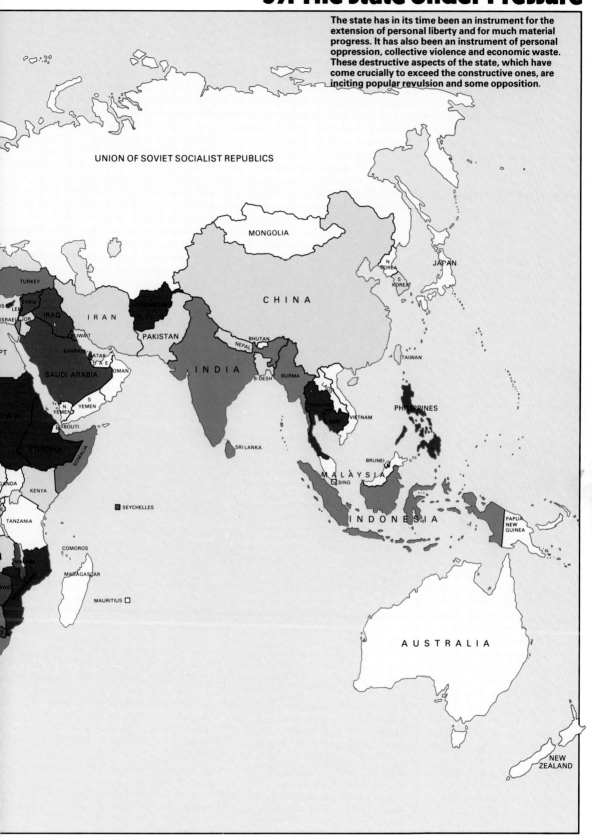

UNION OF SOVIET SOCIALIST REPUBLICS

MONGOLIA

CHINA

N KOREA

S KOREA

JAPAN

TURKEY

SYRIA

LEB

ISRAEL JOR

US

IRAQ

IRAN

AFGHANISTAN

PAKISTAN

BHUTAN

NEPAL

TAIWAN

KUWAIT

BAHRAIN QATAR

U.A.E

SAUDI ARABIA

OMAN

INDIA

B-DESH

BURMA

LAOS

THAILAND

PHILIPPINES

VIETNAM

N YEMEN

S YEMEN

DJIBOUTI

ETHIOPIA

SOMALIA

SRI LANKA

BRUNEI

MALAYSIA

SING

ANDA

KENYA

TANZANIA

COMOROS

SEYCHELLES

INDONESIA

PAPUA NEW GUINEA

MADAGASCAR

MAURITIUS

AUSTRALIA

NEW ZEALAND

NOTES TO THE MAPS ▬▬▬

1

We identify as states those territories which are recognized as such by most governments and inter-governmental agencies, although not always by some or even most of their inhabitants.

Taiwan is included as a sovereign state, although both its own government and that of mainland China insist that it is an integral part of a single Chinese state. Similarly, the South African 'Bantu homelands' and the Ukraine and Byelorussia are excluded; the first are recognized by South Africa alone and the second two, while represented at the United Nations, are not deemed sovereign by any member state. Namibia and Western Sahara are designated as states, although occupied by other countries, because their independent existence is widely accepted within the community of states. Such acceptance applies as well to East Timor, occupied by Indonesia but not designated as an occupied territory on the map. Greenland is not an independent state, although its measure of autonomy is such that it was able to withdraw from the European Economic Community (EEC) on 1 February 1985, while its metropolitan country, Denmark, remains a member. Several states, such as Martinique, Guadeloupe and French Guiana, are legally Overseas Provinces of France, with representation in the metropolitan political institutions. Puerto Rico is a so-called 'free state' but with the United States continuing to control its defence policy and foreign affairs. Puerto Ricans are held to be US citizens and so able to emigrate freely to the USA, but they have no representation in the US Congress. An elected governor is the primary political authority, though with various restrictions on his power.

The two Germanies are shown as new states, since neither existed in its present form before 1945; even though we recognize that historical continuity runs essentially through West Germany.

2

The world would look very different if the sizes of states corresponded to their populations. It would also change shape continuously as populations in the rich states shrink relatively to populations in the poor ones.

Counting people is not an exact science. In some states, important sections of the community do their utmost to avoid being noticed. Obvious examples are the illegal immigrant populations in employment-promising countries such as France, the USA and Venezuela. In others, political arrangements are so closely involved with the results of the population census that the census itself becomes the product of politics and not only its determinant. In Nigeria, for instance, it has long been believed in the south that the census is so organized as to inflate the population figures in the north. In the Lebanon, a census of the different religious communities has long been avoided, since that country's distinctive political arrangements were based on a communal ratio that is increasingly historical. In many states, there are simply no provisions made for a separate census administration; population figures are supplied by officials who are engaged in other, seemingly more pressing business, and who have not necessarily been appointed for their numeracy.

In consequence of the local poverty in statistical services, many of the figures used in the cartogram are estimates from the Population Division of the United Nations Secretariat. Externally-generated figures promote international comparisons. These increase the political importance of national statistics, which, in turn, provoke political interference in their collection or manufacture. The result is even greater reliance on the services and authority of the international agencies.

Forty-nine territories with populations below one million each are excluded from the cartogram. They are: Andorra; Antigua & Barbuda; Bahamas; Bahrain; Barbados; Belize; Bermuda; Brunei; Cape Verde; Comoros; Cyprus; Djibouti; Dominica; Equatorial Guinea; Fiji; French Guiana; Gambia; Gibraltar; Greenland; Grenada; Guinea-Bissau; Guyana; Guadeloupe; Guam; Iceland; Kiribati; Liechtenstein; Luxembourg; Macao; Maldives; Malta; Mauritius; Martinique; Monaco; Netherlands Antilles; Qatar; Reunion; St Lucia; St Vincent and the Grenadines; San Marino; Sao Tome & Principe; Seychelles; Solomon Islands; Surinam; Swaziland; Vanuatu; Vatican City; Western Sahara; Western Samoa.

Five states, from comfortable Northern and Central Europe, actually lost population, for social rather than political reasons, in the five year period with which the map deals. They were West Germany (– 0.9%), Hungary (– 0.7%), East Germany (– 0.6%), UK (– 0.3%) and Denmark (– 0.2%).

THE STATE INVADES ANTARCTICA

3

Antarctica is rich in resources. It is already a major source of protein in the form of fish, whalemeat, and increasingly krill (the many species of oceanic shrimp, which constitute the basic food of whales). It promises to be a major source of many minerals already mined in Southern Africa, Australia, and South America, with which Antarctica shares a common geological past. It is thought to be rich in mineral oil and gas deposits. It harbours 70 per cent of the world's fresh water, in the form of ice. It is also tempting the military planners in many states.

The Antarctic Treaty was signed in 1959. Its purpose is to ensure the peaceful administration of the southern polar region. But history suggests that there is nothing quite so pregnant with the possibilities of conflict as the treaty arrangements made by states for professedly pacific purposes. Already alarm bells are sounding. And there are moves to transfer the administration of Antarctica from the haphazard collection of treaty states to an international authority of general membership such as the United Nations.

Greenpeace, the international environmentalist organization, is sponsoring a scientific station at Cape Evans, Ross Island (a few hundred metres from the base set up by Captain Scott for his polar expedition), to monitor the environmental impact of the human presence, their own and others', in the area; and claim a place, as observers, in the conclave of the Antarctic Treaty signatories.

THE STATE INVADES THE SEA

4

Although it is unlikely that the required number of states will ratify the Treaty in the foreseeable future, the 1982 Convention on the Law of the Sea is shaping an inter-state oceanic regime. Littoral states are claiming Exclusive Economic Zones (EEZs) extending 200 nautical miles off-shore or 350 miles and more into the continental shelf. It is obvious that in the process of establishing and extending EEZs, even the smallest of island territories has enormous value. One third of the seas (which themselves cover 70 per cent of the world's surface, all of its off-shore oil and mineral resources, and most of its seawater fish) is being attached in this way.

The many areas where EEZs overlap are areas of potential conflict. Some of these have caused, or exacerbated, existing disputes, the most important of which are shown on the map. One of these grew more menacing when, in 1987, Britain began enforcing its declaration of a 150-mile Falkland Islands Interim Conservation and Management Zone (FICZ), one third of which overlaps waters claimed by Argentina as part of its own 200-mile zone.

The general acceptance of EEZs and the more narrowly conceived but similar Exclusive Fishing Zones has restrained the rush to extend territorial waters, which are the recognized preserve of state law. The normal limit for territorial waters now appears to be settling at twelve nautical miles. This is substantially more than the traditional three miles still asserted by the old maritime powers (UK, USA and others) but far less than the claims of some Latin American and African countries which extend to the limit of their EEZs.

SPACE INVADERS

5

Most satellites are designed and dispatched for purely military purposes: early warning, communications, navigation, surveillance and, increasingly, the midflight guidance of ballistic missiles. But it is unwise, if not impossible, to distinguish at all precisely between military and commercial satellites, since some of each also perform functions associated with the other. The furthest that one authority will go is to estimate that around 60 per cent of total launchings have been primarily military in purpose. And this proportion will much increase if President Reagan's Strategic Defense Initiative (SDI) or 'Star Wars' project takes off, on some sort of flight path, as it looked like doing at the start of 1987.

The commercialization of space was inaugurated in 1962, when the US Congress established the Communications Satellite Corporation (Comsat) as a private company to be the country's basic 'common carrier' for satellite communications. A decade later, the US Federal Communications Commission declared that the US industry should develop further in a 'free enterprise mode'. US business was not slow to explore the new possibilities.

Commercial satellites are used for the transmission of telephone, telex and data services. They are used for the internal communications of corporations; for facsimile transmission of newspapers and documents; for entertainment. Six years after Home Box Office, the US cable TV company, transmitted its first program by satellite, 12 million homes in the US alone were paying $1 billion a year for cable television.

The USA was the first country to use space for commercial purposes. And, for many years, it was the sole supplier of commercial satellite launches. There are now others, in ever fiercer competition with one another.

Such competition took a gruesome turn when the US space shuttle Challenger exploded shortly after launch in January 1985. France responded by expanding its programme of launches based on the Ariane rocket; only to suffer a damaging failure in September (the first of three). In October, China announced an agreement with Teresat of Houston to place two satellites in orbit. Then, at the start of 1987, the USSR entered the market by signing up India as a launch client. Meanwhile NASA, the US space agency, had retired from the commercial launching business.

BIG BROTHER

6

Military bases are 'foreign' in one of two respects: they are either in the territory of another sovereign state, or in that of a dependency or near-dependency. A French base in Guadeloupe (effectively a French dependency) or the British base on Ascension Island (a British dependency) are as 'foreign' in this sense as are US and USSR bases in the sovereign states of West and East Germany respectively; or the US base on Diego Garcia (a British dependency).

These bases are protected by a secrecy far more effective than their perimeter fences. Even where the presence of the bases is publicly recorded, as in Britain, Norway and Sweden, peace researchers have been arrested and tried, essentially for drawing attention to this. For that reason, our map is not as comprehensive as we would like it to be. Furthermore, the symbols on each country distinguish only particular kinds of base belonging to a foreign state, where several or even many such bases may exist. We show, for instance, only one set of symbols for US bases in the UK, although more than a hundred such bases are located there.

The presence of military advisers and trainees indicates a relationship between states that goes far beyond mere technical training. It embraces trade ties, the convergence of attitudes, political lobbying and influence, along with many other aspects of inter-state relations in an increasingly militarized international order.

It is obvious that the presence of foreign military bases and advisers for the proclaimed purpose of defence against a common external enemy can easily become intervention to sustain an unpopular and threatened regime, as the Russians have demonstrated in Afghanistan or the Americans in El Salvador.

The pattern of military bases and alignments is far from fixed. There are Russians in bases originally built for Americans in Vietnam; Americans using Russian-built facilities in Somalia; Cubans sleeping on Portuguese beds in Angola.

We define a major air base as one which normally contains more than two squadrons of combat aircraft or more than one hundred personnel; a major naval base as one which is regularly used by major warships; a major army base as one with more than 10,000 soldiers.

MILITARY SPENDING

7

Military spending is a term beset by problems of definition, verification, and comparison between states and between periods. The problems are greatest with the two giant spenders, the USA and USSR: responsible respectively for 30.9% and 22.1% of total military expenditure in 1985 (or 53% together); up from respectively 27.4% and 21.9% (or 49.3% together) in 1982. We have used the latest figures supplied by the Stockholm International Peace Research Institute (SIPRI), updated, where necessary, from other sources. SIPRI itself is the most authoritative non-government source for such information.

The inset map on the military share of central government expenditure is based on official US estimates, themselves ultimately derived from the Central Intelligence Agency (CIA). Not surprisingly, these tend to exaggerate the military bias of the Soviet budget. They are, however, the most comprehensive available. While they may be distorted in detail, such figures present as accurate a statement as one could wish of all governments' predilection to invest resources in the instruments of destruction.

SHARES IN THE APOCALYPSE

8

Since the bombs dropped on Japan in 1945, no nuclear weapon has been exploded, outside of test programmes. But this has been as much a matter of luck as of anything else. It is known that the US strategic early warning system produced more than eight false alarms monthly on average in a year and a half from around the beginning of 1980. One British data-base lists 98 serious accidents, which caused or might have caused firing of, or damage to, a nuclear weapon. These include 53 cases in which the delivery system was destroyed; 14, of radioactive release; 13, of damage to the delivery system; 9, of fire; 6, of weapons damaged; along with 5 transport accidents, 5 false warnings of attack, 3 weapons destroyed, and 2 weapons lost.

More and more 'near nuclear-weapons states' are gaining the technical competence to manufacture such weapons. An important component of their capability is the use of a nuclear reactor for either research or electricity production.

There are many more missiles than missile launchers. In NATO, for example, the ratio for short-range missiles is six or seven to one. Similarly, there are more nuclear bombs than nuclear bombers and more nuclear shells than nuclear cannon. We have adopted the convention of counting missile launchers while designating them as missiles. It is misleading, but our sources leave us with no choice.

We have sited nuclear weapons in the states of their deployment, not in the states that own or control them. In Europe, only France and the UK independently possess such weapons. The USA or the USSR control all other nuclear weapons, including every type of cruise missile.

The approach of the apocalypse is as much a matter for those countries that do not yet have nuclear weapons as for those who keep on adding to the stockpiles they already possess. The diffusion of the technology has made it increasingly cheap and easy for states to join the nuclear club without an invitation from its existing members to do so.

CONVENTIONAL KILLING

9

While the threat of nuclear war commands the headlines, the many thousands killed and maimed in battle every year are victims of a more accepted but increasingly horrible conventional weaponry.

The arsenal is the state's assertion of statehood. But the profusion of armaments is not necessarily the measure of effective military power. Some weapons are more sophisticated and accordingly more destructive than others; or more sophisticated than the capacity of the society to service them and so keep them operational. Some military forces are more impressive for their equipment than for their loyalty or morale. Some weapons, expensively accumulated in enormous quantities, have the drawback of rapidly becoming obsolete. Nonetheless, alongside these reservations, the relative strength in major weapons is an indication of relative military power: always excepting the new dimensions produced by the possession of nuclear weapons.

In the first edition of this atlas we employed air power as a measure of conventional military strength. In this third edition, as in the second, we have used land power for the same purpose. The picture that emerges is much the same, since the hierarchies of land and, to a lesser extent, sea power are similar to those of their air equivalent.

There has been an alarming increase in the tank armouries of states during the last few years. No fewer than 21 states which were reported to be without tanks in 1981 were known to possess them in 1985. And with few exceptions, states were deploying more – and heavier – tanks in 1985 than in 1981.

There are three tank superpowers: the USA, the USSR and China, with 10,000 or more each; although China's tank force is more impressive for numbers than as a modern fighting force. Those in the next rank of tank power are small by comparison, with none of them possessing more than 5,000.

This map does not allow for the increasingly refined distinctions between one method of killing and another, any more than it allows for a measure of the waste, in human intelligence and resources, that is involved in their design and production.

WAR IN OUR TIME

10

This map seeks to identify the wars fought during the past 15 years or so: the different kinds of war; and the potential occasions or pretexts for future wars, in active or dormant border disputes.

War itself we define as a series of connected armed clashes in which at least one of the contenders employs regular, uniformed forces.

A border war we distinguish as one which normally – though not necessarily – involves a conflicting claim to territory and which is limited to fighting along the border. It does not include simple boundary demarcation disputes. A general war between neighbouring states is one which may well begin as a border war but which spreads so as to involve virtually the total armed forces of the belligerents and, if only through air attacks, territory far from the border, as in the Gulf War between Iran and Iraq. It is easy to cite instances where a war may appear to be neither of these but contains elements of both, and we have used our own judgement to determine which term most usefully to apply.

A state in general war with a non-neighbouring state and a state with major military engagement in a foreign conflict constitute separate categories that allow even more room for confusion. And again, of course, determination is a matter of judgement. It seems to us clear that, in the late 1960s and early 1970s, the United States was waging in Vietnam and Kampuchea, by the sheer scale of its military operations within those countries, a general war, while its military operations in Laos were closer to a massive military engagement. This definition of general war accordingly applies to a belligerent state even when, as with the United States, its own territory remains untouched.

The difference between a major and a minor military engagement in foreign conflict is, obviously, arguable. In our view, it depends on the scale and/or implications of the engagement. Clearly, French and Libyan engagements in the Chad civil war are major more for their implications than for their scale, while the Cuban engagement in Angola is major both by scale and implication. The Russian engagement in Afghanistan presents a particular problem, since in scale it amounts to a general war. We have classified it as a major military engagement only because, strictly, the war in Afghanistan is not one between states but a civil war. It is not, therefore, the same as the US involvement in Vietnam and Kampuchea, where the war was an interstate one as well as a civil war.

Not least, the definition of civil war bristles with difficulties. It is general, in our view, when its operations or contending forces involve, actively or passively, by impetus or design, the issue of sovereignty throughout the state; regional when a particular area, usually though not always for separatist objectives, is alone involved, even if operations spill over into other areas. Thus, South Africa has general civil war, even though the scale of operations is not yet remotely comparable with that in Afghanistan, for instance; while in Spain we have used the designation of regional civil war, even though Basque separatism is partly manifested by armed acts in the country's capital.

General civil war is shown in Poland, on the basis that there has been widespread conflict between a large sector of the population and the armed forces of the government.

The distinction between interstate and civil wars is frequently blurred. We have excluded as interstate wars, wars in which foreign intervention is of a disguised or 'technical' kind (as is the USA's in El Salvador); but have included wars in which foreign troops have been committed against the existing authority (e.g. Turkey in Cyprus).

We have distinguished anti-colonial wars, since the description of such conflict as civil war misleads more than it illuminates.

Active border disputes are those in which a government maintains an overt claim to all or part of a neighbouring territory. A dormant dispute may be very unlikely to become an active one but remains a dispute while there are those – as in West Germany over the very division of Germany – active in promoting the issue. The border between Poland and East Germany is designated as the subject of a dormant border dispute because its settlement relates to the division of Germany, and the symbol could scarcely have been placed on a border between West Germany and Poland.

States are depicted as they were at the end of 1986; they may not have existed, or existed in their current form, at the time of some of the conflicts shown. For example, most of the interstate clashes associated with Zimbabwe on the map predate the transition, in 1980, from white minority Rhodesia to the present regime.

MINERAL POWER | **11**

Power does not necessarily result from the substantial production of a particular mineral. Some minerals may be in general over-supply; allowing consumers to determine the price or play off one supplier against another. Some are marketable only or chiefly in a processed form, which may invest the processors themselves with more power than the producers can exercise. In all such cases, it is often the transnational corporation, with interests in both mining and processing, and with operations in numerous countries, that is effectively more powerful than the governments to which it pays formal obeisance. To illustrate this, we have included in the map processing centres; identifying states where the processing of particular metals and minerals or their ores substantially exceeds existing, if any, production from mining. A few states – notably the USA and USSR – are both major processors and major producers. They are identified as processors only for those metals which they produce in significantly lower quantities than they process.

Power attaches as well to the marketing of minerals and the manipulation of their price. The map accordingly shows the centres of trading and speculation for particular metals and minerals. The importance of such centres was strikingly illustrated in October 1985, when the International Tin Council in London ceased support operations for the price of tin, with debts running into hundreds of millions of pounds sterling, and the London Metal Exchange (LME) suspended all trading in tin. As the price of tin in minor or makeshift markets plummeted, to less than half the level before the LME suspension, mines in tin-producing countries were shut down as no longer economic. In Malaysia alone, half the 400 mines were closed or began operating at part-capacity.

Nonetheless, the possession of minerals can and does confer power; when cyclical conditions produce the reality or appearance of scarcity; where, as with platinum and chrome, there are very few producers; or where particular countries are so rich in different minerals that their dependence on any one market or corporation is correspondingly reduced. In this last regard, the map distinguishes the five mineral powers, each of which produces significant proportions of more than five major minerals.

Since this map was produced, Australia has become an important source of both gem and industrial diamonds. Gold and oil are excluded since each is considered elsewhere (*Map 13: Oil Power* and *Map 52: The Gold Rush*).

On a technical note: bauxite ore is reduced to alumina powder which is refined to aluminium, in the ratio of 4:2:1 by weight.

ENERGY POWER 12

This map is mainly concerned with commercial energy: energy produced for sale rather than for direct use. Such energy accounts for some 85 per cent of all human energy use.

Most of the commercial energy produced is from non-renewable sources; and most of the renewable energy sources, notably wood and charcoal, are used directly by the producers – poor rural populations in the poor states.

But there is gathering interest, over much of the rich world, in renewable energy sources from sun, wind and waves, as at least an eventual substitute for the ultimately scarce, intermittently expensive, and environmentally polluting fossil fuels.

Certainly, the use of nuclear power has ceased to be widely accepted as the panacea that it was once believed to be. Doubts of its safety were seriously reinforced by the accident in March 1979 at the Three Mile Island nuclear power plant in the eastern United States; by a succession of relatively minor mishaps to such installations elsewhere in the USA and other countries subsequently; and most frighteningly by the still not fully measured human and environmental damage produced by the explosion at the Chernobyl nuclear power station near Kiev, USSR, in April 1986.

The first beneficiary of public disquiet seems likely, however, to be coal. In West Germany, for instance, where the debate about a total nuclear *Ausstieg* or exit is in progress, an estimated DM 28 billion (over $14 billion at the early 1987 exchange rate) will be spent up to 1993 in lowering the pollution levels from coal-fired power stations.

In Britain, remarkably, given its enormous natural resources of coal and its record of mishaps at nuclear power stations, the Layfield Public Inquiry in early 1987 recommended proceeding with the construction of a new nuclear power plant at Sizewell. One week after the verdict, major design faults at two other stations, still in construction, were reported. Nonetheless the government quickly adopted Layfield's recommendations.

Comparison between coal and other sources of energy is based on calorific value. One tonne (metric ton) of coal is equivalent to 1.47 tonnes of crude petroleum or 1.67 tonnes of natural gas liquid. As the inset map demonstrates, there is already a large international trade in hard coal, the staple for electricity generation.

OIL POWER

13

Since the last edition of this atlas, the price of oil has come under substantial market pressure, with increasing supplies from important new producers outside of OPEC; with price discounting and concealed production increases from among members inside it; and, not least, by the decision of Saudi Arabia to abandon its role as 'swing producer' and go for a larger market share rather than price stability. Until 1986, the price decline was relatively gradual. The average spot market price of the benchmark Arabian light crude for the final quarter of each year, in US$ per barrel, was 38.35 in 1979; 38.40 in 1980; 33.75 in 1981; 31.75 in 1982; 28.35 in 1983; 27.77 in 1984; and 27.79 in 1985. Then the decline accelerated sharply, with the price falling below $20 a barrel in January 1986; below $15 in February; and below $9 in the summer. By late in the year, Saudi Arabia had decided to switch policy, and members of OPEC agreed on production cuts to boost the price; setting a figure of $18 a barrel. In the cause of securing this price, OPEC negotiated the agreement of other major exporters – notably Mexico, Norway and the USSR – to production cuts of their own.

Nowhere, perhaps, was the impact of the price decline likely to prove more fateful than in the United States, where many uneconomic wells were sealed so as to be taken permanently out of production. In 1986, domestic oil production fell by 3.4 per cent, to an average 8.7 million barrels a day, compared with a daily domestic consumption of 16.2 million barrels, so that imports rose by 22 per cent. Even without a scramble for supplies that would send the oil price soaring, the dependence of the world's leading industrial economy and military power on increasing imports of oil must have serious implications for international stability and, not least, the stability of a world financial system whose central currency is the US dollar.

FOOD POWER

14

The equivalent map in the first edition of this atlas dealt with all designated foods, including such non-nutritional 'beverages' as coffee, cocoa and tea. We pointed out in the notes that this produced an essentially distorted view of the subject: with Africa, a region of widespread undernourishment and even starvation, emerging as possessed of an overall surplus in the food trade, through massive exports of beverage crops and tropical fruits. In this edition, as in the previous one, we have rejected the general food category altogether and employ instead the category of cereals, the paramount source of nourishment for the vast majority of people.

While the dominance of the export trade by the USA continues, it is coming under increasing pressure from other surplus countries, and especially those in the EEC, which competes the more vigorously as the cost of carrying and still augmenting its enormous stocks mounts. With greater efficiency, partly promoted by subsidies to accommodate the political pressures of the farmers, agriculture in the EEC is more productive. Britain, for instance, has moved from being an historically major importer to the status of a surplus country, which accounted for some 2.6 per cent of the export trade in 1984. Furthermore, after the short-lived but traumatic US embargo against all sales of domestic grain, not already pledged by contract, to the USSR, the world's largest importer has increasingly sought to secure its supplies from elsewhere; making more difficult the endeavour of the USA to dispose of its huge surplus. The fall in its share of world exports, from some 48.5 per cent in 1981 to some 44 per cent in 1984, is an indication of this difficulty which, along with the plight of many US farmers suffering from the decline in cereal prices, has fuelled protectionist pressures in the USA.

Indeed, it may be argued that in a world market glutted by stocks and persisting surpluses, there is no longer much meaning in the phrase, 'Food Power'. But alongside the surpluses are large areas of dearth and even famine. And in this context of contrasts, subsidized sales or grants of grain can all too easily become instruments of political manipulation.

Our map, in dealing with the cereal trade, does not indicate any ranking in production. In fact, the USA itself is far outstripped by China, which produced in 1984 some 365 million tonnes, compared with the 314 million in the USA.

One last feature of the cereal trade is worth remarking. South Africa is one country which has used its cereal exports as a form of political and economic pressure. In the three years, 1982-84, its situation changed dramatically, due largely to drought. In 1982, it imported 301,930 tonnes and exported 3,931,610; in 1983, it imported 1,517,090 and exported 1,475,790; in 1984, it imported 3,239,490 and exported only 175,270.

INDUSTRIAL POWER

15

Industrial power is the paramount source of much other power, from military to financial, that the state possesses. It is also the measure which most dramatically demonstrates the economic disproportion between one state and another.

There is no rigid correspondence between industrial performance and investment, as is all too apparent from the record of the USSR. But in general, states with a consistently high level of investment make progress as industrial powers, to catch up with or leave behind those with a consistently lower level. We have combined, therefore, two measures – relative current output and relative rates of investment in manufacturing – so as to indicate the likely pecking order of states as industrial powers in the future as well as their present relative positions.

We have chosen to present this comparison by relation to the performance of a single state. And what better state may be employed as a benchmark than the United Kingdom. It deserves recognition as historically the first industrial state. It is, among the industrially developed, a small enough power to constitute a suitable target for industrial aspirants to reach, while recording a low enough level of investment to excite confidence that this aspiration will not be disappointed.

As so often in such exercises, there is the problem of converting an immense variety of products, measured physically in different ways for different purposes by different authorities, into a single measure of value. The conversion of this measure, from the national to an international currency – the United States dollar – provides further room for fallibility: even where there is something resembling free trade, if only for a small proportion of total output. Where trade is restricted in price and quantity, as between East and West, conversion often borders on an act of faith.

Nonetheless, we have undertaken the exercise. Most national currencies have been given dollar values at the average annual rates provided by the IMF.

Most problematical of all exchange rates are those provided for the countries in Comecon: the USSR and its associated states. To be consistent, we have used the rates listed in the *UN Monthly Bulletin of Statistics*. But these suggest a weighting for East Germany which seems disproportionately large in comparison with a number of other industrial countries. The 1981 rate for the East German Mark in the *UN Bulletin* is given as 2.2 to the US$. The US Department of Commerce, in its *Trading with the German Democratic Republic*, 1982, asserts that a 1981 rate of 3.34 East German Marks to the US$ came close to actual value for statistical purposes. As always, we must warn that statistics, while not usually an exercise in organized lying, provide only a rough-and-ready comparison.

The graphic on advertising is included here because advertising is so closely connected with the distribution and sale of goods in industrial society. We have used the UK as a benchmark for much the same reason as before.

Figures for advertising expenditure cover different types of advertising in different countries. In many, the cost of cinema advertisements, direct advertising, exhibitions and demonstrations, of display material and sales promotion and reference publications, is excluded. We have not been able to allow for such variations.

NUCLEAR POWER

16

The enthusiasm demonstrated by states for the development of nuclear power depends on the interplay of several factors: the price and security of conventional energy sources, especially oil; the pressure from the military for research and production facilities that might be used for the development of nuclear weapons; the projection of electricity needs and the extent of facilities for the expansion of conventional electricity production; the issue of safety and the related intensity of public protest.

The issue of safety has become increasingly acknowledged. The US Nuclear Regulatory Commission released its own study of the subject in 1982. Having considered 19,400 accidents in nuclear power plants between 1969 and 1979, it selected 169 for detailed review. It found 52 of these to have been significant; that is, potentially contributing to a melt-down of the nuclear core in the plant. The study concluded that the likelihood of a major accident was around one in every ten or twenty years. Following the Three Mile Island accident in March 1979, changes made in nuclear reactor operating procedures are claimed to have reduced the chances of serious accident but not, it should be stressed, to have eliminated them.

The public alarm that followed the accident at Three Mile Island in the eastern USA was beginning to abate, when an explosion wrecked one of the reactors at the Chernobyl nuclear power plant near Kiev, USSR, in April 1986. Within days, a radioactive cloud had passed over most of Europe. Within weeks, food products were destroyed or diverted to other uses, not always successfully. And within months, the anti-nuclear Green Party was triumphantly recording, in the West German general election of January 1987, the largest proportionate increase in votes.

The possibility of accidents is far from being the only source of public concern. Throughout Europe and North America, and occasionally elsewhere, there is spreading disquiet at evidence that the operations of nuclear power plants might be responsible for abnormally high rates of cancer in nearby populations. The disposal of nuclear waste, active for thousands of years, has stirred considerable controversy over the use of the high seas, let alone mines and quarries in and near inhabited areas, as burial grounds.

The cartogram here provides background information, showing shares of world electricity production; while colour is used to indicate shares of installed nuclear capacity.

In general the biggest producers of electricity are also the biggest investors in nuclear power. But the present degree of correlation may not persist. The drive to develop nuclear power has significantly slowed down in the West as a whole, with the notable exception of France, while it proceeds heedlessly apace in the USSR and the countries of the Western Pacific.

FINANCIAL POWER

17

The International Monetary Fund (IMF), with its headquarters in Washington DC, is indisputably the world's largest and arguably its most important interstate financial organization. The Bank for International Settlements, with headquarters at Basle in Switzerland, is a closed club of certain central banks from rich Western countries and plays a more reticent – if certainly influential – role in interstate financial decisions, including whether or not and in what measure to provide support for states in economic difficulties. But the IMF remains the paramount immediate source of loans and lines of credit, as well as being the only interstate financial authority that issues what may be termed supranational money in its Special Drawing Rights (SDRs). Moreover, though a few states, notably Switzerland and the USSR, are not members, the extent of its importance may be gauged from the membership of Hungary, Poland and Romania, all three close economic associates of the USSR.

The IMF acquires much the most of its resources from the subscriptions of its members. These subscriptions are equivalent to what are termed 'quotas'. And the size of a member's quota determines that member's voting power, the extent of its potential access to fund resources, and its share in allocations of SDRs.

In March 1983, the IMF's Board of Governors decided to increase the total value of quotas by 47.5 per cent, from SDR 61,060 million to SDR 90,035 million. In the process, the relative shares of member states were readjusted, so as to reflect, if still only in part, changes in relative economic strength.

Two particular features of the readjustment should be noted. The share of the USA (down from 20.64% to 19.902%) still leaves it with a blocking vote, since a minimum of 85% is required for all essential decisions. And largely for historical reasons – a proportion of any quota increase is related to existing shares – the United Kingdom and some other 'old' members emerged from the readjustment with quotas and so voting power still disproportionate to their relative economic strength. Thus the UK, with 6.88%, would continue to have more weight than West Germany, with 6.002%, and Japan, with 4.691%. Canada, with 3.267%, emerged as holding almost 70% the voting power of Japan.

The decision of the IMF's Board of Governors required ratification from member governments, and this did not have an easy ride. Crucially, the US Congress contained a considerable body of opposition, much of it suspicious of a measure that seemed directed in the main at rescuing the world's big commercial banks from the consequences of imprudent lending to states now unable to repay their debts. After months of pressure from the US Administration and dire warnings of a world-wide collapse of credit if the IMF were denied augmented resources, Congress ratified the changes; and such other governments as had waited for this decision soon followed suit.

Not all the hostility shown to the IMF has been due to an alleged subservience to the interests of the banks. There has been increasing criticism, not least in poor countries, of the Fund's loan criteria, which have more to do with policies of economic restraint than with considerations of social development. But then the IMF represents the prevailing financial order and is, naturally, more preoccupied by the need to sustain that order than to undermine it.

TRADE POWER | **18**

The dominance of world trade by the member countries of the European Economic Community (EEC) is in part due to their considerable trade with one another. And it is arguable that such trade is more internal than international. But the EEC is still no more than a qualified economic association, and it is accordingly reasonable to accept the conventional classification of its internal trade as international, or different in kind from the trade, for instance, among the constituent states of the USA.

Certainly, there is a remarkable disproportion between the importance of these individual EEC countries as trade and as economic powers. But then such a remarkable disproportion is far from uncommon. The USA, with around a quarter of the world's aggregate of gross national incomes, accounts for around an eighth of world trade. Even more striking, the USSR has a share of world trade virtually the same as that of Switzerland, with more than 20 times the national income.

Yet this does not deny the meaning or relevance of trade power, which is a measure of the relative part played by a state in the world economy and which derives from such factors as industrial specialization and sophistication, the command of particular commodities, and the development of competitively priced products.

As the map demonstrates, there have been substantial changes in the relative shares of world trade enjoyed by particular countries. There are various reasons for this. The large declines in the share of many oil-exporting states, notably Kuwait and Saudi Arabia, are essentially due to the substantial drop in their oil exports, with declining demand in the industrial states, the emergence of other important oil producers, and production cuts by some OPEC members to help sustain the oil price. For Iran and Iraq, of course, there was the added factor of their increasingly ferocious and destructive war. Communal warfare accounts for much of the huge decline (some 81 per cent) in Lebanon's trade; the flight of the large white community, South Africa's economic sabotage, and a South African subsidized rebellion, for the even larger decline (some 84 per cent) in Mozambique's; doctrinal fanaticism, then military intervention and civil war, for the still larger (94 per cent) decline in the trade of Kampuchea. Civil war or disorder affected production and trade in a number of other countries, such as Chad, El Salvador, and Poland. A different factor was the substantial decline in the price of major raw materials. The fall in Zambia's share of world trade (58 per cent), for instance, is largely to be explained by the fall in the price of copper during the period.

Japan's particular rise in share of world trade (54%) was equivalent overall, at an absolute 3.55% of all trade, to the declines experienced by many countries together. And marked rises were recorded by some of the so-called new Japans: notably Singapore (119%), South Korea (132%), and Taiwan (111%). Not least, China's new Open Door policy was reflected in a 1.7% share of world trade for 1985, compared with a share of 0.77% a decade before, or a rise of 120%.

The inset map on export income per head of population is included for the staggering contrasts it reveals. It is necessary, however, to point out that countries with tiny populations but thriving tourist and financial sectors may have an export revenue per head that is out of all proportion to their relative trading power.

DEPENDENCE AND DIVERSITY

19

This map demonstrates how many states are dependent, for the bulk of their export income, on the sale of either one product or a very few products. The extreme case is Libya, where the total export income comes from oil.

The economic weakness of a state dependent upon a single major export is evident: especially when the state is poor, in competition with other poor states and even with rich ones, and when the product is an agricultural commodity. Not only is there the persistent threat of bad or too bountiful harvests, there is also the danger that access to major traditional markets may, for one reason or another, be denied. In particular, when major customers are also themselves producers – as with sugar, for instance – they may proceed to protect their own production at the expense of traditional suppliers.

Some poor countries seem to have a stronger, more diversified economic base than really exists, since their principal export takes more than one form. Bangladesh provides a striking example: 15% of its export income comes from raw jute; another 24% comes from textile products that are made mainly from jute; and a further 19%, from 'woven non-cotton textiles', i.e. jute. A rare example among rich states is New Zealand, three-fifths of whose exports are animal products.

Finally, it must be stressed that oil constitutes an important export even where it does not account for the bulk of export income. In seven countries – Cameroon (46.83%), Tunisia (43.3%), USSR (38.8%), Norway (28.2%), Panama (22.6%), Peru (17.3%) and the UK (15.4%) – it is the largest single export. In many others, it is an important, if not the leading, export commodity.

SCIENCE POWER

20

We have used an unusual measure to depict science power; one which is based on the number and citations of articles published in science journals, classified by the country in which the author lives (or the first author, when there is more than one). It is far from satisfactory, for it seriously understates the concentration of science power. We have chosen this measure because the relevant information is by far the best that is generally available.

Only some 35 per cent of the articles by Third World authors are published in Third World journals. The great majority are published in the West, particularly in the USA and Britain. Indeed, the USA ranks as the largest single publisher of Third World science articles. India is second and Britain is third.

This map is a telling example of the phenomenon highlighted in *Map 27: Languages of Rule*. About 88% of all science articles published are in English, as are no less than 92% of all science articles in the Third World.

Not all science journals are equal. One fifth of all science articles in the world are published in 60 journals, which constitute a mere 0.12% of the total; while 400 journals, still a mere 0.8% of the total, account for half of all such articles.

Added to this, the impact of articles published in the West is far greater than that of articles published elsewhere. In the mid-1970s, science articles published in the Netherlands were cited on average 3.9 times; in the USA, 3.6 times; in Britain, 3.3; Denmark, 2.8; Switzerland, 2.7; West Germany, 2.3: in contrast with 1.2 for articles published in Costa Rica; 1.1 in India; 0.2 in Brazil and 0.1 in Venezuela.

India is an anomaly in the science world. It is a considerable science power; accounting for half of all science articles published in poor countries and for 60 per cent of all poor country science publishing. Its scientific research reaches beyond the clinical and biomedical fields on which science in the poor countries concentrates, to biochemistry, physics, chemistry, and – especially – chemical physics. Yet its impact is relatively small.

NATIONAL INCOME

21

The information available on gross national products must be treated with a great deal of caution. The value of subsistence production is inadequately measured. The value of unpaid domestic labour is wholly ignored. Variously thriving so-called black economies, where goods and especially services are sold or exchanged privately in order to escape taxes, are excluded.

The measure of value is the US dollar, and movements in exchange rates for the dollar have a corresponding impact on the figures for other countries. In an era of exceptional monetary excitement, amounting at times to hysteria, such movements can have a grotesque effect. It is manifestly absurd that a country's income should be considered to have shrunk by one per cent in a few days or even hours because its currency has, under the influence of rising interest rates in the USA, fallen by that proportion against the dollar.

Not least, the methods by which the gross national product is calculated differ so markedly in certain states from those commonly employed that comparison of any real precision becomes impossible. The World Bank, which is a major source for these statistics, does not provide any for a number of states, such as Afghanistan, Angola, Iran, Iraq, Kampuchea, Lebanon and Mozambique, where war or social upheaval has made the collection of comparable figures virtually impossible. Moreover, for the centralized economies, it has ceased publishing estimates, 'until a broadly acceptable methodology is developed'. We have had nervous recourse to *The World Factbook* of the US Central Intelligence Agency, which has its own, scarcely secret, in-built bias, but whose estimates have a certain consistency and value. In consequence, the cartogram is somewhat more comprehensive than before: including, for instance, Iran and Lebanon.

For the colour differentiations, on growth or decline during the decade to 1983, we have, however, had the sole general source of the World Bank, and there are, accordingly, more white patches than in the last edition. It should be noted that, within the limited information available, there were no less than 22 states where the annual real rate of movement in gross national income was actually downwards during the period; and this may well have happened in some of the 22 states – Lebanon among them – for which information was not available. One explanation for the average annual decline in several Latin American states – Argentina, Bolivia, Peru, Venezuela – was almost certainly the debt crisis, which led to imposed programmes of austerity and effective economic contraction as a condition for the supply or sanctioning of credit by the IMF.

| **THE FIRST SLICE OF THE CAKE** | **22** |

All governments take slices of national income for themselves. Some take larger slices than others. This map depicts broad bands of difference in government appetite, along with relative shares of states in the aggregate government income of the world. Further comparisons are evident from viewing this map alongside *Map 21: National Income*. There are some remarkable discrepancies. Italy, with a gross national product (GNP) some 19 times the size of Israel's, had a government income that was actually smaller in the years covered. The USA, with a GNP more than two-and-a-half times that of the USSR, had a government income of around four-fifths the size.

As so often, there are reservations to be recorded. The most recent years for which figures are available is not the same for every state. And the conversion of national currencies into the US dollar, as the common measure of value, gives rise to distortions. Some states have been excluded because no relevant information is available. Relative shares of aggregate government income in the world are accordingly very approximate, and the cartogram is more indicative than definitive.

Figures for Eastern European countries were derived from: the CIA, for estimates of GNP (on the basis of standard Western national income accounting concepts); national statistical yearbooks or their equivalents; and the conversion of currencies at 'effective' exchange rates for the period, as provided by Pick's *Currency Yearbook*.

| **COMPLEXIONS OF GOVERNMENT** | **23** |

The authors do not pretend to be providing a definitive differentiation of governments throughout the world. We offer only a rough guide to various broad categories of distinction.

It may be argued that all parliamentary regimes are more or less restricted. The designation 'restricted parliamentary' is here applied to the considerable variety of governments whose parliamentary institutions are patently qualified by controls or limitations of one sort or another. In Bangladesh, for instance, the military do not rule directly but in practice choose which candidates for office should be selected or excluded. In Singapore, there is a parliamentary opposition, but one circumscribed by difficulties and tolerated only for as long as it has only a token presence. In South Africa, conventional parliamentary government is effectively, where not legally, restricted to the minority white population; and even within the white context, the power of the state president is enormous and increasing.

The designation 'despotic' is applied to a government where a single personal authority is in such overriding control that any other institutionalized form of power, whether restricted parliamentary, one-party bureaucratic or military, is essentially a mere instrument of the despotism. It is on this basis that we have designated Paraguay as having a despotic rather than a military, and North Korea or Romania as having a despotic rather than a one-party, regime. Some despotisms are, of course, a great deal worse than others. The despotism in Malawi or Zaire, for instance, is more oppressive, not least for being so arbitrary, than the despotism in most of the monarchical despotisms, such as Kuwait. Beyond the identification of 'monarchical', such distinctions are not the subject of the map.

For some countries, we have been forced to find a special category, the praetorian state, in which essentially military or para-military rule is exercised through civilian institutions. We have placed in this category such states as Guatemala, where it is the armed forces that are ultimately in charge, and Panama, where it is the National Guard.

For those who question the implicit judgements of our categories, we offer the words of Rosa Luxemburg, writing in some alarm at the course of the revolutionary government in Russia:

'Freedom for supporters of the government only, for the members of one party only – no matter how big its membership may be – is no freedom at all. Freedom is always freedom for the person who thinks differently. This contention does not spring from a fanatical love of abstract "justice", but from the fact that everything which is enlightening, healthy and purifying in political freedom derives from its independent character, and from the fact that freedom loses all its virtues when it becomes a privilege. . . Without general elections, freedom of the press, freedom of assembly, and freedom of speech, life in every public institution slows down, becomes a caricature of itself, and bureaucracy rises as the only deciding factor.' *The Russian Revolution*.

HARMWORKERS AND HEALTHWORKERS

24

The morally repulsive priorities of the state can be illustrated in many ways; but perhaps nowhere more eloquently than in the comparison between expenditure on preparations to promote injury or death and expenditure to heal and sustain life. Most states spend more on their armed forces than on their medical services. The states that deploy fewer military than medical personnel are outnumbered more than eight to one by those that prefer the bullet to the bandage.

Military expenditure is virtually everywhere and always a monopoly of the state. Medical expenditure is, in many countries and often, also part of the private sector. Comparing public outlays on the two pursuits is accordingly less an exercise in the measurement of relative expenditure than a pointer to where the state's own priorities lie.

The same holds true for the deployment of personnel. There are usually more doctors, dentists and nurses at work in a society than are employed in its public sector. Moreover, there are peculiarities in the published statistics that tend to understate the number of public service personnel in some countries. Thailand and the Philippines, for example, report the numbers of doctors but not those of dentists. Some military establishments are also understated by the exclusion of paramilitary forces; though the exclusions constitute a far smaller proportion of the total in the military than in the medical category.

The figures for military expenditure may not include all the expenditure, as when there is a substantial grant element in arms supplies (for example, Israel). And some of the information on which the comparison is based is very dated; 1979 is the most recent year for relevant information on Iraq, Laos, Vietnam and South Yemen.

Overall, however, and with all reservations duly cited, the contrasts evident from the figures are generally valid.

OURGES OF THE STATE

25

Self-defence takes precedence over any other value professed by the state, as is demonstrated by the results of a survey submitted to the UN Congress on the Prevention of Crime and Treatment of Offenders in 1980. Out of the 125 states for which information was available, 'in 99 . . . homicide is subject to capital punishment, but offences against the state are punishable by death even more frequently – in 113 countries.'

It is this unwavering defence of self-interest that promotes the cruel paradox whereby regimes, most notably in Latin America, deny themselves the use of capital punishment only to engage in state assassination and the 'disappearance' of suspected opponents. This is, for instance, true even of Costa Rica, whose reputation for humanitarian conduct – it does not possess a formal army – is widely accepted.

Nor do all states that reserve the right to kill judicially exercise the right that they possess. In this edition, we have, for the first time, distinguished between active executioner states and those that are merely prepared to become such, or that pass death sentences in the courts but commute them as a matter of course.

Torture in some form, applied by agents of the state to those regarded as its enemies, is widely used as an instrument of policy. But in general, wherever it is used, its use is denied, and not only by the authorities directly responsible for it. Many other people, from sheer incredulity or misguided patriotism, will leap to the defence of their own state against such charges.

It may be thought important to distinguish between states in which torture is both widely used and officially condoned, such as Chile or Iran, and states where, though officially condoned, it has not been widely used, such as Italy or Nicaragua. It is also important to point out the bias in the accumulation of evidence against the rich Western states, where allegations of torture are both more likely to be made and easier to verify than elsewhere.

But the essential point remains: 'if,' as Amnesty International asserts, 'one prisoner of conscience is held, if one single detainee faces torture or execution, this is a violation of human rights that must be confronted.'

It is for this reason that we have included Nicaragua amongst the violators of human rights despite its government's clear intention to renounce state terrorism. Army atrocities in the Pantasma area on the border with Honduras in 1983 and in the Atlantic coast territories inhabited by the Miskito Indians in 1984 were both followed by courts martial and heavy sentences for those found guilty. But there remain instances of torture and attempted assassination by the security forces that the authorities have ignored and, by that token, implicitly condoned. The provocation to lower standards of official behaviour is immense in Nicaragua. The opposition Contras – as reported by Amnesty International – practise widespread torture, execution-style killing of individuals, and general mayhem. But in our view, provocation, however great, is no justification.

It is always heartening to record a retreat from barbarism. Since the last edition of this atlas, Argentina has broken with a past of widespread, systematic torture, and the 'disappearance' of political prisoners and public critics. Uruguay, with its first civilian government after 11 years of brutal military rule, followed suit; as did the Philippines, after a popular upheaval that overwhelmed the corrupt and cruel Marcos regime.

The range of scourges wielded by states against their own and others' citizens is not exhausted by those depicted on the map. Some states, notably the USSR and Romania, use psychiatric hospitals as political prisons, and psychotropic drugs as instruments for the ill-treatment of prisoners. Almost all states inflict on prisoners a degree of ill-treatment that falls little short of torture. Some, even among the privileged states of the rich West, expel and deport political and other refugees to almost certain torture or death in their countries of origin, as did the UK and Switzerland to Tamil refugees from Sri Lanka in 1986. Some, such as Pakistan and Saudi Arabia, indulge in public floggings and mutilation; many arrange for prisoners to die in custody; and many, too, make a practice of arbitrary arrests and detention without trial.

A SORT OF SURVIVAL

26

Our world is an increasingly violent one. There were more refugees in the 1970s than there had been in the 1960s, and there are likely to be more again in the present decade. Some eventually return to their countries, if not their homes; others settle, with more or less difficulty, as citizens or tolerated aliens, in the societies of other countries; many remain for years in special camps or villages, often in appalling conditions, with their lives in a seemingly endless state of suspense.

The very definition of a refugee is the subject of much dispute. The United Nations High Commission for Refugees, the principal interstate agency for refugee relief, deals essentially with those who have fled across state borders. But multitudes of people are displaced, by war or persecution or the fear of either, from one part of their country to another. Furthermore, individual governments, reluctant to provide sanctuary but concerned to protect their humanitarian pretensions, are sometimes peculiarly, sometimes capriciously, exacting in their own definitions of what constitutes a refugee. The US authorities, for instance, have tended to consider Haitians, fleeing an oppressive government and conditions of intolerable poverty, 'economic refugees' and have accorded them a correspondingly cold reception. They have generally been far more liberal in accepting for settlement similarly motivated refugees from Vietnam.

There is much dispute as well over numbers. Some host governments, with an eye to financial assistance from the UN High Commission and other relief agencies, are tempted to exaggerate the numbers in their care. On the other hand, there are many refugees who slip across state borders and, uncertain of their reception, assiduously seek to escape official scrutiny.

In short, it is extremely difficult to determine the numbers of refugees according to the broadly compassionate criteria that we wish to apply. We have included as refugees those displaced within their own state boundaries. We have not attempted to sort out the so-called 'economic' from the so-called 'political' refugees, so as to exclude the former. But we have excluded those who may reasonably be considered migrant workers, themselves the subject of *Map 32: In Search of Work.*

LANGUAGES OF RULE

27

In 1492 Don Elio Antonio de Nebrija dedicated his Castilian grammar – the first grammar produced for a modern European language – to Queen Isabella la Catolica. His declared object was to 'turn the Castilian language from a loose possession of the people into an artifact so that whatever shall henceforth be said or written in this language shall be of standard coinage, of a coinage that can outlast the times.' For Nebrija, this structured language 'has forever been the mate of empire and always shall remain its comrade.'

The future course of Castilian, or Spanish, as of other imperial languages, was to prove him right. And if the great European empires came in time to disintegrate, the imperial languages generally remained, as instruments of rule.

We define a language of rule as one which is used by a political and/or economic elite to sustain its cohesion and control. It effectively excludes from any real participation in power those who do not speak or read it. It promotes, most notably in Africa, a closer association among the elites of individual states than between such elites and the populace of their own societies. The contemporary record shows how widespread such languages of rule still are. The map shows too, the sites of significant linguistic conflict, or those states where the issue of language has manifested itself in serious protest, usually involving some resort to violence. In many – perhaps all – instances, of course, such conflict is essentially an expression of a deeper and often wider social conflict.

In certain states, mainly of the Caribbean, a local or so-called Creole version of the imperial language is widely used. We have identified such cases where we have been advised that it is necessary to do so.

The map is a contemporary rather than historical record. Portuguese, for instance, was brought by conquest to what is now known as Brazil. It then so far displaced the indigenous languages as to constitute no longer a language of rule.

Based as it is on the world of states, the map does less than full justice to the complexities of language and social power within particular ones. China provides a major example. The official language of China is 'Putonghua' or 'common language', based on the dialect spoken in Beijing and widely referred to as Mandarin. It is the language generally spoken in a number of provinces, comprising 70 per cent of the population. These are Heilongjiang, Jilin, Liaoning, Hebei, Henan, Shandong, Shanxi, Gansu, Ningxia, Jiangsu, Anhui, Hubei, Hunan and Jiangxi. In the three provinces on China's southeast coast – Zheijiang, Fujian and Guangdong – and in Taiwan, the dialects spoken are unintelligible to Mandarin speakers, and vice versa. But these dialects are largely identical to Mandarin in written form.

In Inner Mongolia, Qinghai, Yunnan, Guizhou and Guangxi, where the majority speak Mandarin, there are large areas in which non-Chinese languages, with their own scripts and literatures, are spoken, particularly by the rural poor. In Xinjiang and Tibet, the majority speak their own completely different languages. And in Sichuan, there is a clear division between the eastern half of the province, where 'Mandarin' only is spoken, and the western half, where the only languages spoken are non-Chinese ones, related to Tibetan.

In summary, there is a patchwork of linguistic dominance in the country, with Putonghua or Mandarin as the language of rule over China as a whole.

RELIGIONS OF RULE

28

The belief in future fulfilment, peace and happiness; the representation of that belief in ritual; its justification through reference to some holy writ, interpreted by a special category of people; and its involvement with state-associated or -supported institutions: such are the hallmarks of many religions. In this sense, official Marxism-Leninism is such a religion: with its concentration on the benefits of the future through present sacrifice; its ritual parades and ceremonies; its revealed truths, whose texts are to be interpreted acceptably only by those appointed to do so; and its association with the power of the state. Furthermore, like some other religions, it has its own schismatic orthodoxies: mainly the Moscow denomination, but with local variants, primarily the Chinese; and it has its popular low church heterodoxy (Titoism in Yugoslavia), anathematized heresy (Trotskyism), and fundamentalist sects (revolutionary Marxism).

We define a religion of rule as one which is professed by those in power and which sustains their solidarity. Poland provides a celebrated example, with official Marxism-Leninism, of the Moscow denomination, ruling over a population almost entirely Catholic in allegiance. Britain provides another, much more muted, manifestation. There the majority of the population is either secular in persuasion or holds a variety of 'unestablished' religious beliefs. But the Church of England is the 'established' Church or state religion, with the monarch at its head and with its bishops or 'lords spiritual' members of the upper house in parliament.

So spirited has the reaction of readers been to this map that we believe it necessary to make our essential position clear. There is no inexorable coincidence between a religion of rule, professed by those in power, and a popular religion, upheld by the ruled. They may be similar or the same; and they may not.

In dealing with Christianity, we have distinguished between Catholicism and Protestantism only where one of these is clearly dominant, and no distinction is made between different versions of Protestantism. For Islam, the only distinction drawn is between Sunni and Shi'ite.

Sites of current or recent religious conflict are shown on the map only where violence, due wholly or in considerable part to religious differences, has been involved. The incidence of such conflict has markedly increased since the first edition of this atlas. This has partly been due to an upsurge in militant Islamic fundamentalism and to the particular intervention or influence of the Shi'ite regime in Iran. But the resurgent, increasingly violent Sikh separatist movement in India and violent clashes between Tamil and Singhalese in Sri Lanka suggest that the increase is far from being an Islamic phenomenon.

BIG MONEY

29

The size of a commercial bank is conventionally measured by its assets, although these are not, as may be mistakenly supposed, mainly such property, direct investments and cash that it holds, but, overwhelmingly, the loans it has given. By this measure, the world's 500 biggest commercial banks are very big indeed.

The sums involved are all the more extraordinary because these are not central banks, the state institutions that are in general custodians of national reserves and issuers of the national currency. And only a few commercial banks, notably the major French ones, are owned by the state. The vast majority of the world's biggest 500 banks are so-called public companies, owned by individual shareholders.

It is scarcely strange that the world's leading economic power, the USA, should possess, by a considerable margin, more of the world's top 500 banks than any other country. What may be surprising is that Japan, with little more than half the USA's number, should have a larger share of aggregate assets.

The capital and reserves of a bank, as a proportion of its assets (generally its loans), are regarded as its safety margin or reassurance factor, since such may be used to meet large losses on bad debts or a rush of withdrawals by depositors. The sovereign debt crisis of the early 1980s, along with domestic problems, such as those affecting US banks from large loans to the ailing energy and farming sectors, drew the attention of both the public and the authorities to the enhanced importance of this 'primary capital' ratio. We have accordingly used colour in the cartogram to show the average 'primary capital' ratios of banks in the relevant states.

The national reserves, on which the comparisons in the inset map are based, include gold holdings valued at the prevailing free market price. They would, for many countries, be much smaller, if some artificial fixed price for gold, such as that employed by the United States authorities, were used instead. The comparison between national reserves and commercial bank assets is, to be sure, not a conventional one. But it is serviceable as a guide to the enormous financial power possessed and wielded by what are, in the overwhelming main, essentially private institutions.

BIG BUSINESS

30

The world's largest industrial companies are conventionally ranked by annual sales income, and such income is very large. The top 500 had aggregate sales in 1985 equivalent to almost one quarter (23.6 per cent) of the world's whole annual income in the previous year. Within these 500, the US ones have together, since such measures began to be taken, held a clearly dominant position. Since sales income is, for purposes of comparison, measured in US dollars, whatever the domicile and corresponding currency of particular companies, exchange rate movements can commensurately affect the ranking and number of US or other companies in any composite list. But this factor, however temporarily material, affects the extent rather than the fact of a US dominance in big business that is distinctly disproportionate to the relative size of the US economy.

In 1985, there were 212 US companies in the top 500, or 42.4 per cent of the total; and their share of the aggregate sales income, at some $1,551 billion out of $3,225 billion, was even larger, at some 48.1 per cent, or little short of half. The average size of the US companies, however, while higher (at $7.3 billion of sales income) than the average of the 500, was dwarfed by the single representative of Mexico (at $20.4 billion) or the five representatives of the Netherlands (at $16.9 billion apiece).

31

This map is based on a study prepared by the UN Centre on Transnational Corporations and published in 1983. It is a study that deals with 382 such transnationals among the thousands that exist.

The distribution of subsidiaries applies to the year 1980, as does the distribution of domiciles. The outflow of payments applies to 1979.

The proportions of gross national product represented by payments on foreign direct investment may seem so small as to be meaningless in many instances. They are not. For a poor country in need of capital to develop its economy, the export of any hard currency at all represents a serious loss. For one, such as Honduras, to be exporting more than $2 out of every $100 generated by all economic activity in a year – let alone a Botswana which exports more than $11 of every $100 – is a recipe for increasing dependence and deprivation.

Furthermore, such payments are concerned only with 'foreign direct investment'. They exclude the enormous drain in interest charges and capital repayments for foreign commercial bank and government loans. They take no account of the incalculable economic loss caused by the recruitment for export of trained people, an activity in which the transnationals are greatly involved.

The United Nations study of transnationals indicates the degree to which the once virtual monopoly of such enterprise by the advanced industrial states of the West has been eroded. Japanese representation among the 382 transnationals examined is exactly twice the French and not far from twice the West German. South Korean representation is exactly the same as the Belgian and some four-fifths that of the Netherlands. The operations of these Eastern transnationals are not, of course, limited to the poor countries of the so-called Third World. Their subsidiaries are planted in the heartlands of the system, Western Europe and North America. Increasingly, Japan – in receipt of enormous funds from its annual surpluses on trade and confronted by mounting pressures for protection against its competitiveness – has been buying or building companies and plant abroad.

The inset cartogram depicts the extent of Japan's direct investment overseas in 1985, generally through the instrument of the transnational corporation: an investment whose $12.2 billion in that year alone was not far from twice that of its total investment for the period 1951-72 (at $6.8 billion).

Japan's Direct Overseas Investment, 1951-85

	cases number	US $millions
1951-72	6,411	6,773
1973	3,093	3,494
1974	1,912	2,396
1975	1,591	3,280
1976	1,652	3,462
1977	1,761	2,806
1978	2,393	4,598
1979	2,694	4,995
1980	2,442	4,693
1981	2,563	8,932

	cases number	US $millions
1982	2,549	7,703
1983	2,754	8,145
1984	2,499	10,155
1985	2,613	12,217
total	36,927	83,649

The immense economic power wielded internationally by a relatively few companies must be considered alongside their general hierarchical structure. In effect, a few thousand executives, nearly all of them men, are responsible for decisions that have a considerable impact on the lives of countless millions.

32

Labour is essentially a commodity, bought and sold, in the international marketplace. It is true that many states take measures to impede the trade in labour. But then, similarly, they take measures to impede the trade in other commodities. What distinguishes labour is that it is not inanimate. People can move to jobs across state frontiers, regardless of measures to prevent them; and if some are discovered and expelled, others successfully evade the interventions of authority or are discovered but nonetheless allowed to remain because their labour is more useful than the law. Contributory crucial factors in the flow are the increasing lack of employment opportunities for much of the population in most countries, together with the availability of low paid or disagreeable jobs in others.

Figures for labour migrations are notoriously difficult to determine. The line between migrant labourers and refugees from oppression is frequently blurred. Estimates for that large component of migrant labour which is illegal can be no more than educated guesses.

We have drawn on such information and informed opinion as we encountered. The numbers given on the map apply to the workers themselves and not to the family members that accompany or follow them.

The term 'major', for exporting and importing states alike, is used only where at least 1 per cent of the country's work force and at least 100,000 workers are involved. Some countries designated as exporters are also considerable importers. Italy, for instance, is estimated to have around 500,000 foreign workers, legal and illegal: from Algeria, Egypt, Ethiopia, Libya, Portugal, Somalia, Spain, Tunisia, Turkey, Yugoslavia and other countries. In all cases, the designation of importer or exporter applies to the net flow.

The dynamic of migrant labour is most tellingly illustrated by the attraction of the USA for multitudes of Mexicans. The estimated real wage differential between the USA and Mexico averages around 7 to 1 for unskilled labour, and around 13 to 1 for such labour in agriculture. Above all, there are jobs in the USA and many people without the prospect of a job in Mexico. The huge flow of illegal migrants across the border is easy enough to explain. The official list of Mexican nationals applying for US visas to migrate legally contains about one million names, and it takes an average of seven years for someone on the list to obtain a visa.

With little or no economic growth in the industrialized world, corresponding high unemployment, and anti-immigrant sentiment exploited by reactionaries of almost every political persuasion, the numbers of legal immigrant workers have generally fallen there. But this has almost certainly been accompanied by a significant increase in the numbers of illegal migrants, who find a home in the flourishing 'black economies' and who are protected by employers unable to find indigenous workers prepared to do the available jobs at the wage rates that such employers are prepared to pay.

The fall in the price of oil may have produced some restraint in the labour-importing practices of some oil-exporting states. But the reliance on imported labour, for jobs which the indigenous cannot or will not do, means that overall there is unlikely to have been much, if any, decline in the migrant component of the labour force.

EXPLOITATION

33

Ideally a measure of exploitation would compare the output of all productive workers – those workers whose labour provides essential ingredients for further production – with their disposable income. Such a measure does not exist and cannot be created from the information available. Productive and unproductive workers are not differentiated, analytically or statistically. Inessential is not differentiated from essential output. Statistics do not cover all relevant activity; are not everywhere reliable or even pertinent; and vary in scope from state to state.

We cannot accordingly use the formula we would have wished: value added in productive activity divided by wages in cash and kind for productive activity. We have had to settle instead for: value added in manufacturing (the value of output less the value of bought-in goods and services) divided by the wages and salaries of the people directly engaged in its production.

The data present certain problems. Some states report estimates for value added, some do not: and comparable estimates have had to be derived by using a different coefficient for rich (OECD) countries, middle-income (Comecon) countries and poor countries, from figures for gross output in manufacturing. Similarly, some states report estimates for operatives' pay; some do not, and the figures have had to be derived from those for employees' emoluments. Sometimes statistics for manufacturing cover only a particular range of industries; sometimes they are stretched to include the output of utilities and services. In most cases, a five year average (1976-80) has been used; sometimes a four or three year average; sometimes three or four non-consecutive years have been used to establish an average; and sometimes whatever year or years were available.

The results reflect the inadequacy of the data. In particular, the association of high exploitation rates with poor states is valid only because productivity in manufacturing is partly insulated from, and does not fully reflect, the general level of productivity there.

The range, given on the key to the map – from Rwanda, where the rate of exploitation is seemingly the highest recorded, to the USSR, where it is seemingly the lowest – should alert readers to the complexities of the issue and the difficulties of interpretation. The two states ought not to be seen as exemplars of hell or heaven for workers. In the first case, manufacturing scarcely exists, and the result is due to a statistical quirk. In the second, it results from institutional structures and official dispositions which make the wastage of human resources a most attractive option in many cases.

THE LABOUR FORCE

34

The economically active population is conventionally defined as that sector which receives wages or salaries in cash or kind. It accordingly excludes most women in most states; and, by definition, those in the unrecorded 'black economy'. It includes, if somewhat erratically, the unemployed, or at least those regarded as such, on the basis that they are no more than temporarily inactive. It is this economically active labour force from which we calculate the ratio between those engaged in agriculture and in industry.

In some poor states, a surprisingly small proportion of the population seems to be employed in agriculture, together with an unsurprisingly small proportion working in industry. This is because in such states, much of what is termed the 'economically active population' is actually unemployed or is engaged on the fringes of the economy in a multitude of elusive 'service' capacities.

A high ratio of industrial to agricultural workers is not always a corresponding index of industrial advancement and power. Britain, as the map demonstrates, has a higher ratio than Japan. Japanese industry is in general more advanced and efficient than British industry; while British agriculture is more mechanized and large-scale in its operations than is Japanese.

The existing map applies in general to the early 1980s. Using different sources, we have found figures that are different for around a third of the countries on our map. Some of the differences may be due to real changes reflected in more recent statistics; but others simply reflect the new sources and the basis of their particular calculations. We provide below these new and different figures – relating in general to 1984 – often so unreliably exact.

Afghanistan 665; Albania 53; Algeria 224; Belgium 12; Belize 309; Benin 3,500; Bolivia 891; Botswana 850; Bulgaria 65; Burma 773; Cameroon 653; Costa Rica 126; Cuba 29; Dominican Republic 173; El Salvador 181; Fiji 700+; French Guiana 195; Gambia 400+; Greece 125; Guatemala 484; Hungary 74; Iran 157; Iraq 111; Jordan 113; North Korea 198; Kuwait 16; Malawi 578; Malaysia 285; Maldives 800+; Mauritania 336+; Mexico 180; Mozambique 1,371; Nigeria 4,243; Oman 2,480; Panama 231; Philippines 495; Poland 103; Romania 81; Sao Tome 864; Seychelles 116; Sri Lanka 396; Surinam 45; Swaziland 257; Syria 208; Taiwan 42; Thailand 820; Togo 355; Tunisia 159; Turkey 519; USA 15; Vanuatu 3,482; Venezuela 80; North Yemen 1,368; and Zimbabwe 433.

WOMEN WORKERS

35

Women workers are peculiarly invisible to official enumerators, whose scrutiny ignores the world of domestic labour. When noted at all, even women agricultural workers in poor countries or women working at home in the production of marketable goods are likely to be described as 'not economically active' or 'unpaid family workers'. Only when active in the male-defined world of paid jobs do women have a chance of being recognized statistically.

Our map is, of course, as much a geography of ideology as of women's work. And this explains some of the wide regional differences in the ratio of women to men workers: the generally low ratio in Islamic countries; the generally high one in Eastern Europe, where far more women have jobs outside the home.

We have retained in this edition a small and very old study of child labour: small not because the subject is so, in incidence or importance, but because there is so little statistical information. We include it here, in what seemed to us the most suitable conjunction, since like so many unpaid working mothers, some four fifths of recorded working children are unpaid family workers. The data available have forced us to accept the conventional narrow definition of child labour, which excludes the millions of regular workers below the age of 10.

THE FORCE OF LABOUR

36

Modern trade unions were generally formed to secure independent sources of social power. A few trade unions in a few states are still essentially dedicated to that purpose (with yet fewer dedicated to an internationalist perspective). Many are committed to it formally, but in practice are concerned with making the best available material deal for their immediate members. And many, perhaps most, have no commitment at all, beyond serving their requirement to function as creatures of the state or its governing party.

The categories and definitions were determined on the advice of leading international trade union officials. Trade unions that are totally controlled, as in the USSR, Eastern Europe, and parts of Africa and Asia, are essentially organs of government, with no independence of decision. Trade unions that are tightly controlled have independence of decision in form, but are in fact permitted such independence only when it involves no conflict with major government policies. There is, very occasionally, a twilight zone where this category merges into that of independent unions free of government control. Given the unstable relations between state power and union independence in Kenya and Ghana, we have placed the trade union movement of these countries in both categories.

We have not revised the main map, since relatively few changes would need to be made. Argentina, Brazil, Grenada, Guinea, Hong Kong, Philippines, Rwanda, Sierra Leone, Thailand, Togo and Uganda should be transferred to the category of 'independent unions effectively free of government control.' Gabon, Mauritania, Sudan and Zimbabwe should be placed in the cross-hatched or intermediate category, between the category of effectively free unions and that of unions nominally independent but tightly controlled. Afghanistan and Indonesia should belong to the category of 'unions nominally independent but totally controlled.' Namibia, South Africa, Surinam and Turkey should be placed in the category of 'unions nominally independent but severely repressed.'

On the whole, therefore, the situation at the end of 1986 was rather better overall than it had been in mid-1983.

UNEMPLOYMENT

37

We are, once again, including a map on unemployment. We have used the latest official figures or estimates wherever they appear to bear, with all their faults, some relation to reality; and where figures were not available or were manifestly absurd, we have used estimates contained in more or less independent reports from political correspondents and other commentators. We are convinced that the results beg as many questions as they answer and mask as much as they reveal.

Unemployment is essentially a product and feature of industrial and urbanized society. It should reflect the proportion of those who are capable of economic activity but who are, for one reason or another, excluded from it. In such societies, where there are relatively refined procedures of research and analysis, it might be supposed that official figures for unemployment would be reliable. It is not a supposition that bears serious scrutiny. Apart from political engineering through special training schemes or even military service to deflate the figures, Western authorities define unemployment in various ways which all tend to understate the real extent of the problem. In a number of countries, those people who have searched for work, failed to find it and as a result stop trying, are no longer included in the figures. In all such countries, the figures take no account of many adults, generally women, who would prefer to be employed for a wage or salary but who never are; sometimes because they accept a role which excludes such activity, sometimes because they simply despair of finding acceptable employment.

In the centralized economies of the USSR and Eastern Europe, the distortion is a different one. The political dedication to full employment is reflected in the absence of any unemployment figures. The USSR, for instance, concedes only the existence of 'free hands'. Work is provided without corresponding production, in a form that crowds factory floors.

In other, less 'developed' countries, conventionally defined unemployment is a phenomenon of the urban sector. But the urban sector contains a minority of the total population. In Brazil, for instance, there is – or at least was, at the last available estimate – an unemployment rate of just under 10 per cent for six urban centres. But it has been estimated that there is in the countryside a rate of what is described as 'underemployment' upwards of 25 per cent.

Underemployment itself is a complex and disputed concept. There is no serviceable purpose in making it mean merely the measure of some timing device, so that only people who work for less than an arbitrarily defined number of hours must be considered underemployed. It should reflect the extent of the shortfall between the labour required to produce a decent standard of living and the actual payment given for labour of all kinds. By this definition, which provides a virtual poverty index, studies by the International Labour Organization suggest a rate of underemployment in the so-called developing world of from just under 32 per cent to 42 per cent, and an underemployed population of almost 500 millions (all estimates excluding China).

RICH AND POOR PEOPLE | 38

Measuring disparities in income between rich and poor members of the same society is an exercise usually limited to a few Western states. Measures or at least estimates of such disparities within other states are generally irregular and infrequent. A co-ordinated world-wide survey of such disparities is rare indeed. The figures we use are old ones. And they are old because no one with the requisite resources seems interested any longer in undertaking the exercise. We owe what we have to a brief period when the World Bank, under the direction of Robert McNamara, was concerned about investment in social infrastructure such as education and funded some research into this and related subjects of social development.

But wherever and whenever any measuring exercise is undertaken, the disparities that emerge are almost certainly less wide than they really are. For the rich have ways of obscuring their incomes. In the West, they use company-owned apartments and transport, company-subsidized medical care and company-subsidized education for their children, company-paid entertainment and leisure activities, to redefine personal income as business expenses. Furthermore, they (or their accountants) arrange their affairs so as to translate what is essentially earned income into capital gains – the acquisition of stock options is a common device – with the object of reducing their tax liabilities. In the East, they carve private domains out of public provisions: apartments, transport, medical care, education, entertainment, leisure. In the South, they surround themselves with a privacy that is normally impenetrable by officials, including statisticians. In all parts of the world, much of what is earned is simply not reported.

The disparity in income between rich and poor states is measured often, but it is seldom appreciated in its full enormity. We hope that our inset map will do a little to dramatize the disparities, by showing that half the people in the world enjoy – if that is a suitable word – an income equal to that of one middle-sized rich country, West Germany.

OUR DAILY BREAD | 39

An adequate intake of calories is the most common and the most important measure of adequate nourishment. The minimum calorie intake regarded as adequate by the World Health Organization differs from state to state; taking into account climatic conditions, patterns of work, the average weight of inhabitants, and other relevant factors.

Figures for deficit countries inevitably understate the nutritional deficiency suffered by many inhabitants, as figures for surplus countries mask altogether the existence of any such deficiency. For the figures apply to average calorie intake, and average intake can obscure extremes of self-indulgence and deprivation. There are inhabitants of surplus states who do not have enough to eat, and inhabitants of deficit states who eat as abundantly as do the rich and powerful elsewhere.

Far from being relieved since the last edition, the horror of mass starvation would seem only to have spread and strengthened its hold.

But if the vagaries of the weather contribute to visitations of famine, they are far from accounting for nutritional deficiencies over much of the world. Food production per head in Africa has been falling in general throughout the 1970s and 1980s.

Food Production in Africa

	base 100 annual average 1969-71	base 100 1974
1972	97.0	–
1973	94.5	–
1974	96.7	–
1975	94.7	99.0
1976	95.0	100.0
1977	91.3	94.5
1978	92.6	96.3
1979	89.4	92.7
1980	87.8	89.9
1981	90.3	92.7
1982	–	92.7
1983	–	86.2
1984	–	86.2
1985	–	89.9

The pressures of population growth might have been relieved by appropriate social policies and economic development. Instead, a rapid urbanization has drained human and material resources from the countryside. The new urban elites have acquired a taste for foods, such as wheat and rice, which are not traditional crops and have had to be imported in increasing volume at increasing cost. Shortages of foreign exchange, in part arising from the cost of providing the elites with the foreign consumer goods they demand, have promoted government concentration on encouraging the growth of non-nutritional cash crops for export. And policies to keep food cheap for the appeasement of the urban populace deprive farmers of resources and accelerate the drain of population from the countryside. Not least, warfare – whether waged by discontented peoples against the artificial unifications of the state, as in Ethiopia, or promoted by foreign intervention, as in Angola and Mozambique – has devastated vast areas of once richly productive agriculture.

But the mounting plight of Africa is only an extreme example of preoccupations and policies so distorted and distorting across the world of states that many hundreds of millions are permanently undernourished, while certain governments are agitated by the problem of what to do with their accumulated surplus stocks of food. There seems little doubt that the world is perfectly capable of feeding decently all its inhabitants. That it is so conspicuously not doing so at present is the product not of human necessity but of choice.

WITHOUT DUE CARE AND ATTENTION

40

The incidence of hospital beds is generally related to the facilities provided for conventional Western medical treatment. It is not exclusively so. In China or Sri Lanka, for instance, a substantial hospital provision exists for medical treatment by traditional methods. But the common use of hospital bed provision as a measure of comparative commitment to medical care in different states essentially reflects the international dominance of conventional Western medicine. In employing this measure ourselves, we are directed by the course of available statistics. We do not imply any belittlement of the unconventional Western or traditional non-Western treatments that avoid hospitals. We simply have no means of determining any comparative social commitment to such treatment.

Such statistics as we have found in later or different sources, for the ratio of hospital beds per 100,000 people, are as follows:

Denmark should be switched from over 800 beds to 600-800; France, from over 800 to 400-600; India from under 100 to 100-200; Israel, from 200-400 to 400-600; Jordan, from under 100 to 100-200; Kampuchea, from no data to 100-200; Kuwait, from 400-600 to 200-400; Laos, from no data to 200-400; Lebanon, from no data to 200-400; Malaysia (Sarawak), from 100-200 to 200-400; Oman, from 200-400 to 100-200; Switzerland, from no data to over 800; Taiwan, from no data to 200-400; United Arab Emirates, from 400-600 to 200-400; and Yugoslavia, from 200-400 to 600-800.

Figures for life expectancy are, in a number of instances, evidently vague estimates. The coincidence of identical figures – such as 44.4 years for males and 47.6 years for females in well over a handful of African states – must excite a certain doubt.

Life expectancy has generally increased since the last edition; though we would maintain that the quality of life has generally deteriorated. But in 33 of 157 countries for which more recent figures than those shown in our map are available, life expectancy has fallen. And in 16 of these, life expectancy fell by a month or more for every year of life. These were: Afghanistan, Benin, Burkina Faso, Central African Republic, Chad, Gambia, Guyana, Jamaica, Jordan, Kampuchea, Kenya, Madagascar, Nigeria, Sierra Leone, South Africa and Togo. By contrast, life expectancy rose, by a month or more for every year of life, in 11 countries: Bangladesh, Botswana, Brunei, Ethiopia, Laos, Mali, Oman, Pakistan, Saudi Arabia, Vietnam and North Yemen.

THE RIGHT TO LEARN · 41

Most of the world is poorly furnished with facilities for formal education. And in general, the poorer the state, the smaller are the resources devoted to such facilities. Even then, much home produced training and talent is ultimately diverted to the rich states, in what is now known as the brain-drain (the migration abroad, or recruitment by foreign business, of those with the most valuable skills and exploitable experience). The educational system in poor states is often largely irrelevant to their own needs; being too closely modelled on imported curricula which reflect other demands and priorities. The consequences are socially wasteful and explosive.

Facilities for primary education are much the cheapest and easiest to develop; but pressure for places in primary schools and economic or other pressures outside them mean that not all who enter stay the course. For the multitudes who do, finding a place in the tiny sector of further education needs exceptional social standing, influence or ability. At every stage, many are forced to leave with their expectations frustrated.

Some states, it must be stressed, score badly because their educational reporting has not kept pace with their educational activity.

Formal education can be good or bad. It is certainly not the same as knowledge or understanding. Its presence or absence indicates, above all, degrees of popular access to the ruling culture in any given state, whatever the value of that culture may be.

THE LONGER REACH · 42

There are few ways in which the individual citizen can reach out to give and receive news, ideas and opinions, in exchanges which reflect our mutual dependence. Hesitantly and unevenly, these exchanges are growing; though discouraged or even forbidden by not a few governments, which see them as a source of mischief and even danger. As before, we have chosen the incidence of letters and radios as our measure, while providing an inset map with updated statistics on access to telephones.

In many states, it is poverty that above all accounts for the low levels of access. In some others, notably the USSR, it is government policy rather than economic backwardness that is largely responsible.

Access is, of course, no guarantee of free communication. Telephone calls can be tapped and interrupted. Letters can be opened and 'lost'. Radio receivers can provide only limited reception, and foreign broadcasts can be jammed. The very fear of discovery may inhibit the enjoyment of access. But surveillance is not infallible. Even in the most closely policed societies, human ingenuity can find ways to give and receive news, ideas and opinions, by telephone, radio and mail.

The statistics for the distribution of telephones are woefully incomplete. Many reporting authorities simply do not know how many telephones there are in their own countries.

Some countries provide figures not for radio receivers but only for licences issued. In those few cases where the figures for both are given, the number of radio receivers is usually around double the number of licences. We have revised upwards our categories of incidence, to take account of the phenomenal spread of radios throughout the world.

CRUMBS FROM THE CAKE | 43

In the first edition of this atlas, we pointed out that assistance received from the state by those of its citizens officially recognized as being in need had, in the early 1970s, declined as a proportion of total state outlays in the whole of Africa, all of Asia except Japan, and all of South America apart from oil-rich Venezuela. Since then, the old principle – from those who do not have, it shall be taken – has gained impetus and excuse from world-wide economic recession.

This recession has dragged more people and larger proportions of the population into poverty traps of one sort or another, while governments, attempting to restrain public expenditure, have in general sought to reduce the real value of individual welfare payments. Nearly all the exceptions of the early 1970s have, in the early 1980s, joined the rule.

The cruel truth remains that, for many countries, welfare payments exist, if at all, for very few of the needy.

If information is unavailable for many countries, it is because the best measures we have found and have chosen to use are ones for which many countries do not provide figures. Happily, we have been able to improve our coverage in this edition.

LAW AND DISORDER | 44

Interpol warns against the use of its crime statistics for purposes of comparison, even though these are the least incomplete generally available. The statistics are supplied by the countries themselves and accordingly represent what the various authorities in such countries are able to identify, competent to compile, or willing to admit.

The Interpol statistics, indeed, invite suspicion. It seems highly improbable, for instance, that Nigeria should have virtually no incidence of fraud. If such were true, then the society is certainly maligned by its reputation, or the activities of the business community have been generically excluded.

The particular crimes of murder and serious assault present, of course, some difficulties of definition for the authorities in various states. It is unlikely, for instance, that the figures for the Lebanon, high as they are, fully reflect the incidence of deaths directly due to the protracted civil conflict in that country. It is absurd to believe that the moderate figures for Chile reflect the deaths and serious assaults directly due to those serving the security of the military regime.

Even among the advanced industrial states, whose statistics are widely regarded as less than usually unreliable, it is difficult to understand how France should have by far the highest rate of fraud (at 1,449 cases per 100,000 inhabitants) and neighbouring

Belgium, with a society so similar in so many respects, one that is around one hundredth (at 14.6).

Once again we have not included information on rape on the map. The statistics at our disposal are sketchy, quirkish and ideologically coloured. This said, it is heartening to note a shift in official attitudes; more countries are filing statistics on rape with Interpol, and more rapes are being recorded. This last indicates the change in official policies as much as it reflects the deterioration in behaviour as a consequence of economic recession, and of the strains engendered by unplanned social change in poor countries.

For what they are worth, these are the statistics on rape for various countries, as supplied to Interpol, per 100,000 inhabitants: Angola 5.97; Australia 13.79; Austria 5.26; Bahamas 38.94; Barbados 25.39; Belgium 5.67; Bermuda 16.18; Botswana 44.73; Brunei 2.86; Burundi 1.26; Cayman Islands 25; Chile 10.58; Colombia 4.39; Congo 0.78; Cyprus 0.56; Denmark 7.67; Dominica 10.67; Dominican Republic 3.76; Ecuador 5.89; Fiji 5.5; Finland 6.48; France 5.21; Gabon 0.32; West Germany 9.73; Greece 0.93; Hong Kong 1.63; Hungary 6.11; Indonesia 1.23; Ireland 1.98; Israel 5.45; Italy 1.77; Ivory Coast 5.06; Japan 1.6; Jordan 0.93; Kenya 1.93; South Korea 10.02; Kuwait 0.53; Lebanon 1.13; Lesotho 48.21; Libya 10.53; Luxembourg 2.75; Malawi 2.72; Malaysia 3.17; Maldives 11.14; Malta 1.21; Mauritius 2.43; Morocco 3.41; Netherlands 7.19; New Zealand 14.42; Niger 0.46; Norway 4.24; Papua New Guinea 19.07; Philippines 2.63; Portugal 1.97; Qatar 1.14; Senegal 1.35; Singapore 4.15; Spain 3.56; Sudan 4.03; Swaziland 5.81; Sweden 11.93; Syria 0.99; Tanzania 0.3; Thailand 5.26; Togo 0.13; Trinidad & Tobago 9.17; Turkey 0.19; UK – England & Wales 2.69, Northern Ireland 5.04, Scotland 4.35; USA 35.67; Venezuela 17.38; Zambia 5.83; Zimbabwe 28.99.

FOULING THE NEST

45

There are still very few national surveys of land, water and air pollution, and none worldwide; only the most localized surveys of sound, sight and smell pollution; and no commonly accepted criteria of measurement. But some state authorities, impelled by the increasing concern of their long-suffering people, have recently begun to take the subject seriously. In state-crowded Continental Europe, with its rich traditions of mutual blame and the use of science in the service of aggression, there has been a marked advance in the monitoring of air-borne pollution.

Thirteen out of 24 reporting countries trace more than half of the sulphur depositions on their territories to foreign sources. In 1984, some 93% of such depositions in Norway originated abroad: 7% each in East Germany, Poland and the UK; and 6% in the USSR. Switzerland imported 89% of its sulphur depositions: mainly from Italy (38%), France (7%) and West Germany (6%). Romania's 87% came largely from Hungary (13%), the USSR (11%), Bulgaria (10%), Yugoslavia (9%), and Czechoslovakia (6%). Sweden's 84% came largely from East Germany (10%), Poland (9%), and the USSR (6%). And similar patterns of imported sulphur pollution are identifiable for Austria's 81%, Finland's 74%, Netherlands' 74%, Portugal's 70%, Denmark's 69%, France's 60%, Yugoslavia's 58%, Belgium's 53%, and West Germany's 53%.

The criterion chosen for measuring land pollution – chemical fertilizers applied – is crude but serviceable enough. It does not, however, take into account those few areas of modern agriculture which conform to the best practices of humus renewal even while using chemical products.

The criteria for measuring air pollution are unsatisfactory on two counts: by substance (they do not cover lead, the most pervasive and among the most dangerous of pollutants); and by geography (they are confined to selected urban areas only). The World Health Organization very cautiously suggests, as guidelines for 'exposure limits consistent with the protection of human health', 40-60 micrograms per cubic metre on average per year in the case of sulphur dioxide (SO_2, the main suspected source of 'acid rain'), and 60-80 micrograms per cubic metre for dust ('suspended particulate matter'). We have taken the mid-point in each range to illustrate these two aspects of urban air pollution.

We have had to make some crude assumptions about the relative values produced by the two major testing methods for sulphur dioxide and about the relative importance of the sites chosen. In general, we have opted for City Centre Commercial sites, when available; otherwise, for City Centre Residential; and thirdly for Industrial; before using suburban sites.

Oil spills are reported primarily on a voluntary basis, although Lloyds of London supplements the reports with their own. Predictably, more information is available for the rich Western states than for the rest of the world. The map includes oil spills on inland waterways.

URBAN BLIGHT

46

In September 1980, within two weeks of reporting that only 30% of city-dwellers in Bolivia were served with water and only 31% covered by sanitation services, the United Nations Secretary-General published a second report which revealed that the fortunate Bolivian city-dwellers were covered to the extent of 100% in both respects. The two reports (A/35/341 of 5 September and A/35/367 of 18 September) gave the coverage of urban sanitation in Brazil as 65% and 35% respectively; in Chile, as 50% and 66%; in Cuba as 46% and 97%; in El Salvador, as 34% and 79%; in Ethiopia, as 'low' and 'not available'; in Haiti, as 0% (sic) and 67%; in Jamaica, as 33% and 95%; in Mozambique, as 'low' and 60%; in Nicaragua, as 38% and 92%; in Uruguay, as 54% and 94%; and in Zaire, as 8% and 80%.

We do not for a moment suppose that the Secretary-General's Office was doctoring the evidence. We cite such figures merely to demonstrate that available evidence, even in respect of such public, measurable properties as safe water and sanitation pipes, is highly suspect.

The two most recent sources for the proportion of people served with safe drinking water – the *World Health Statistics Annual* 1985 and the UN's *Compendium of Human Settlement Statistics*, 1985 – give widely different statistics in some cases. In North Yemen, the WHO figure is 100%, compared with the UN figure of 6%. Other conflicting figures are those for India (80% and 67%), Malaysia (97% and 65%), Pakistan (78% and 58%), Sri Lanka (76% and 47%). Similarly, for the proportion of city dwellers covered by sanitation services, the World Health Organization records 90% for Botswana compared with the UN's 37%. For Chile, the figures are 100% and 65%; for Cuba, 100% and 68%; South Korea, 100% and 37%; Libya, 100% and 53%; Malaysia, 100% and 26%; Mauritius, 100% and 34%; Mexico, 78% and 45%; Pakistan, 53% and 25%; Peru, 57% and 46%; Singapore, 100% and 64%; Sri Lanka, 80% and 16%; Thailand, 50% and 3%; Venezuela, 90% and 14%.

With the world's urban population growing, both absolutely and as a proportion of the total, and with this population crowding into ever more gargantuan centres, the pressure on services to provide even the rudiments of a safe and sane environment will grow well beyond what is currently planned, let alone likely to be implemented. Add to this the social strains resulting from a polarization of city dwellers, in rich and poor countries alike, into those who have the means, the skills or the sheer luck to participate in the growing world urban economy and those who do not, and there is no escape from urban social conflagration – inner city in the rich countries, shanty town in the poor – on a terrifying scale.

THE DYING EARTH

47

It has taken thousands of years for large tracts of desert and semi-desert land to develop out of what were once fertile regions; years in which haphazard human encroachment has often been responsible for upsetting the delicate balance on which ecological renewal depends.

Recently, this encroachment has become more rapid and violent. In many parts of the world, population pressure, patterns of landownership, government economic policies, war — or some combination of these — have destroyed or blighted huge areas of land, to produce, particularly in much of Africa, expanses of endemic famine.

A report of the UN Conference on Desertification (1977) concluded that although more than one third of the earth's land is already arid, this is very far from the full extent of the problem. Declining land fertility, caused by current pressures, will in due course affect the livelihood of well over 600 million people, most of whom live in poor states.

Tropical moist forests cover only 6 per cent of the world's land area but have a special significance in the world's ecological balance. They harbour as much as half of the world's animal and plant species, along with the people who know best about such species, their behaviour and possible uses; they are essential for the world's oxygen supply; and they are of immeasurable climatic importance. Yet they are being felled – to make way for farmland, roadbuilding, cattle ranching, mining, and to support the appetite of the timber industry – at the rate of 40 hectares or 100 acres every minute. By the mid-1970s, they had been cleared from some 40 per cent of their natural habitat. And little was, or is, being done to repair the damage. Successfully established tree plantations represent a mere 2.5 per cent of the annual loss.

With the trees, go the inhabitants. Brazil, with one third of the world's total tropical forest area, had a forest population of some 6-9 million people three centuries ago. Its present estimated forest population is 200,000 people. In some cases, such declines have resulted from ruthless methods of elimination or displacement. In Brazil, the Indians have been bombed, poisoned, and deliberately infected with tuberculosis, influenza and smallpox. In Bolivia, they have been forced into debt bondage. In Paraguay, they have been the target of military manhunts and imprisoned in reserves. In the Philippines, they have been swept off the land and into armed rebellion.

PROTECTION AND EXTINCTION

48

According to the International Union for the Conservation of Nature and Natural Resources, about a thousand species of mammals and birds are currently threatened with elimination; as are many more, one in ten, species of flowering plants. The number of entire species under threat of extinction may seem relatively small. But the extinction of any must represent an irreparable loss and one, moreover, which may have damaging consequences for those that are left. Besides, the number of provenances (subpopulations) of species that are threatened with severe genetic depletion or extinction is large. These endangered provenances are often at the limits of their particular species range and have developed, through natural selection, corresponding characteristics – such as tolerance to drought or cold or other adverse environmental conditions – that are of immense potential value to humanity.

We have used data for 1978 and 1979 in preference to those for later years because the coverage by our main source, the IUCN's Red Data Books, is greater for the earlier period. But even that coverage is far from evenly distributed around the world. North America and Northern Europe feature disproportionately, not because they are exceptionally lethal environments for living species but because they are monitored more closely and cited more systematically than are other regions.

The 214 Biosphere Reserves in 58 countries are representative habitat types, established to protect genetic and ecological diversity for research, monitoring, education and training. The World Natural Heritage Sites are areas of international significance. They were selected because they represent a major stage in evolution; an important continuing geological process, biological evolution or social/natural interaction; contain unique, rare or superlative natural phenomena, formations or features, or areas of exceptional beauty; or contain habitats for populations of rare or endangered plant and animal species.

More has been done to protect animal and plant life since the map was first prepared. By the end of 1985, there were 61 recognized World Natural Heritage Sites in 27 countries, compared with the 1982 figures of 29 in 15 countries. Among the new hosts are Australia (5), Bulgaria (2), Costa Rica (1), Ecuador (2), Guatemala (1), Honduras (1), India (3), Ivory Coast (3), Malawi (1), Panama (1), Peru (2), Turkey (1) and Zimbabwe (1). More countries too, are hosting internationally recognized Biosphere Reserves. Among the newcomers are Chile, Cuba, Czechoslovakia, East and West Germany, Mauritius and Rwanda.

The picture is less clear for protected areas. If we accept that the changes recorded are real ones and not merely changes in reporting practice or convention, then the states that have moved from a higher to a lower category of protection are more or less matched by the ones that have moved in the opposite direction. Those that are reported as having moved in the wrong direction include Angola, Benin, Burma, Central African Republic, Chad, Cyprus, El Salvador, France, Gambia, Jamaica, Lebanon, Lesotho, Mali, Papua New Guinea, Paraguay, Peru, Qatar, Sudan, Sweden, Uruguay, Zimbabwe. States that seem to have moved in the right direction and increased their protected areas are Algeria, Austria, Burkina, Chile, China, Ecuador, East Germany, Ghana, Honduras, Hungary, India, Indonesia, Italy, South Korea, Liberia, Malawi, Pakistan, Philippines, Portugal, Sierra Leone, South Africa, Spain, Switzerland, Vietnam.

INDUSTRIAL DROOP | 49

In the previous edition, this map provided two instances – Venezuela and Zaire – of states whose industrial production in the period 1970-80 had declined absolutely, so that any measure of declining industrial growth from the period 1960-70 was impossible to calculate and, indeed, a contradiction in terms.

The map in this edition, which compares 1975-80 with 1980-85, shows that no fewer than 15 states recorded absolute declines in the second period, while two, Cyprus and Sweden, had recorded absolute declines in the first.

In most other states for which figures are available, there were declines in industrial growth rates. In the case of Greece, the decline amounted to 100%; which means that in the second period industrial production did not grow at all.

No more eloquent testimony is needed to the gathering economic crisis in the world.

A regional survey by the World Bank shows that over a period of 20 years, there was an overall decline in the growth rate for both the rich states (industrial market economies) and the poor (developing) ones, with the decline sharpest in Africa.

Industry growth rates, percentages

	1965-73	1973-80	1980-84
rich states	5.1	2.3	1
poor states	8.5	6	2.2
Africa	8.1	1.3	−1.2

THE PAPER CHASE | 50

The phenomenon of inflation reflects both the power and the vulnerability of the state: its power to extract resources, by providing a means of payment which is worth less than the value assigned to it; its vulnerability to public protest which rejects the deception by assigning its own value to the means of payment. In the process, there is usually a substantial and socially disruptive redistribution of wealth, from the poor and weak, who are helpless victims of the process, to the rich and strong, who manipulate it to their own benefit.

The decline in the rate of inflation across much of the rich world during the first half of the 1980s was due in part to the tighter monetary policies pursued by the governments concerned; in part to the related rising rates of unemployment which affected wage pressures; and in part to the declining price of important commodities, especially oil. But this decline was far from being matched in much of the poor world, where rates of inflation generally continued to rise. And within the Comecon bloc of the USSR and its associated states, where inflation rates have historically been low, social unrest contributed to a rate of inflation in Poland that rose beyond an annual 15 per cent in 1985.

The dangerous discrepancy between rich and poor worlds has widened considerably year by year.

Inflation rates, percentages

	1982	1983	1984	1985
rich states	7.4	5.0	4.8	4.2
poor states	28.3	39.3	46.6	48.9

A QUESTION OF TERMS

51

The emergence of the sovereign debt crisis in 1982, caused by the manifest inability of states in the developing world to repay their enormous debts on time, if at all, or even continue paying the interest charges, led to widespread public concern with the problem, since it involved the stability of the whole international banking system. For the capital possessed by the banks (see *Map 29: Big Money*) was inadequate to meet the scale of potential losses involved.

Alarmed at the financial implications of the crisis, the IMF, with its dominant Western members, promoted a series of negotiated debt reschedulings; or what Britain's Lord Lever has characterized as 'exchanging an incredible and defaulted promise to pay for another incredible promise to pay later.'

The extent of the problem is indicated by the size and number of reschedulings that took place: from those involving 10 states and a total of $2.2 billion in 1982; through 30 countries and $51.1 billion in 1983; to 34 countries and a total of $116.2 billion in 1984.

But if the burden of debt repayments and servicing charges was relieved for the while, the problem was merely postponed. The flow of new money from the banks, more than ever needed by the poor, sharply diminished; indeed, net bank lending to Latin America actually fell in 1984. In 1985, Peru's new president announced that his country simply could not afford the servicing of all its accumulated debt and would limit payments to 10 per cent of export receipts. In 1986, the governments of Nigeria and Mexico made similar statements on the inability of their countries to meet all payments in full. Increasingly, the economic and social costs of pursuing such policies of austerity as the creditors of the poor demanded were proving popularly explosive.

THE GOLD RUSH

52

The world market in gold is veined with apparent contradictions. Some countries – notably, the richest of all, the USA – value the gold holdings in their reserves at a fixed price that is a tiny fraction of the free market value. But they will sell none of their gold at such a price and indeed, when they do sell, sell it at the prevailing price on the free market. The USA has long been in the forefront of a campaign to reduce the importance of gold as a monetary instrument – has even sold gold from its official stocks to counteract the gold rush – yet continues to possess by far the largest single holding in the world and to be one of the very few states with more than three quarters of its reserves, by value, in gold.

Unlike such alternative, supposedly 'safe' investments as bank deposits and government or top quality corporate bonds, gold earns no income and even costs money, in insurance and other security charges. In fact, given the high prevailing rates of interest during the last ten years, an investment in gold rather than in such other instruments has cost both states and individual citizens a substantial measure of lost income each year. Yet states have been generally reluctant to sell their gold holdings even at high free market prices and have preferred, when in need, to dispose rather of interest-bearing investments in foreign currency; while private citizens have, if erratically, persisted in purchasing gold, and on a massive scale overall.

Such was the rush into gold during the high inflation years of the 1970s that the free market price rose from $35 an ounce in the early months of 1970 to peak at over $800 an ounce in March 1980. What followed was, perhaps, even more surprising. Given that so enormous a rise in price had been fuelled by fears of a total collapse in the monetary system and a hysterical degree of speculation on some such prospect, the deepening of economic recession and the sharp drop in rates of inflation across most of the advanced industrial world might have been expected to end in a return of the gold price to somewhere near the level of the old days. But after a brief dip below $300 an ounce, the price recovered to hover above $400 in 1986. Demonstrably, fears of revived inflation had been far from excised, while the difficulties of the commercial banking system, with the effective bankruptcy of large sovereign borrowers, had added a new element of instability to the financial system.

But if the gold rush is primarily promoted by such considerations, there are other factors. Gold is an alluringly anonymous form of wealth for those who are concerned to keep their financial dispositions secret, especially from tax or other officials. It is supremely negotiable, and without risk of any capital loss, across state frontiers, in a way that very few paper currencies are. And at times of social upheaval – as people seeking to escape from Vietnam knew or were to discover – it may be the only acceptable medium of exchange. In summary, the rush into gold is a measure not only of financial instability but of the wider political instability in the world of states.

GREEN REVOLUTION | 53

For some people, the way humanity relates to the rest of nature is the most important and pervasive issue of our time, since on it hinges our judgement of all social and political arrangements. For others, the defence of a village green, a threatened tree or a stray animal has no wider implication; however passionately the particular cause is felt or fought.

This map attempts to represent green consciousness in all its forms – the broad and the narrow, the official and the unofficial – at least for as far as our informants could take us.

Its central conclusions were reached through a version of the so-called Delphi method, whereby a number of people actively engaged in the study of a subject are asked to evaluate relevant phenomena according to commonly agreed criteria. This approach has its dangers, in proportion to the homogeneity of background and of view among the participating experts. We make no pretence of having cast the net very wide, geographically or philosophically. Where our informants disagreed with one another, we adopted the view with the largest measure of support. Where disagreement was balanced, we in general opted for the more generous judgement.

Such generosity was not rewarded by the critics. One informed and representative opinion judged that we had underestimated the level of green consciousness in five cases – Bhutan, Mongolia, New Zealand, Norway, Papua New Guinea – but had exaggerated it in no less than nineteen: Brazil, Bulgaria, Cameroon, Czechoslovakia, Ecuador, Egypt, Ethiopia, East Germany, Hungary, Indonesia, Ireland, Malaysia, Madagascar, Nepal, Poland, Switzerland, Uruguay, USSR and Vietnam.

The existence of a 'green' party is not necessarily an indication of substantial public sensitivity to environmental issues. Nor, equally, should its absence be taken to indicate public insensitivity. Green parties do not exist in one-party states or in many other states with a high degree of political intolerance. Where a Green party does exist, this may reflect the closed minds of the traditional parties rather than an acute public awareness of the issues involved. But political success for such a party can itself create a space for environmental concern within the existing political structures; as has been evidenced in West Germany, with the election to the Bundestag of Green deputies.

In many states, especially the poorer ones and those with highly centralized economies, green consciousness is more likely to course through university departments, scientific institutions and particular government ministries than through the offices of pressure groups. In such countries, action is more likely to follow pressure from international bodies, such as the World Bank or the IUCN, than to result from spontaneous indigenous pressure. For this reason we have included *all* organizations listed in the Environment Liaison Centre's Directory. This has resulted in a massive underrecording of the numbers in some countries, notably the USA.

Official endorsement of green policies, as indicated by a state's adherence to international conventions on environmental protection (our inset map), may mean very little in practice. Of the 37 states that had, by September 1983, considered the IUCN's World Conservation Strategy since its publication three and a half years earlier, only three had established a special task force to implement some of the strategy's provisions.

WOMEN'S RIGHTS

54

The right of women to control their pregnancy is variously abridged by male-dominated law. The particular laws on abortion indicate, albeit imperfectly, one aspect of this abridgement, and restrictive changes in such laws show how tenuous is the hold of women on such limited rights as they have won.

The map demonstrates widespread differences in legal provision on abortion. In most states some right to abortion is recognized, but on more or less restricted criteria, and always by leave of a predominantly male authority. In no state does a woman have an unrestricted right to abortion. Even in the Netherlands, perhaps the most liberal in practice, abortion on demand is available only in a few private, 'non-profit' clinics, and then with *formal* legal sanction only on narrow medical grounds. In Cuba, another liberal state in this respect, abortion on demand is available in government hospitals, but only for certain categories of women and/or for the initial stages of pregnancy.

Some 24 per cent of the world's 4.9 billion people live in countries where abortion is permitted only to save the life of the pregnant woman or, in a few cases, not even then. These include most Muslim countries in Asia; two-thirds of the countries in Latin America; half of those in Africa; and, in Europe, Belgium, Ireland and Malta. Some 13 per cent live in countries where abortion is permitted on broader medical grounds, to avert a threat to the woman's health rather than her life; sometimes on eugenic grounds, when the foetus is damaged or likely to be damaged; or on juridical grounds, when pregnancy is the result of rape or incest. A further 24 per cent live in countries where social factors, such as income, housing, marital status, can be taken into account in evaluating the threat to a woman's health (social-medical grounds); or when adverse social conditions alone, unrelated to health, may justify an abortion (social grounds). In most of these countries, abortion is permitted virtually on request. Finally, 39 per cent of people live in countries which permit abortion on request within parameters provided by time (usually the first three months of pregnancy); though 'conscience clauses' exempt physicians, nurses or other staff from performing or aiding the operation if they have religious or philosophical objections to it, or even objections based on the age of the woman.

Very often, legal provision and social practice are far apart. A statute permitting abortion on social-medical grounds may define the threat to the woman's health narrowly or broadly; for example, by specifically mentioning mental health. Social grounds may be defined or interpreted narrowly, as in Uruguay, or broadly, as in Japan or Poland. In many countries, abortion law is not strictly enforced: for instance, abortions can be obtained openly from private physicians in South Korea, a restrictive state. In other countries, liberal laws may have to contend with a lack of medical provisions or with conservative attitudes among physicians and hospital administrators, which affect poor women in particular, as in parts of Austria, France, West Germany, India, Italy and the United States.

Where a state's laws cover more than one category of grounds for abortion, we have adopted the more or most liberal: as in the cases of Australia, Bulgaria, Burundi, Czechoslovakia, Ecuador, Finland, West Germany, Hong Kong, Hungary, Iceland, India, Japan, North Korea, Luxembourg, Mexico, Poland, Spain, Taiwan, the UK and Zambia.

In some states with a federal system of government, national legal provisions are moderated by state law and range from extreme liberality (California in the USA, Slovenia in Yugoslavia, and South Australia) to extreme restrictiveness (Louisiana in the USA, Queensland in Australia).

We add below a table recording the dates on which women first achieved equal status as voters. When denied, equality of franchise presents a challenge to the strength and purpose of women. Once attained, it constitutes perhaps the first milestone in the journey towards a society of equals.

Year	Country	Year	Country	Year	Country
1893	New Zealand		Sri Lanka		Costa Rica
1902	Australia	1935	Burma		India
1906	Finland	1936	Puerto Rico		Syria
1913	Norway	1937	Philippines	1950	El Salvador
1915	Denmark	1942	Dominican Republic		Haiti
	Greenland	1944	Bermuda	1951	Antigua & Barbuda
	Iceland		France		Barbados
1917	USSR		Guadeloupe		Nepal
1918	Luxembourg		Jamaica	1952	Bolivia
	Poland		Martinique		Greece
1919	Austria	1945	Hungary	1953	Mexico
	Czechoslovakia		Indonesia	1954	Belize
	Germany		Italy		Nigeria
	Netherlands		Japan	1955	Ethiopia
	Sweden	1946	Albania		Ghana
1920	Canada		Korea		Honduras
	USA		Liberia		Nicaragua
1922	Ireland		Panama		Peru
1924	Mongolia		Trinidad & Tobago	1956	Bangladesh
1928	UK		Yugoslavia		Benin
1929	Ecuador	1947	Argentina		Burkina Faso
1930	South Africa		Bulgaria		Cameroon
	(whites only)		China		Central African Republic
1931	Spain		Malta		Chad
1932	Brazil		Venezuela		Congo
	Thailand	1948	Belgium		Egypt
	Uruguay		Israel		Gabon
1934	Cuba		Romania		Guinea
	Turkey	1949	Chile		Ivory Coast

	Kampuchea	1960	Zaire		Guyana
	Laos	1961	Burundi		Lesotho
	Madagascar		Gambia		Namibia
	Mali		Paraguay	1967	Dominica
	Mauritania		Sierra Leone		Grenada
	Niger		Tanzania		St Christopher-Nevis
	Pakistan	1962	Bahamas		St Lucia
	Senegal		Rwanda		St Vincent-Grenadines
	Togo		Uganda	1968	Nauru
	Vietnam	1963	Iran		Swaziland
1957	Colombia		Kenya	1970	South Yemen
	Djibouti		Libya	1971	Switzerland
	Lebanon	1964	Afghanistan	1973	Guinea-Bissau
	Malaysia		Iraq	1975	Angola
1958	Algeria		Malawi		Cape Verde
	Mauritius		Zambia		Mozambique
	Somalia	1965	Guatemala		Papua New Guinea
1959	Cyprus		Singapore		Portugal
	Morocco		Sudan	1980	Zimbabwe
	Tunisia	1966	Botswana	1982	Jordan

GAY SURVIVAL, GAY ASSERTION

55

In the nineteenth century, the word 'gay' was used to describe 'loose women' and prostitutes. By the 1920s, it was coming to be used within the homosexual sub-culture as a term of self-identification. In 1968, the term was adopted by the Conference of Homophile Organizations in the United States.

In the rich West, public and official attitudes towards homosexuality have long reflected a generally restrictive approach to sexuality. Homosexual behaviour was, until recently, commonly illegal; and, when exposed, prosecuted. Then, in the 1960s, with the liberalization and secularization of attitudes towards sexuality and personal behaviour, attitudes towards homosexuality softened, and it began to be freed from legal restrictions, though not from social pressures and condemnation.

In the USSR, Eastern Europe, and other parts of the 'communist' world, homosexuality is officially considered a Western capitalist corruption that is incompatible with 'communist' morality and needs to be strictly controlled. Even at their most enlightened, official attitudes view homosexuality not as a natural expression of individual personality but as a disease or the product of a congenital defect.

Across the mass of states in the poor world, the legal regulation of homosexuality is often a relic of colonial rule, with its religious and educational accompaniments. But if the laws have survived into independence, their prosecution has in general not done so. Homosexual behaviour is usually tolerated or disregarded.

Lesbianism is seldom mentioned in the law, because women are usually not expected to have an independent sexual identity. And indeed, in a male-dominated world, relatively little is publicly known about it. The gay movement is itself male-orientated and finds it difficult to get lesbians to participate. Even the feminist movement, which has played so crucial a part in promoting the emancipation of women, has tended to avoid any identification with lesbianism; so that many lesbians have felt themselves under pressure to deny their sexuality for the cause of emancipation. Nonetheless, and partly under the influence of the growth in homosexual consciousness and assertion, the 1970s saw the growth of a lesbian consciousness and a lesbian liberation movement.

The special category in our map, 'lawful but repressed', suggests some of the difficulties still confronting gays. In some states, for instance, gay sex in private between consenting adult men is not illegal, but homosexual organizations and information are banned. And the law as such remains a threat, if only indirectly, since it is universally biased towards maintaining the primacy of the conventional family as the basic social building block.

But whatever the differences in legal regime from state to state, the gay experience is much the same in many of them, with the assertion of gay conduct encountering social discrimination, risk to employment, and a sense of alienation. It has led to the widespread development of gay organizations, events, newspapers, that transcend cultural, racial and political differences.

A new threat to gays and their free expression has come from the Aids epidemic. In 1981, following the discovery of unexplained but related breakdowns in the immune systems of some homosexual and bisexual men, the US Centre for Disease Control revealed the existence of a new disease. Now known as Aids (Acquired Immune Deficiency Syndrome), the term describes the rare and often fatal illnesses produced by a virus first isolated in 1983. This life-threatening disease speedily came to be seized upon – notably by some major newspapers – to attack homosexuals and their life-styles. Patients in the USA and elsewhere, already under enormous stress because of the disease's fatal nature, faced the additional burden of extensive legal and social discrimination. With few exceptions, public figures remained silent or acquiesced in this new turn against gays. It was left to the gay organizations themselves to mobilize support for the massive research and care programme needed to deal with what was fast becoming an international epidemic.

It is abundantly clear that Aids is not an American 'gay plague', but an alarmingly virulent and fast-spreading sexually-transmitted disease among heterosexual as well as homosexual men and women throughout the world. It has been widespread – unrecognized and untreated – since the early 1970s at the very least, in central Africa, where the virus is almost exclusively heterosexually transmited. Yet anti-gay prejudice still informs social and official attitudes to the disease and so inhibits effective action to combat it. Not least, the careful nurturing of an association between gays and the disease encourages or supports an authoritarian reaction that calls for a sacrifice of civil liberties in the cause of containing the disease.

MINORITY VIEWS

56

Virtually every state in the world has within it a minority or minorities: racial, religious, linguistic, cultural, or some combination of these. This sort of social minority is not the same as a political one, though the two may often be effectively the same.

This map does not deal with all such social minorities, but in general only with those that are known to be suffering discrimination of some kind. Our information is very far from adequate. Despite the research undertaken by various concerned organizations, most notably the Minority Rights Group in London, much remains to be found out and made known about social conflict and, in particular, discrimination against minorities around the world. This is not surprising. Too many governments patrol their internal affairs to prevent the escape of embarrassing information.

The nature and even existence of an organized movement within minorities that suffer discrimination is often largely a matter of inference and judgement. We have followed – and are grateful for – the advice afforded us by those with specialist knowledge. But in the end we have sometimes had to draw conclusions of our own, from such scraps of information or reports of relevant events as have come our way.

In some states, the regime itself is based on some social minority, and it is the majority that suffers discrimination. We have considered it appropriate to provide such information on the map.

In some states too, there are substantial minorities – in a few cases, even majorities – that are regarded as more or less temporary, since they consist in large measure of immigrant labour and refugees (see *Map 32: In Search of Work* and *Map 26: A Sort of Survival*). Here we have provided only a few extreme examples, where large immigrant populations are denied political rights.

Where a significant armed movement exists, we have given it priority over any peaceful one, on the principle that the organized resort to violence indicates a further stage of discontent or despair. The siting of an armed movement in a particular state must not, accordingly, be taken to mean the absence of an organized peaceful one. Indeed, the peaceful movement of protest may be – and usually is – the larger of the two.

THE STATE
UNDER PRESSURE

57

Identifying the existence of significant pressure on the state is a difficult exercise. The category of 'other states' is a catch-all, both for those (such as the Western parliamentary democracies) where opposition is directed at a particular government rather than the regime, and those where we have had to accept that our information could not sustain any sort of sensible judgement.

In the process of preparing this most disputable because most judgemental of maps, we found ourselves deciding to ditch one differentiation after the other, for categories that seemed more defensibly to fit the reported facts and the advice of experts we consulted.

The first current category, 'states unable to exercise control over all their territory', is both wider and more relevant than the previously used 'disintegrating or divided state'. To the extent that a state fits into this new category at all, it fails to perform its essential function of commanding its domain. Inevitably it contains considerable degrees of failure: from Thailand, where a relatively small portion is beyond the power being exercised by the state; through Cyprus, where the state is effectively partitioned; to Lebanon, where the capital itself is largely under the control of forces independent of the state.

The second category is no longer limited to 'separatist or irredentist pressure', but shows 'significant popular movements of armed opposition'. These may be separatist or irredentist, as is the case with the Irish Republican movement in the Northern Ireland province of the United Kingdom, or concerned with the conquest of state power for the purpose of exercising it in a radically different way, as is the case with the Shining Path guerrilla movement in Peru. The qualification of 'significant' is, of course, a matter of judgement. But we would defend a judgement that, for instance, places the UK and Spain in this category, but France and West Germany in others; despite the existence of organized violence by a separatist Corsican movement in France and that of a radical group pursuing violent methods in West Germany.

Two important anomalies require mention here. Namibia is universally regarded as an independent state under illegal occupation by South Africa; Western Sahara, generally regarded as an independent state, under illegal occupation by Morocco. In both instances, the 'significant popular movement of armed opposition' is, of course, directed against the occupying state.

For the third category, 'states under serious external pressure', inclusion may mean the warring presence of another state power within the borders, as is the case with Iraq, or the exercise, actual or threatened, of military and/or economic pressures by a foreign state, such as confronts Botswana, Lesotho, Swaziland and Zimbabwe from South Africa.

The final category, 'states with regimes under significant domestic pressure', includes threats from sources as different, sometimes within the same state, as organized labour and the armed forces.

In the categorization of all states, we have been careful to check one expert's judgement against another's. But the final adjudication has been our own.

Finally, we have, in this edition, removed the symbols for 'active ecological movement' and 'active peace movement' that we previously employed. This is not because we consider such movements unimportant or irrelevant, but because their very spread has made them less of a distinguishing factor. And where they represent a serious pressure on the state, they are accommodated in the fourth category, as in West Germany.

SOURCES FOR THE MAPS ■

Ambio: a Journal of the Human Environment, Stockholm, bi-monthly
American Bureau of Metal Statistics, *Non-Ferrous Metal Data 1981*, New York: American Bureau of Metal Statistics, 1982
Amnesty International, London, *Newsletter*, monthly
—, *Report*, annual
Anuarul Statistic al Republicii Socialiste România 1981, Bucharest: Directia Centrala de Statistica Romania, 1981
Ashman, Peter, and Paul Crane, private communications
Ashworth, Georgina (ed), *World Minorities*, Sunbury, Middx: Quartermaine House; vol. 1, 1977; vol. 2, 1978
—, *World Minorities in the Eighties*, Sunbury, Middx: Quartermaine House, 1980
Atlas of Earth Resources, London: Mitchell Beazley, 1979

Bank of China, private communications
The Banker, London, monthly
Birks, J.S, and C.A. Sinclair, *International Migration and Development in the Arab Region*, Geneva: ILO, 1980
—, *The Kingdom of Saudi Arabia and the Libyan Arab Jamahiriya*, Geneva: ILO, 1979
BIS [Bank for International Settlement], *53rd Annual Report*, Basle: BIS, June 1983
Boggan, E.C., *et al, The Rights of Gay People*, New York: Bantam Books, 1983
BP [British Petroleum], *BP Statistical Review of World Energy 1982*, London: BP, n.d.
Bridgman, James C, 'Who gets what resources in the EEZ: the top twenty-five', in John J. Logue (ed), *Villanova Colloquium on Peace, Justice and the Law of the Sea*, photocopy supplied
British Telecom, private communications
Buzan, Barry, *A Sea of Troubles? Sources of Dispute in the New Ocean Regime*, Adelphi Papers 143, London: International Institute for Strategic Studies, 1978

China Official Annual Report, Hong Kong: Kingsway International Publications, annual
CIA [United States Central Intelligence Agency], *Handbook of Economic Statistics 1982*, Washington DC: CIA, 1982
—, *Soviet GNP in Current Prices*, SOV 83-10037, Washington DC: CIA, August 1979
—, *The World Factbook*.
—, *The World Oil Market in the Years Ahead*, ER 79-10327U, Washington DC: CIA, August 1979
Commodity Research Bureau, *Commodity Yearbook 1982*, New York: Commodity Research Bureau, 1982
Consolidated Goldfields, *Gold*, London: Consolidated Goldfields, annual
—, private communications
Council of Europe, Parliamentary Assembly, Strasbourg, 29 September-7 October 1982
Couper, Alistair (ed), *The Times Atlas of the Oceans*, London: Times Books, 1983

Deutsches Institut für Wirtschaftsforschung, *Handbook of the Economy of the German Democratic Republic*, Farnborough, Hants: Saxon House, 1979

Earthscan, London, 'Press Briefings', occasional; see also: Mitchell
—, *Tropical Moist Forests*, Press Briefing Document no. 32 by Catherine Caufield, April 1982
ELC [Environmental Liaison Centre], *Environmental Activities of Non-Governmental Organizations (NGOs) related to UNEP Programmes: Report and Directory*, prepared for the Eighth Governing Council of the United Nations Environment Programme, Nairobi: ELC, April 1980
Europa Publications, *Africa South of the Sahara Yearbook*, London: Europa Publications, annual
—, *Europa Yearbook*, London: Europa Publications, annual
—, *Far East and Australasia Yearbook*, London: Europa Publications, annual
—, *Middle East and North Africa Yearbook*, London: Europa Publications, annual
European Advertising and Media Forecast, *International Advertising Statistics, December 1986*, Volume II, London: Advertising Association and the European Advertising Tripartite, 1986

FAO [United Nations Food and Agricultural Organization], *Fertilizer Yearbook*, Rome: FAO, annual
—, *Fourth World Food Survey*, Rome: FAO, 1977
—, *Production Yearbook*, Rome: FAO, annual
—, *Trade Yearbook*, Rome: FAO, annual
Financial Times, London, daily
Flood, Michael, *Energy without End*, London: Friends of the Earth, 1986
Fortune, New York, fortnightly

Garfield, Eugene, 'Mapping Science in the Third World', *Science and Public Policy*, vol. 10, no. 3, June 1983
Grinyer, Anne and Smoker, Paul, *It Couldn't Happen – Could it? An assessment of the probability of accidental nuclear war*, University of Lancaster, Department of Politics, November 1986
Guide to World Commodity Markets, 3rd edn, London: Kogan Page, 1982

Harrison, Jeremy, Kenton Miller and Jeffrey McNeely, 'The world coverage of protected areas: development goals and environmental needs', *Ambio*, vol. 11, no. 5, 1982
Hopkins, Michael, 'Employment trends in developing countries: 1960 and beyond', *International Labour Review*, vol. 122, no. 4, July-August 1983

IAEA [International Atomic Energy Agency], *Research Reactors in Member States*, Vienna: IAEA, 1986
IBRD [International Bank for Reconstruction and Development], *World Tables*, 2nd edn, Washington DC: IBRD, 1980
IEA [International Energy Agency], *World Energy Outlook*, Paris: Organization for Economic Cooperation and Development, 1982
IISS [International Institute for Strategic Studies], *The Military Balance*, London: IISS, annual
ILO [International Labour Office], *The Cost of Social Security*, Geneva: ILO, 1981
—, *Labour and Discrimination in Namibia*, Geneva: ILO, 1977
—, *Labour Force Estimates and Projections 1950-2000*, Geneva: ILO, 1977
—, *ILO Social and Labour Bulletin*, 3 & 4/1982, Geneva: ILO, 1983
—, *Yearbook of Labour Statistics*, Geneva: ILO, annual
IMF [International Monetary Fund], *Direction of Trade Annual*, Washington DC: IMF, annual
—, *Direction of Trade Statistics Yearbook*, Washington DC: IMF, annual
—, *International Financial Statistics*, Washington DC: IMF, monthly
—, *International Financial Statistics Yearbook*, Washington DC: IMF, annual
International Tanker Owners Pollution Federation, private communications
Interpol [International Criminal Police Commission], *International Crime Statistics*, Paris: Interpol
IUCN [International Union for Conservation of Nature and Natural Resources], *The IUCN Invertebrate Red Data Book*, Gland: IUCN, 1983
—, *The IUCN Mammal Red Data Book*, part 1, Gland: IUCN, 1982
—, *Red Data Book*, vols. 1-4, Morges: IUCN, 1972-9
—, *World Conservation Strategy: Living Resource Conservation for Sustainable Development*, prepared by the IUCN with the cooperation of UNEP and WWF, and in collaboration with FAO and UNESCO, 1980

Jain, Shail, *Size Distribution of Income: a Compilation of Data*, Washington DC: IBRD, 1975
Japan, Ministry of Finance, International Finance Bureau, unpublished papers

Kaplan, Frederic M, and Julian M. Sobin (eds), *Encyclopaedia of China Today*, 3rd edn, London: Macmillan, 1982
Keesing's Contemporary Archives
Kidron, Michael, and Dan Smith, *The War Atlas: Armed Conflict, Armed Peace*, London: Pan Books and Heinemann Educational Books, 1983; New York: Simon & Schuster, 1983
Kidron, Michael, and Ronald Segal, *The Book of Business, Money and Power*, London: Pan Books, 1987; or, *What You Need to Know about Business, Money and Power*, New York: Simon & Schuster, 1987
Kurian, George Thomas, *The Book of World Rankings*, London: Macmillan Press, 1979
—(ed), *World Press Encyclopedia*, London: Mansell, 1982

Lloyds Bank, *Economic Report on Taiwan*, London: Lloyds Bank, 1983

McHale, M.C, and J. McHale, *Children in the World*, Washington DC: Population Reference Bureau, 1979
Minority Rights Group, London, occasional publications; see also: Ashworth
Mitchell, Barbara, and Jon Tinker, *Antarctica and its Resources*, London: Earthscan, 1980

Newland, Kathleen, *Refugees*, Worldwatch Paper 43, Washington DC: Worldwatch Institute, March 1981

Philippine Statistical Yearbook 1982, Manila: National Economic and Development Authority, 1982
Pick, Franz, *Pick's Currency Yearbook 1977-9*, New York: Pick Publishing Corporation, 1981

Rocnik Statystyczny 1981, Warsaw: Gatowny Urzad Statystyczny, 1982
Royal Aircraft Establishment, Farnborough, Hants, private communications

SCAR [Scientific Committee on Antarctic Research], *Bulletin*, Cambridge (UK): Scott Polar Research Institute, 3 times a year
Scherer, John L, *China Facts and Figures Annual*, vol. 5, Gulf Breeze, Fla: Academic International Press, 1982
—, *USSR Facts and Figures Annual*, vol. 7, Gulf Breeze, Fla: Academic International Press, 1983
Science, Washington DC, weekly
Singh, Jyoti Shankar (ed), *World Population Policies*, New York: Praeger, 1979
SIPRI [Stockholm International Peace Research Institute], *Yearbook*, London: Taylor & Francis, annual
Sivard, Ruth Leger, *World Military and Social Expenditures*, Leesburg, Va: World Priorities, annual
South, London, monthly
Soviet National Survey, vol. 1, no. 1, London: Suchasnist Publishers, January 1984
Spanish Yearbook, Madrid: Instituto Nacional de Estadistica, Anuario Estadistica de Espa6a, annual
Starch INRA Hooper, *World Advertising Expenditures*, 17th edn, New York: Starch INRA Group of Companies and International Advertising Association, 1983
Statesman's Year-Book, London: Macmillan, annual
Statistical Yearbook of the Czechoslovak Socialist Republic 1982, Prague: Federal Statistical Office, 1982
Statistical Yearbook of the Netherlands 1978, The Hague: Central Bureau of Statistics, 1978
Statisticki Godisnjak Jugoslavije 1982, Belgrade: Savezni Zavod za Statistiku, 1982
Statisztikai Évkönyv 1981, Budapest: Központi Statisztikai Hivatal, 1982

[Taiwan] Statistical Yearbook, Republic of China [Taiwan]: Directorate-General of Budget, Accounting and Finance, Executive Yuan, annual
Terre des Femmes, Paris: Maspero, 1983
Tietze, Christopher, *Induced Abortion: a World Review*, 5th edn, New York: The Population Council, 1983
Tietze, Christopher and Henshaw, Stanley, *Induced Abortion a World Review*, 6th edition, New York: The Alan Guttmacher Institute, 1986

UK CEGB [United Kingdom Central Electricity Generating Board], *World Energy Background to 2030*, Sizewell document CEGB/S/331, 1983
UN [United Nations], *Compendium of Human Settlement Statistics*, 1985
—, *Demographic Yearbook*, New York: UN, annual
—, *Energy Resources Development Series*, no. 25, ST/ESCAP/219, New York: UN, 1982
—, *International Drinking Water Supply and Sanitation Decade: Present Situation and Prospects*, Report of the Secretary-General, A/35/367, Geneva: UN, 18 September 1980
—, *International Migration Policies and Programmes: a World Survey*, New York: UN, 1982
—, *Monthly Bulletin of Statistics*, New York: UN, monthly
—, *Patterns of Urban and Rural Population Growth*, New York: UN, 1979
—, *Regional Reviews of Activities Pertaining to the International Water Supply and Sanitation Decade*, Report of the Secretary-General, A/35/341, Geneva: UN, 5 September 1980

—, *Statistical Yearbook*, New York: UN, annual
—, *World Map of Desertification*, 1977
—, *Yearbook of Industrial Statistics*, New York: UN, annual
—, *Yearbook of National Accounts Statistics, New York: UN, annual*
—, *Yearbook of World Energy Statistics*, New York: UN, annual
UN Centre on Transnational Corporations, *Transnational Corporations in World Development, Third Survey*, New York: UN, 1983
UNCTAD [United Nations Conference on Trade and Development], *Handbook of International Trade and Development Statistics*, New York UN, annual
UNCTAD VI, *Protectionism, Trade Relations and Structural Adjustment*, policy paper, Belgrade, June 1983
UNEP [United Nations Environment Programme], *The World Environment 1972-1982*, Dublin: Tycooly International Publishing, for UNEP, 1982
UNESCO [United Nations Educational, Scientific, and Cultural Organization], *Yearbook*, Paris: UNESCO, annual
UN High Commissioner for Refugees, *Report of the UNHCR to the General Assembly, 37th Session*, New York: UN, 1982
USACDA [US Arms Control and Disarmament Agency], *World Military Expenditures and Arms Transfers 1971-1980*, Washington DC: USACDA, 1983
US Bureau of Mines, *Minerals Yearbook 1981*, Washington DC: US Bureau of Mines, 1982
US Congress, *World Refugee Crisis: the International Community's Response*, Report to US Senate Committee on the Judiciary, Washington DC: USGPO, 1979
US Department of State, Bureau of Intelligence and Research, *Status of the World's Nations*, Washington DC: USGPO, June 1983

Veliz, C. (ed), *Latin America and the Caribbean: a Handbook*, London: Blond, 1968

WHO [World Health Organization], computer-stored data, 1983
—, *Air Quality in Selected Urban Areas 1979-1980*, Geneva: WHO, 1983
—, *Sulfur Oxides and Suspended Particulate Matter: Executive Summary*, Environmental Health Criteria 8, Geneva: WHO in conjunction with UNEP, [1981]
—, *World Health Statistics*, annual
Wilkie, James W. (ed), *Statistical Abstract of Latin America*, vol. 20, Los Angeles: University of California Press, 1980
Wint, Guy (ed), *Asia Handbook*, Harmondsworth, Middx: Penguin Books, 1969
Women at Work, ILO unpublished paper, 1983 no. 1, Geneva: ILO
World Bank Atlas, Washington DC: IBRD, annual
World Bank, World Development Review, annual
World View, London: Pluto Press, annual
WRI/IIED [World Resources Institute/International Institute for Environment and Development], *World Resources 1986*, New York: Basic Books, 1986

ACKNOWLEDGEMENTS ████

We would like to record some of the many people and institutions to whom we are beholden for information and guidance who are not recognized elsewhere in these pages. They are (in London unless otherwise stated):

ASH Films; Janet Barber, World Wildlife Fund, Godalming; Mr Barnett, Department of Transport; Kate Bateman, US Embassy; P.A. Bliss-Guest, UN Environment Programme, Geneva; Roger Böhning, International Labour Office, Geneva; Susan Boxall, Marine Biological Association of the UK, Plymouth; Penny Brooks, Great Britain-China Centre; Dave Bull, Oxfam, Oxford; Jeff Canin, Greenpeace UK; Terry Cannon, Thames Polytechnic; Ian Carter, World Health Organization, Geneva; Catherine Caufield, International Institute for Environment & Development; Clive Challis, DMB&B; Philip Chrimes, Royal Institute of International Affairs; Fred Clairmonte, UN Conference on Trade and Development, Geneva; Roland Clarke, Ecology Party; Andrew Cornford, UNCTAD, Geneva; Elana Dallas, Amnesty International; Nigel Dudley, Earth Resources Research; Pat Farquhar, UN Information Centre; Gerry Foley, IIED; F. John Frizell, Greenpeace International; Nicole Gallimore, Royal Institute of International Affairs; Dan Gallin, International Union of Foodworkers, Geneva; Maurice Goldsmith, Science Policy Foundation; Mark Halle, International Union for Conservation of Nature and Natural Resources, Gland; Nigel Harris, Development Planning Unit; Jerry Harrison, Protected Areas Data Unit, Kew; Richard Helmer, WHO, Geneva; Linda Holman, UN Information Centre; Don Holtum, formerly Morgan Guaranty Trust Company; Alfred Homberger, Blick Rothenberg and Noble; Mike Hopkins, ILO, Geneva; Martin Ince; Paul Ingram, DMB&B; Paul Jeorett, Zoological Society; Denis Jones, RIIA; Margaret Julian, RIIA; Michael Kaser, St Antony's College, Oxford; David Kewley; Henk de Koening, WHO, Geneva; Albert Köhler, World Meteorological Organization, Geneva; Joelle Kuntz, Geneva; Robert Lamb, IUCN, Gland: John Logue, Villanova University, Philadelphia; David Long, British Telecom; Jeffrey McNeely, IUCN, Gland; Alfred Meyer, Shearson/American Express, Geneva; John Montgomery, RIIA; François Nectoux, Earth Resources Research; Kurt Noll, Union Bank of Switzerland, Vevey; Rhona O'Connell, Consolidated Goldfields; Janet Paice, UK Atomic Energy Authority; Walt Patterson, Oxford; Vela Pillay, Bank of China; Clarence da Goma Pinto, Third World Foundation; Peter Richards, ILO, Geneva; Ms Saurwein, UN, New York; Joe Schwartzberg, University of Minnesota, Minneapolis; Clare Seabrook, International Tanker Owners Pollution Federation; Charles Secret, Friends of the Earth; Susan Segal, Walton-on-Thames; Judy Sharpe; A. Sivanandan, Institute of Race Relations; Ruth Leger Sivard, World Priorities, Washington, DC; Dan Smith, Brighton; Paul Smoker, Richardson Institute for Conflict and Peace Research, Lancaster; David Somerville, Scottish Campaign to Resist the Atomic Menace, Edinburgh; Malcolm Spaven, Armament and Disarmament Information Unit, University of Sussex; Odyer Sperandio, WHO, Geneva; Kaye Stearman, Minority Rights Group; H. Suzuki, ILO, Geneva; Malcolm Swanston, Derby; Jon Tinker, Panos Institute; Louis Turner, Royal Institute of International Affairs; Basker Vashee, Transnational Institute, Amsterdam; Ruth Vermeer, International Organization of Consumer Unions, The Hague; Hazel Waters, Institute of Race Relations; Paul Wachtel, World Wildlife Fund, Gland; Rita Ward, International Planned Parenthood Federation; Ben Whitaker, Minority Rights Group; Joseph Woodall, WHO, Geneva; Lissie Wright, Conservation Monitoring Centre, Cambridge.

The staffs of the following London libraries, public or with privileged access, have been gracious and willing collaborators: British Library Science Reference Library; Department of the Environment; Department of Transport; Family Planning Information Service; Foreign Office; Home Office; International Institute for Strategic Studies; International Labour Office; London Business School; London School of Economics; Morgan Guaranty Trust Company; Natural History Museum; Royal Aircraft Establishment (Farnborough); Royal Institute of International Affairs, Chatham House; St Pancras Reference Library; School of Oriental and African Studies; United Nations Information Centre; USSR Trade Delegation; Westminster Reference Library; Women's Research and Resources Centre; Zoological Society.